"Before this book came out, good information on 529 plans was hard to find. Joseph Hurley has done a terrific job of making it easy to get all the details on these plans. It's well researched and authoritative, yet easy to read. Best of all, there's a thorough analysis of features in every existing plan. You'll learn what these features are, and find the plan that's right for you. This is a must read for anyone who is thinking of using one these plans—or considering an alternative, such as a custodial account or Coverdell account. It has my highest recommendation."

> KAYE A. THOMAS, ESQ.
> Fairmark Press Tax Guide for Investors,
> Fairmark.com

"Fortunately, this book is exactly what the title states: a comprehensive and clearly written guide to saving for college."

> THE CPA JOURNAL

"The leading book on 529s"

> JEFF BROWN
> The Philadelphia Inquirer

"This book will prime you about one of the best education deals around."

> AMY GRANZIN
> Morningstar.com

"Finally, a book explaining college savings programs in a way we can all understand."

> DEENA B. KATZ
> President, Evensky, Brown & Katz, named one of the
> Best Financial Planners by Worth magazine and
> author of Deena Katz on Practice Management
> (Bloomberg Press, 1999)

"This highly informative book is for any parent seeking the best way to save for a child's college expenses. Even the most novice reader on college-investing options will find Hurley's guide to 529 plans easy to understand . . . Parents will get the data they need to make an informed decision in this comprehensive guide."

REVIEW, TODAY'S LIBRARIAN

"Hurley writes very clearly about the details, advantages, disadvantages, pitfalls, etc. about the plans"

DAVID KINCHEN
The Register-Herald

"Your book is great—I bought two copies, one for my attorney."

LYNN DAVIS, CALIFORNIA

"I recently acquired your book, and I think you have done a fantastic job in dealing with the subject in depth and clarity. It is one of the finest handbooks of its type I have ever seen."

BRUCE BERGER, WRITER

Unsolicited Comments Found on the Web:

"The best book ever written about saving for college! This book unlocks the secrets of saving for college like the 401k plan did for saving for retirement. A real must for all families to understand."

"A fantastic summary of 529 plans. This book should be read by anyone planning to send a child to college."

"Terrific guide to a new way to save for college. Highly recommended. This is the first comprehensive analysis that I've seen of an extremely important and relatively new way to save on a tax-deferred basis for your children's or grandchildren's college expenses. It's well-written, comprehensive, and objective, and it gave me enough information to make an informed decision."

THE
BEST WAY
TO SAVE FOR
COLLEGE

A COMPLETE GUIDE TO 529 PLANS

THE
BEST WAY
TO SAVE FOR
COLLEGE

A COMPLETE GUIDE TO 529 PLANS

2002/2003 EDITION

Joseph F. Hurley, CPA

BonaCom Publications
Pittsford, New York

Published in the United States by:
BonaCom Publications
Corporate Crossings Office Park
171 Sully's Trail, Suite 201
Pittsford, NY 14534
TELEPHONE: (800) 400~9113
INTERNET: www.savingforcollege.com
E-MAIL: bonacom@savingforcollege.com

Copyright © 2002 by Joseph F. Hurley
First Printing
Library of Congress Card Catalog Number: 2001099609

Additional copies of this book may be ordered directly from the publisher.

Publisher's Cataloging-in-Publication
(Provided by Quality Books, Inc.)

Hurley, Joseph F.
    The best way to save for college : a complete guide
to 529 plans / Joseph F. Hurley. — 2002/2003 ed.
    p. cm.
    Includes index.
    LCCN 2001099609
    ISBN 0–9670322–6–1

    1. Prepaid tuition plans—United States.
2. Education, Higher—United States—Finance.   3. College
costs—United States—States.   I. Title.

LB2340.94.H87   2002   378.3'8'0973
                                  QBI02–200094

Disclaimer

The author has endeavored to research and write this book with the greatest accuracy possible and with the necessary factual depth to serve as a general guide. However, the reader should understand that there may be both typographical and substantive mistakes within the text of this book. Consequently, this book must be employed as a general guide and not as the rendering of legal, accounting, tax, investment, or other professional services. The reader should, when required, seek the proper professional services in these areas.

The views and opinions expressed herein are those of the author and do not necessarily represent the views and opinions of any professional organization of which the author is a member.

The intent of this book is the education and entertainment of the reader. The author and publisher will not be liable or responsible, if the content of this book causes, or allegedly causes, directly or indirectly, any losses or damages to any person, organization, or entity.

If any purchaser of this book does not want to be obligated by the disclaimer above, you may request your money back in full except for international shipping and handling costs.

All comments received will be considered in future revisions of this book.

Table of Contents

Section One

529 Plans Explained

Section Two

State by State Comparisons

About the Author

Joseph F. Hurley, CPA

Joe Hurley is generally regarded as one of the top section 529 experts in the country. After the first edition of this book was published in 1999, he founded and is currently CEO of Savingforcollege.com LLC, an Internet-based publishing and consulting company that focuses on 529 plans. He is a frequent speaker at conferences around the country and is editor of a newsletter targeted to professional advisers called "The 529 Plan Report."

Joe has practiced as a certified public accountant for over 20 years providing tax planning services to individuals, businesses, and tax-exempt organizations. He remains a partner at Moore Stephens Bonadio LLP, a CPA firm headquartered in Pittsford, New York. Joe is a member of the American Institute of Certified Public Accountants, the New York State Society of Certified Public Accountants, and the Financial Planning Association.

Joe became interested in the unique benefits of 529 plans in the wake of the Taxpayer Relief Act of 1997. He wrote several articles and appeared in hearings before the IRS and Treasury in Washington D.C. to provide comments on the proposed regulations issued in 1998 under Internal Revenue Code section 529. In addition to a professional interest, Joe and his wife Virginia have a personal interest in planning for college costs, with two children ages 16 and 12. To date they have established accounts in over twenty different 529 plans (the large number justified only by the purpose of research).

Aside from offering books, newsletters, and other information services, the author, his company Savingforcollege.com LLC, and his accounting firm are independent with respect to the states and program managers that operate 529 plans. The views and opinions expressed in this book are not conditioned on, or influenced by, the approval of any state official or other employee associated with these programs.

The author does not render personal investment advice. Requests for other consulting and speaking services, and comments about this book, can be directed to Joseph F. Hurley at Savingforcollege.com LLC, 171 Sully's Trail, Suite 201, Pittsford, New York 14534. You may also contact him via e-mail at jhurley@savingforcollege.com.

Visit www.savingforcollege.com

Here's Why

The *Internet Guide to 529 Plans* at www.savingforcollege.com is the perfect complement to this book. Here is what you will find when you visit:

+ News about developments in Washington and the states affecting 529 plans.
+ Exclusive "5-Cap Ratings" judging the overall usefulness of each state's 529 plan.
+ An active message board for those with questions, and for those with answers.
+ Joe Hurley's "529 E-ditorials" expressing opinions on a range of topics.
+ Investment performance for many of the 529 savings programs.
+ Up-to-date descriptions of the programs with links to their official Web sites.
+ Huge listing of useful articles and links.

"Hurley updates his site before the states update their own."

ANDREW TOBIAS
Demystifying Finance,
AndrewTobias.com

"There is quite a bit of insightful data here. Hurley clearly knows his stuff."

FORBES "BEST OF THE WEB"
Forbes.com

"Savingforcollege.com provides the most comprehensive look at the relatively new state-sponsored 529 Plans for college savings."

SENSIBLE INVESTOR'S HONOR ROLL 2001
Sensible-Investor.com

Preface

It has been four years now since I first took up the cause of section 529 plans, and more than three years since the first edition of this book was published. The journey so far has been exciting and gratifying, although at times I feel like I am in the middle of the tornado that brought Dorothy to the Land of Oz. The 529 sector has become a point of convergence for the states, the federal government, the private investment industry, and our institutions of higher education. It seems that nothing in the "World of 529" stands still for long.

In 1998, I suggested that the future evolution of 529 plans would be both dynamic and interesting to watch. It was clear that many states would be adopting new 529 plans, and it was just as obvious to me that the states with 529 plans already in place were not going to be able to just sit still. "These programs must change in order to remain strong," I wrote. "The formerly insular relationship among state programs will be challenged and the forces of free-market competition will dictate the future."

We are now squarely in the grip of that competition. Every state realizes that its residents have a choice when it comes to college savings, not only among different investment vehicles, but also among the increasing number of states that invite nonresidents to participate in their 529 plans. On top of that we find private enterprise becoming increasingly anxious to partner with the states, sensing opportunity in a higher education marketplace that involves tens of billions of dollars each year.

With approximately $17 billion in assets coming into the year 2002, the 529 industry is still relatively small. But the potential is very large.

Most parents who assume responsibility for their children's college education know they should be saving for this expense, just as they should be saving for retirement. State-sponsored college savings plans may well follow the path of the 401(k) industry, which over the past twenty years has grown to nearly $2 trillion in assets.

My decision to jump "out of the box"—latching onto section 529, writing this book, and launching a Web site—is certainly a decision I am happy I made. Having worked for over twenty years in relative, but comfortable, obscurity as a practicing CPA, I am thankful for the opportunity to be a source of help for families around the country, as well as for their professional advisers, in understanding the workings of 529 plans. My pursuit of section 529 has been a whole-hearted effort, born of the belief that state-sponsored college savings plans are not only an effective tool for the important goal of sending children to college, but also a den of confusion for people trying to make sense of it all.

I am also thankful for all of the friends and associates who have provided their assistance and support along the way. They include my partners at the accounting firm of Moore Stephens Bonadio LLP; Jeffrey Clark, Terri Robson, Kelly Dolan, Jared Fine, Cheryle Kulikowski, Caroline Crocker, Libby Gallis, Marie Osypian and the other fine people who work with me at Savingforcollege.com LLC; fellow authors Kaye Thomas, Esq. and Rick Darvis, CPA; all the dedicated and enthusiastic individuals working for the states, and their vendors, who have been so cooperative with my many requests and intrusions; and the many people around the country who have shared their enthusiasm and support through e-mail and Internet message boards.

Most importantly, I thank my best friend and wife, Ginny, who has been a source of unwavering support, a valued adviser, and a wonderful mother to our two children.

To Megan and Christopher.
Keep up the good work in school.

Special thanks and love to
Ginny, my wife,
without whom none of
this would be possible.

Introduction

Religion, morality, and knowledge, being necessary to good government and the happiness of mankind, schools and the means of education shall forever be encouraged.
NORTHWEST ORDINANCE, enacted by Congress July 13, 1787

For many young people in our society, a college degree is the key that unlocks the door to opportunity. We know this from studies that show a wide (and increasing) disparity between the incomes of those who graduate from college and those who do not.[1] We hear it from our elected officials as they place college accessibility high on the nation's political agenda. We even know it from our own college experiences; many of us have seen our lives enriched and improved by the formal recognition of our academic achievements.

But college is expensive. And it will only get more expensive in the future. This means that parents face a formidable challenge in paying for the higher education expenses of their children. Although a considerable amount of assistance is available to ease this burden, in the form of government support, student aid programs, private scholarships, and perhaps some help from grandparents or other relatives, most parents cannot eliminate the need to prepare for the cost of sending their children to college. It becomes a matter of saving.

---

1. One study found that between 1979 and 1999 the earnings of the average full-time college-educated worker rose 16 percent (after inflation), while the earnings of full-time workers with only a high school diploma dropped by 8 percent. U.S. Department of Education, *The Condition of Education 2000.*

1

This book is all about a remarkable and relatively new savings program available to American families facing future college costs. Its name is the qualified tuition program, sometimes abbreviated as QTP, but more often referred to as a "section 529 plan" or just plain "529 plan." Originally developed by the states, and given special status under federal tax law, it is a savings program you should know about. If you are looking for an effective way to save for your children, your grandchildren, or even yourself, a 529 plan may be a large part of the solution.

Section 529 refers to the specific provision in the Internal Revenue Code, our federal tax law, that describes this particular type of college savings vehicle and lays down some rules that the programs must abide by in order to assure their participants of its tax-beneficial treatment. Until recently, section 529 required that a qualified tuition program be established and maintained by a state. Now it can include a prepaid tuition plan offered by one or more post-secondary educational institutions, albeit with additional restrictions. (The word "tuition" in any of these titles can be a little misleading, because many 529 plans can be used to save for several categories of higher education expenses beyond tuition.)

All 50 states and the District of Columbia have authorized one or more 529 plans, although a few of these programs are still in the development stage at the beginning of 2002. As you will see, many of these 529 plans extend an open invitation to you no matter which state your family lives in. In addition, we should expect one or more institution-sponsored 529 plans to come along before the end of 2002. This all adds up to a great deal of choice in your selection of a college savings program, and more than a little confusion. By reading this book, you will be better prepared to make the right decisions for you and your family.

How much does college cost?

According to the College Board, the price of one year at the average four-year private college including room and board and other expenses now exceeds $26,000, and the price for a resident student at the average public college or university is approximately $12,000. The rate of increase over the past ten years has been more than 5% per year.[2]

Since 1980, college prices have been rising at a rate two to three times the increase in the Consumer Price Index. If this trend continues, the price of a degree at a four-year private institution for the student enrolling ten years from now will exceed $160,000, and the price of four years at a public institution will be more than $70,000. More troubling is the fact that median family income has not been keeping pace with rising college costs.

The future cost of college is difficult to predict. There are some factors that point to increases that continue to outpace the general inflation indices: high demand as more high school graduates choose to enter college immediately; the second baby boom; and increasing costs relating to technology and faculty salaries. Other factors may suggest a slowdown in average increases, including the nascent trend of "distance education."

For those who lack sufficient financial resources, the traditional means of outside assistance—federal, state, and institution-based financial aid programs—will still be available. Indeed, the money available for student aid has picked up considerably in recent years after a long decline through the 1980s and early 1990s. Since 1992, the federal government's investment in student aid through college scholarships and student loans has more than doubled.[3] But much of this increase is needed just to keep up with higher costs. Moreover, the use of averages fails to reflect the fact that the income disparity between high and low earners has widened over time, so that the problem of "unmet need" among lower-income students has been growing, not slackening. Future levels of aid from state and local governments will depend largely on budgetary considerations, while institutional grants will depend to some extent on investment performance of endowment funds.

---

2. Based on data from *Trends in College Pricing 2001*, The College Board (a nonprofit association serving students, schools and colleges). These figures are for students who are living away from home while attending college.

3. U.S. Department of Education, *Expanding College Opportunity: More Access, Greater Achievement, Higher Expectations*, 2000.

How are other families coping with this?

There is no shortage of surveys showing how families view the challenge of saving for college, or how they respond to that challenge. Depending on which survey you read, many Americans do not feel adequately prepared.

+ Most Americans believe that a college degree is absolutely essential or very important for young people today (Peter Hart and Associates, 2000), and consider saving for a child's college education to be a top savings priority. (Richard Day Research, 1999)
+ 50% of parents, however, do not have a good grasp of the expected cost of college. (Yankelovich Partners, 2000)
+ 50% of parents with young children (i.e., in pre-school), believe they are currently saving enough to meet college savings goals. One-quarter of parents haven't started to save at all. (Richard Day Research, 2000)
+ One-third of parents with older children (i.e., in high school), feel they are meeting college savings goals. Only 20% of them, however, expect to foot most or all of the bill for college expenses. (Richard Day Research, 2000)

Where is higher education on the nation's list of priorities?

Clearly, we have entered an era where higher education is regarded in the halls of Congress and state capitols as a national priority worthy of public subsidy. The nature of the subsidy has shifted to one that provides incentives to individuals, rather than the direct support of institutions. More than ever before, our federal and state governments are using the tax laws as a means of distributing education incentives. These tax law provisions are meant to encourage individuals to save on their own for college. Over the past five years, we have seen federal tax law changes that will undoubtedly result in much more money being invested in dedicated college savings plans than ever before. Soon, many families with children in their junior and senior high school years will have significant sums of money set aside for college, and they will be looking for the best education that money can buy.

The turnaround in education-friendly tax legislation has been remarkable. Before 1996, there were only a few tax breaks aimed at helping individuals pay for their own or their children's college expenses. One such break is the exclusion of interest on the redemption of certain U.S savings bonds used to pay for college costs. Another tax break is the employer-provided educational assistance plan whereby an employee can receive up to $5,250 to pay for undergraduate (and beginning in 2002, graduate) school costs as a tax-free benefit. Finally, there have been income exclusions allowed for certain qualified scholarships received by an individual and, in narrow circumstances, for student loan forgiveness.

Other parts of the tax law became downright anti-education in the late 1980s, including the treatment of interest on student loans as non-deductible personal interest, the penalization of taxpayers under 59 ½ years old for taking distributions out of a qualified retirement plan or an individual retirement account to pay for college costs, and the imposition of a "kiddie tax" on investment income of children under the age of 14. For most people, these rules left only one real way to save for future college costs—putting money aside after-tax in a savings or investment account.

Certainly, many families who could afford to set aside savings for education purposes have done just that. Investment accounts have been established for children and grandchildren, either in the parents' or grandparents' own names; in the child's name under the Uniform Gifts or Transfers to Minors Acts; or in special education trusts drafted by attorneys and trust companies. These are not tax-advantaged vehicles, however, and so the selection of investments has often been influenced by the tax impact. Zero coupon municipal bonds, stock mutual funds, and even life insurance have been favored investments for this type of saving.

The traditional approaches to college saving will continue to be popular with many people, particularly now that the capital gains tax rates have been lowered. The Taxpayer Relief Act of 1997 reduced the maximum rate on the net adjusted capital gain for an individual from 28 percent to

20 percent, with an even lower 10-percent rate for someone in the 15-percent bracket. Reduced capital gains rates of 18 and 8 percent will apply to the sale of certain property held more than five years. The new capital gains rates should stimulate even more long-term investing as a means to save for future college expenses, since the tax cost to be paid when cashing in those investments will be dramatically decreased. In addition, the education savings bond program and employer-provided educational assistance plans remain viable for taxpayers who can take advantage of them.

But now we have a greatly expanded menu of alternatives in saving for future college expenses. Since 1996, Congress has created three new and very significant ways to invest for college and save taxes at the same time:

+ using an individual retirement account (or Roth IRA),
+ saving with a Coverdell education savings account (formerly the Education IRA), and
+ saving with a 529 plan.

And there's even more. In addition to the new savings alternatives, the tax law now offers new government tax subsidies in paying for college costs, including the Hope Scholarship credit, the Lifetime Learning credit, and the renewed deductibility of interest on college loans.

How confusing are all these programs?

Very confusing. The good news in all of this is, of course, that tax breaks will help pay for the increasing price of a college education. There is a negative aspect, however, and that is the unprecedented level of complexity faced by families who may wish to take advantage of the new incentives. There are now so many alternatives available that you are likely to have a difficult time selecting the ones that are most appropriate in your circumstances. The difficulty is compounded by the fact that some of these options are mutually exclusive. Your use of one program may restrict or eliminate the use of another.

Why focus on 529 plans?

The reason for focusing on 529 plans is that they provide some powerful and unique tax advantages not available with the other options you have in saving for college. What other tax-advantaged program allows everyone to participate, without regard to age or income level? What other program allows the accumulation of over two hundred thousand dollars in a tax-sheltered account for one child's future college costs? What other mechanism allows someone with a large estate to immediately reduce that estate by $55,000 per child (or grandchild) without triggering gift tax, and without losing control of the assets?

The answer is that there is no other tax-advantaged program that provides the combination of benefits that a 529 plan does. 529 plans are unique and wonderful creations that come in as many different forms as there are states and institutions that sponsor them. A 529 plan is intended to serve one purpose—providing a way for families of any income level to save for future college costs in the most effective way possible. But in so doing, the 529 plan actually has investment, tax, retirement, and estate planning implications that reach far beyond this one purpose.

This book will provide you with guidance on how to make the most effective use of the savings opportunity presented by the 529 plan. There are many strategies to consider, and choices to make, before the decision to enroll in a 529 plan is made. Once enrolled, your account continues to need attention, despite the fact that one of the advantages of a 529 plan is that your account is managed by professionals. This book will also compare 529 plans with the other alternatives available to a family in saving for college, so that the best options can be selected from the bewildering array of choices.

Glossary

There are a number of terms used in this book that deserve some explanation. An effort is made to use the most common terminology, although not necessarily the language found in tax law, and to be as consistent as possible in the use of the terms. You will find, however, that the various state programs and other descriptive resources are not consistent in this regard.

529 plan—a **qualified tuition program** described in section 529 of the Internal Revenue Code. Also referenced throughout this book as the **program**. Referred to in some sources as a **Section 529 Plan** or **QTP**.

Account owner—the person with ownership and control of the 529 account, usually the **donor** or **contract purchaser**. Many 529 plans refer to the account owner as the **participant**.

Basis—the sum of all prior cash contributions, plus the contributions portion of any qualifying rollovers to the account, less the contributions portion of any distributions previously taken. Also known as the **principal** of the account. Tax law refers to basis as the **investment in the account**.

Designated beneficiary—the individual for whom the account or contract is established for the purpose of paying future college costs. Both 529 prepaid programs and 529 savings programs will have a designated beneficiary for each contract or account (with the possible exception of accounts established by state or local governments or 501(c)(3) organizations).

Distribution—an amount of cash withdrawn from a 529 account, or the value of educational benefits provided by a 529 plan. Most 529 savings programs use the term **withdrawal**. If a distribution is used to pay for qualified higher education expenses it is called a **qualified distribution** or **qualified withdrawal**. If a distribution is made for any other reason its is called a **non-qualified withdrawal** or **refund**.

Earnings—the total account value less the basis. A distribution is comprised of an **earnings portion** and a return of principal.

Prepaid program—one variety of 529 plan, describing a program that will pay for one or more years of future college tuition and other specified costs pursuant to the **prepayment contract** that you purchase. The person who purchases the contract is known as the **contract purchaser**. The owner of the contract is known as the **contract owner**. Some prepaid programs offer **units**, with each unit representing a fixed percentage (often 1%) of one year's tuition. These programs are referred to as **unitized** prepaid programs, and the purchaser is called the **unit purchaser, unit owner,** or **unit holder.** Tax law refers to an interest in a prepaid program as a **prepaid educational arrangement or contract,** to the purchaser as the **contributor**, and to the contract owner as the **account owner.**

Private prepaid program—a 529 plan operated by an eligible educational institution (not by a state), as authorized under the Economic Growth and Tax Relief Reconciliation Act of 2001.

Qualified higher education expenses (QHEE)—the post-secondary education expenses incurred by a designated beneficiary that are counted in determining the tax treatment of distributions from a 529 plan. Tax law describes the types of higher education expenses that qualify, generally tuition, fees, books, supplies, equipment, and a limited amount of room and board.

Rollover—a transfer of funds between 529 accounts that is not treated as a distribution because it satisfies certain conditions under section 529.

Savings program—the other variety of 529 plan, describing a program in which a **donor** makes a **contribution** to an **account** that grows in value over time from the investment of the contribution, or by pegging the value of the account to a tuition index. The person who owns the account in a savings program is known as the **account owner.** Tax law refers to the donor as the **contributor**, and to an interest in a savings program as an **educational savings account.** Some states will refer to their 529 savings program as an **investment program** to underscore the fact that accounts can lose value.

ONE

History of 529 Plans

In his January 1986 State of the State Address, Michigan Governor James J. Blanchard proposed that Michigan adopt a new state-run prepaid tuition program "designed to help parents guarantee to their children the opportunity of a Michigan college education." Such a program would address the concern that many had about soaring tuition costs during the first half of the 1980s. The result of this proposal was the Michigan Education Trust (MET), developed in 1986 as the first program of its kind. Under the program any resident of Michigan could pay a stipulated amount into the trust to cover the future tuition of a particular beneficiary at a Michigan public college or university.

Before issuing any prepaid tuition contracts, the state of Michigan requested a ruling from the Internal Revenue Service regarding the tax aspects of this arrangement. The IRS responded with both good news and bad news.[1] The good news was that the purchaser of a prepaid tuition contract would not be taxed on the accruing value of the contract until

---

1. IRS Letter Ruling 8825027

funds were actually distributed or refunded in the future. The bad news was the IRS' determination that the trust itself would be subject to income tax on earnings from invested funds. In short, the IRS concluded that the trust was taxable as an association.

Lacking an exemption from federal income tax, the MET went ahead anyway and began entering into prepaid tuition contracts with residents of that state. Fifty-five thousand individuals signed up for the program. The MET paid tax on its investment income, and then filed suit for refund in 1990 against the IRS. The case was first decided in favor of the IRS, but on appeal in 1994, the Sixth Circuit Court of Appeals reversed the district court judge's decision and found in favor of Michigan.[2]

The irony of the Michigan experience is that the MET was forced in 1990 to stop issuing new contracts, due not so much to the burden of paying income taxes, but because it had been selling the prepaid tuition contracts at prices that were discovered to be too low. When originally establishing contract pricing, program administrators had relied on overly optimistic projections of the rate of return on invested funds in relation to the trust's obligation to pay for rising tuition prices. The trust was on its way to becoming insolvent. (The program later resumed with more appropriate pricing and remains today as one of the largest prepaid programs.)

Not long after its defeat in the Sixth Circuit, the IRS retrenched and considered challenging the beneficiaries in prepaid programs. A proposal was made to tax beneficiaries each year on the increasing value of the prepayment contracts. Concerned that such treatment would be a disincentive for savings, Congress passed new legislation authorizing "qualified State tuition programs (QSTP)" as part of the Small Business Job Protection Act of 1996. Section 529 was added to the Internal Revenue Code by the Act, conferring tax exemption to qualifying state programs, and deferring tax on participants' undistributed earnings. Substantial changes were made to section 529 as part of the Taxpayer Relief Act of 1997 to add room and board to the list of qualifying expenses and provide special estate and gift tax treatment for participants in a 529 plan.

---

2. Michigan v. United States, 40 F.3d 817 (6th Cir. 1994), rev'g 802 F. Supp. 120 (W.D. Mich 1992)

The 1997 Taxpayer Relief Act also gave rise to a new tax-advantaged savings vehicle for college—the Education IRA. Unlike the 529 plan, which provided that earnings were taxable when withdrawn for qualified higher education expenses (albeit at the student's tax rate), the Education IRA offered federal tax exemption for the earnings when withdrawn for the same purpose. While this was seen as a significant advantage, the Education IRA was hobbled by age and income restrictions, and by a $500 annual per-beneficiary contribution limit.

Not long after the 1997 Act, Congress undertook consideration of tax-free treatment for qualified 529 withdrawals. In fact, Congress passed legislation in both 1998 and 1999 that would accomplish this objective. Both of the bills granting tax-free treatment were vetoed by President Bill Clinton, but for other reasons. The most objectionable provision being paired with 529 plan tax exemption was one being advanced by Republican Senator Paul Coverdell of Georgia that would include certain elementary and secondary school expenses in the list of qualified expenses for purposes of the Education IRA. The Democratic administration likened this provision to private school vouchers and deemed it unacceptable.

The stage was set for President George W. Bush when he took office in January 2001. New tax bills were crafted in both the Senate and the House of Representatives, and the tax exclusion for qualified withdrawals from a 529 plan was a part of those bills. The proposal had strong bipartisan support as well as the backing of the President. On June 7, 2001 the Economic Growth and Tax Relief Reconciliation Act (EGTRRA) of 2001 was signed into law, making qualified distributions from a 529 plan exempt from federal tax, effective in 2002.

EGTRRA made several other significant changes affecting education savings. Educational institutions would be permitted to establish their own section 529 prepaid programs, without state involvement , although tax exemption for participant distributions would be delayed until 2004. Another change related to "non-qualified" distributions. No longer would the states be required to collect a penalty, as they were under original Code section 529. Instead, the federal 10% penalty already contained in the law (Code section 530) for beneficiaries receiving non-qualified withdrawals from an Education IRA was extended to participants in a 529 plan.

Not only was the 529 plan improved by EGTRRA but so was the Education IRA. Beginning in 2002, the annual contribution limit would be increased from $500 to $2,000. Furthermore, the use of the Education IRA for Kindergarten through 12th grade was approved, and subsequent to the enactment of EGTRRA the name Education IRA was changed to the Coverdell education savings account in honor of the now late Senator who had been the biggest proponent of the K–12 provision.

Why do states start 529 plans?

All fifty states and the District of Columbia now have 529 plans in operation or under development. Even before Congress fully sanctioned these plans in 1996, there were nine states operating prepaid tuition programs for their residents. But why are the states going through all the trouble to establish and maintain these programs? Until recently, there seemed to be little if any net revenue accruing to the sponsoring state. In fact, the unrecovered startup cost in some programs has been substantial (as much as $3.5 million). Each program then requires an ongoing commitment of staff and other resources.

There appear to be several reasons for the great interest on the part of most states in setting up 529 plans. One is the conviction that the education of a state's citizenry is an essential function of state government, and the establishment of tax-advantaged savings programs targeted for education will allow more individuals to obtain a college degree without taking on a crushing load of debt. This argument is subject to some debate, however, since the amount of direct support provided by many states to their public systems of higher education has not kept pace with costs and the schools have been forced to increase their prices.

Another reason for a state to set up a 529 plan is to provide more incentive for its residents to attend in-state public colleges and universities. Obviously, this would help keep the state's own institutions financially strong. Although nearly every 529 plan has "portable" benefits, which means that beneficiaries are allowed to use their account to pay for qualified expenses at eligible private and out-of-state institutions, a number of the older programs provide a better investment return to families who choose in-state public institutions. The newer programs are generally less punishing to account beneficiaries who go out of state for their education, and in many programs, it makes absolutely no difference whether the student attends college within or outside the state operating the 529 plan.

The more cynical among us may believe that the reason the states commit money to establish and maintain 529 plans is essentially a political one. The programs allow elected officials to look good to the voters. Education is a powerful campaign issue. The Governor and Treasurer who champion legislation making it easier for people to afford a college education are able and willing to claim credit for a very "pro-family" program.

Some of the impetus and support for the expanding 529 market comes from the National Association of State Treasurers, which has formed an affiliate, the College Savings Plan Network (CSPN), as a means to coordinate resources among its members and share ideas concerning their state-sponsored programs. Comprised of state officials and program administrators, CSPN meets at least annually to discuss issues and communicate ideas and new developments.

What's in store for the future?

The future is assuredly bright for 529 plans. New programs have been springing up across the country, creating a stir among the professional financial community and attracting the interest of the press. Articles and feature stories extolling the benefits of 529 plans have been appearing at an increasing pace in the national and regional media. While some writers and commentators are appropriately cautionary in their message, very few have projected a negative opinion of these programs.

Substantial dollars are beginning to find their way into 529 plans; the $9 billion invested at the beginning of 2001 was expected to nearly double by the end of that year. It seems certain that, under the recent tax law changes and a recovering economy, we will witness an accelerating pace of investment in 529 plans over the next few years. Polls indicate that public awareness of 529 plans is still relatively low; the majority of families with children likely to attend college are not yet fully aware of this investment option. This situation is rapidly changing, however, due not only to the substantial amount of media coverage, but also because an increasing number of large mutual fund companies and investment brokers are taking on a direct role in the 529 industry.

As recently as June 2000, there were only four large nationally- recognized investment companies that had been selected by the states to manage their 529 college savings programs: TIAA-CREF, Merrill Lynch, Fidelity Investments, and Salomon Smith Barney. Since that time the list has expanded rapidly to include many of the country's largest mutual fund companies and financial services firms. These companies are willing to invest substantial sums in advertising and promoting the programs they represent. They see a direct revenue opportunity with 529 plans, and they also see a new tax-advantaged product that will help to round out a menu of products and services to investors.

A significant number of the newer 529 savings programs are now being marketed as "national" college savings plans, despite their state sponsorship. Many of these widely-available programs are being distributed under commission agreements with brokers, financial planners, and other financial advisers. By partnering with the professional investment community, the states are able to offer 529 plans with the look and feel of mutual fund and annuity products without incurring the associated costs. Financial professionals who are registered to provide investment advice can directly assist families in understanding 529 plans and selecting appropriate investments, whereas state program administrators are unable to provide investment advice.

As people come to realize that they have a choice among 529 plans, "program shopping" will become more prevalent and some states will find many of their citizens jumping the border to obtain better-perceived benefits with another state's program. There will be many individuals who have already enrolled in 529 plans that later seek to change programs by transferring their account balances from one state to another.

In order to protect the viability of their programs, most states appear very willing and even eager to adopt frequent modifications to their 529 plans and provide additional investment alternatives. Several states have added incentives for residents to stay close to home with their college savings, including state income tax deductions for participant contributions, or even a partial match of contributions. Some residents now enjoy a break on fees and expenses in their home state programs.

Most of the older 529 plans were developed by the states as prepaid programs, while the majority of newer 529 plans are savings programs (see Chapter 5 for a discussion of program types). Many of the prepaid programs are restricted to state residents and only cover undergraduate tuition and fees. The savings programs are generally seen as more flexible in their application to all the qualifying costs of higher education, and they are more familiar to American families accustomed to IRAs, 401(k) plans, and other similar investments. This type of program is also easier to administer and less costly to the state, particularly when an outside financial services company is willing to offer turnkey management under attractive financial arrangements with the state.

In states offering both a prepaid program and one or more savings programs, separate trusts are maintained and each program has its own set of rules. However, they are often packaged under one marketing umbrella and administered by the same agency (Illinois is a notable exception). We are even starting to find some states turning over marketing and operational responsibilities for their prepaid programs to the investment firms managing their savings programs.

Despite the more restrictive nature of prepaid programs, many families continue to be attracted to the "tuition guarantee" they offer and the fact that stock market volatility does not have a direct impact on the value of benefits available through those programs. Kentucky launched a new prepaid program in 2001, and a couple of other states are planning to do so. The efforts of Tuition Plan, a not-for-profit national consortium of over 275 independent colleges and universities, should result in IRS' approval to become the first institutional 529 prepaid program. Modeled after the Massachusetts U.Plan (which is not a qualified 529 plan), Tuition Plan will offer tuition certificates redeemable towards tuition at any member institution at a pre-determined percentage.

There has been a rapid evolution in the investment offerings available through 529 savings programs. The earliest such programs offered a single fixed-income investment. In the late 1990s we witnessed the introduction of equity investments in several states as part of an "age-based" investment strategy. This approach, involving a shift in the underlying asset allocation from an equity-weighted portfolio to a fixed income-weighted portfolio as the beneficiary grew older, was viewed as an appropriate "auto-pilot" investment program under a provision in Code section 529 that prohibited investment direction by the participant. Several 529 plans then moved quickly by adding "static" or "fixed-allocation" investment options and creating a menu of investment offerings for the program participant. These options appealed to investors who wanted more control over their asset allocation, despite the continuing prohibition on investment direction. Fair warning was provided to participants, however, that contributions to a particular investment option could not be redirected later on.

The variety of investment offerings has continued to expand. As new savings programs opened, investors became aware of the opportunity to rollover existing accounts in one state's 529 plan to another state's plan at any time, provided the beneficiary of the account was substituted with another family member in the process. The 2001 tax law changes created an even better opportunity by permitting a same-beneficiary rollover between programs, but only once in a 12-month period, beginning in 2002. Finally the IRS, sensing the prohibition against participant investment direction had become a paper tiger in the wake of these changes, issued a notice in September 2001 (Notice 2001–55) announcing that a program could give its participants permission to change their investment option once every calendar year or whenever a beneficiary change took place. Now investors would not have to jump between programs in order to adjust the asset allocation of their 529 accounts.

We also now see an increasing effort to introduce 529 plans into the workplace where employees are given the opportunity to enroll and make contributions periodically through payroll deduction. More and more, 529 plans are looking and acting like 401(k) retirement plans.

Where in the past 529 plans were largely viewed as somewhat quirky and of limited usefulness, they have now broken out into the mainstream. Their tax advantages, investment offerings and near-universal accessibility make them attractive to the majority of families in a position to save for college. The states have ceded much of their direct involvement in running the programs to the large financial institutions that can succeed in marketing and managing an investment product. The collegial atmosphere in which state politicians and agency heads have worked together in developing and promoting the concept of college savings program is being tested by the inevitable forces of free-market competition.

Public policy watchdogs will keep a close eye on these developments and issues surrounding them. They are raising such questions as are state-sponsored college savings programs a good use of public funds? Do they disproportionately benefit socio-economic groups that do not really need these incentives? Are program marketing materials providing full disclosure? Do new rules need to be adopted by the SEC and MSRB (a municipal securities self-regulatory organization) for these investment offerings? Will a program's obligation to pay for tuition influence the pricing decisions of the state's public institutions? Are these institutions becoming too dependent on these programs, and therefore at risk? Will colleges raise their prices, affecting everyone, as more students begin appearing with significant balances in their 529 accounts? Michael A. Olivas and his colleagues at the Institute for Higher Education Law and Governance at the University of Houston Law Center are leading the discussion on several of these issues.[3]

It is likely that our federal lawmakers and the IRS will begin taking a closer look at the developments in the 529 industry as well. It is fairly obvious that 529 plans have progressed far beyond any expectation that Congress may have had when section 529 was enacted in 1996. In fact, the introduction of the Education IRA in 1997, and its improvement with the 2001 tax law changes, is evidence that Congress did not anticipate the rapid evolution of the 529 plan into a conventional, and very powerful, investment vehicle.

---

3. See Michael A. Olivas (ed.), *Prepaid College Tuition Plans—Promise and Problems*, (NY: College Board, 1993), and Barbara M. Jennings and Michael A. Olivas, *Prepaying and Saving for College, Opportunities and Issues*, Policy Perspectives No. 3 (D.C.: College Board, 2000).

This scrutiny will intensify as attention is focused on the scheduled 2010 expiration of the EGTRRA tax incentives. Millions of families, with tens of billions of dollars invested in 529 plans, will be anxious to see these provisions extended. Our institutions of higher education should be interested as well; many of these families will have sizable savings accounts matched by a desire for the best education this money can buy. Even those families without the financial resources to save for college may have reason to support section 529 tax incentives. To the extent that higher-income families are willing and able to increase their own savings, we may find that aid dollars can be more effectively directed to those families that truly need the assistance.

529 Plan Chronology

Years When Operations Began

1986	Wyoming*
1987	Florida
1988	Michigan**
1989	Ohio**
1990	Alabama, Kentucky***
1991	Alaska
1993	Pennsylvania
1995	Massachusetts U.Plan**
1996	Texas, Utah, Virginia**
1997	Colorado**, Indiana, Louisiana, Mississippi**, Tennessee**, Wisconsin
1998	Connecticut, Delaware, Illinois**, Iowa, Maryland**, Montana, Nevada**, New Hampshire, New Jersey, New York, North Carolina, Rhode Island, South Carolina, Washington, West Virginia
1999	Arizona, Arkansas, California, Maine, Missouri, Vermont
2000	Kansas, New Mexico, Oklahoma, Wyoming
2001	Nebraska, Oregon, Idaho, Minnesota, North Dakota
2002	(scheduled) Georgia, Hawaii, South Dakota

*	Prepaid program suspended in 1995
**	A savings program was added in a later year.
***	A prepaid program was added in a later year.

TWO

Why You Should be Interested in a 529 Plan

Simply stated, the 529 plan is likely to be your best option for college savings if you have school-age children or grandchildren and are looking to invest significant amounts of money.

As everyone knows, children "grow up too fast." Yet, at the same time, too few parents really make an attempt to figure out how much it will cost to send their children to college, or consider available options in planning for those costs. Perhaps you expect your child to receive a full athletic or other merit scholarship to a major university. Is your seventh grader already up to six-foot-four and able to hit four out of five from beyond the three-point line? Was she the national champ in her age group for the 200-meter butterfly? Has he been the headline performer at Carnegie Hall? If so, congratulations! College costs should not be a problem for you, assuming your child's injury-free dedication to the sport or other activity continues through high school. If not, welcome to the group of us who cannot count on a full scholarship and need to face the prospect of coming up with the resources to fund our child's education.

Part of the reluctance to pre-fund future college costs stems from the challenge faced by most young families in just meeting everyday expenses, never mind trying to save significant dollars on top of that. The task of putting aside enough money to pay for the college of choice may seem overwhelming. It is difficult to conceptualize the amount that the experts are telling us a private college will cost in eighteen years when today's newborn will be enrolling. A quarter-million dollars? Why even bother to try?

Some of the "savings gap" can also be traced to the feeling that a safety net will exist. "If it turns out that I can't afford to pay the costs when my child goes to college, I know there will be other ways to handle it." To the credit of our educational institutions and government, the safety net currently does exist, in the form of federal, state, and institution-based financial aid programs. With the programs now available to students and their families—including loans, grants, and work-study—few qualified students will be denied a good college education for lack of money. (Unfortunately, however, we see that loans, not grants, are the fastest growing component of financial aid.)

Finally, there has been an unwillingness on the part of parents to establish dedicated college savings accounts even when they have the resources to do so, because they do not like to give up control of assets. Someone can save by putting assets in Uniform Gifts or Transfers to Minors Act accounts, but how do you eliminate the risk that the child will decide to find an "alternative" lifestyle that does not include college, especially if that lifestyle depends on the use of those funds once the child is no longer a minor? The answer may be to place the assets in trust with provisions that prevent unauthorized use of the funds, but the establishment of a trust may involve significant time and money to do right, and then requires annual maintenance. What seems to be the easiest and safest way for parents to save? For many, it's contributing the maximum allowable amount to qualified retirement plans, buying a nice house with some appreciation potential, and, if there is anything left over, putting it away in some mutual funds.

Section 529 plans are designed with many features and tax incentives to overcome the reluctance on the part of families to save for future college expenses. No matter what circumstances a family may be in—large or small, low-income or high-income, decided on a particular college or undecided, transient or settled—there are programs available to accommodate college saving desires in simple, flexible, and tax-efficient ways. In fact, the tax advantages of a 529 plan can be used even if there are no school-age children or grandchildren. Who's to say that the older individual will not want to return to school at some point in the future? There are more and more "nontraditional" students enrolling in post-secondary schools every year, for graduate work, for a change of career, or just for enjoyment and self-improvement. A 529 plan can be a great way to save for this possibility, even if the idea is eventually abandoned.

What's so great about 529 plans?

Here are the advantages, in a nutshell:

Federal income tax advantages

✦ Earnings build up in your account on a tax-deferred basis.
✦ Distributions from your account that are used for certain qualifying college costs are tax-free.

Estate and gift tax benefits

✦ Your contributions to a 529 account are treated as completed, present-interest gifts to the beneficiary for purposes of the federal gift tax and generation-skipping transfer tax. This means that the money comes out of your taxable estate, and the gifts qualify for the $11,000 annual gift tax exclusion.
✦ A special election allows your contributions to be treated as if they were made over a five-year period for gift and generation-skipping transfer tax purposes. This means that $55,000 can be contributed to a 529 plan account gift-tax free (assuming you make no other gifts during that five-year period).

Availability and flexibility

- ✦ Unlike so many tax breaks that are subject to income limitations on the taxpayer, a 529 plan imposes no income limitations. A high-income individual can take advantage of a 529 plan when other alternatives (such as a Coverdell education savings account) are not available.

- ✦ Over $200,000 can be invested in 529 plan accounts for a single beneficiary (and perhaps much more). At $2,000 per year, an IRA or Coverdell education savings account just doesn't measure up.

- ✦ Despite the treatment of your contributions as completed gifts, you still retain ownership and control of the account. This creates powerful and unique advantages. As the account owner it is you, and not the beneficiary, who decides when to take distributions and for what purpose. You can substitute the beneficiary of the account; you can even revoke it. Any concern that you may have about losing control of significant assets is greatly diminished.

Investment benefits

- ✦ Different 529 plans offer different investment approaches, providing the opportunity to select an approach that parallels your own investment objectives. Some 529 plans offer a way for your savings to keep up with increases in tuition costs; others offer a menu of investment options ranging from low-risk fixed income funds to higher-risk stock funds; while still others use portfolios allocated among stocks, bonds and money market investments tailored to the age of your beneficiary. Many programs have no residency requirements, making the range of savings options available to all.

- ✦ You can obtain professional investment management at low cost. While fees and expenses vary considerably, the costs of many 529 plans are remarkably low considering the effort required in establishing, marketing, and administering a 529 plan. Some programs utilizing mutual funds are able to acquire the lowest cost "institutional" shares, thereby reducing the expenses to you.

✦ Many programs accommodate automatic payment plans through payroll deduction or electronic funds transfer from your bank account, making education budgeting simple and providing the discipline that some parents need.

State tax benefits

✦ Many states follow federal income tax treatment in excluding the earnings in your 529 account from state and local income taxes, and several offer a deduction for all or part of your contributions into their programs.

✦ A few states also provide other financial benefits to program participants, such as scholarships, matching contributions, or favorable state-aid treatment.

Asset protection

✦ In some states, the law provides specific protections from the claims of creditors.

Why have I only recently heard about 529 plans?

Many people will find all this hard to believe at first. "If these programs are so great," one may object, "then why doesn't everyone know about them and use them?" The answer is that everyone **should** know about them, and in fact the word is spreading. A survey conducted in 2001 by American Century Investments found that the number of parents having some familiarity with 529 plans jumped from 24% in 2000 to 37% in 2001.

Further evidence comes from data showing an increasing number of accounts and dollars in 529 plans. At the beginning of the year 2001 there were approximately $9 billion in all 529 plans. Preliminary data suggests that at the beginning of 2002 this figure had nearly doubled to about $17 billion, despite an uncooperative stock market. It is reasonable to expect another doubling during 2002. What accounts for all this growth? We can point to several factors:

+ We're just now moving from the start-up phase to wide availability and full public acceptance of 529 plans. Although several states have a tuition savings program dating back to the late 1980s, it was not until 1996 that section 529 was added to the Internal Revenue Code, and the majority of programs now in operation are new since 1997. A few states still have 529 plans under development. We are also likely to see the introduction of a large (with nearly 300 private colleges), centrally-administered, "private" pre-paid tuition program sometime before the end of 2002.

+ There has been an outpouring of media interest in 529 plans, particularly in the wake of the tax law changes in 2001 that granted federal income tax exemption for qualified withdrawals. Many personal finance periodicals, including *Money*, *SmartMoney*, and *Kiplinger's Personal Finance Magazine*, regularly mention 529 plans. Many of the country's top financial writers now recognize the advantages of 529 plans and recommend them through their books, Web sites, public appearances, and columns in national and regional newspapers.

+ Awareness of 529 plans among the professional investment and insurance community is increasing at an even faster rate than in the public at large (as one might expect). Until recently, many brokers, investment advisers, and financial planners had little reason to promote 529 plans over other more traditional investment products, because none of the state programs would pay a commission. That has all changed now. Every segment of the professional planning community—hourly fee-based, asset fee-based, commission-based, or some combination—has a way to introduce 529 plans into their clients' portfolios and be compensated for their advice and guidance. In fact, we now see that broker-sold 529 plans are the fastest growing component of new account growth, reflecting the large number of investors who rely on financial professionals in making investment decisions. For those individuals who wish to conduct their own research and make their own investment decisions while incurring lower fees and expenses, there will continue to be a number of "direct-sold" 529 plans.

✦ Employers appear eager to bring 529 plans into the workplace by facilitating payroll deduction and offering group enrollment into 529 plans. As an after-tax voluntary deduction program, a group 529 program has no payroll tax implications, no discrimination testing, and few, if any, eligibility requirements. Many employers will appreciate the opportunity to offer this additional "benefit" to employees at low or no cost to the company. Special considerations come into play, however, in deciding which particular 529 plan or group of plans to offer under a group enrollment format. Since the dollars being contributed are coming from the employee, it is incumbent upon the employer to consider whether the 529 plans selected are the ones that offer the best benefits to their particular employees.

✦ An increasing number of private companies wish to support the cause of higher education and have recognized 529 plans as a way to help families that are facing the challenge of paying for college costs. One of the most ambitious of these is Upromise Inc., a three-year-old company based in Boston that operates a "rewards" program for its individual members (www.upromise.com). Purchases made through Upromise from participating vendors earn rebates that are directed into a member's account with selected 529 plans. Another rewards program with a 529 emphasis is run by BabyMint (www.babymint.com).

But don't 529 plans require that I send my child to an in-state public school?

This is one of the most common misconceptions about 529 plans. In fact, every state's 529 plan permits your account to be used at colleges and universities located anywhere in the United States (and many foreign institutions as well). Some 529 plans provide better benefits for in-state schools, but none lock you into a specific institution or state public education system.

I've heard about the program in my state and it doesn't really excite me. That leaves me out, right?

Not at all. You should consider other states' programs. Many of the best 529 plans are operated by states that impose no residency restrictions. They are open to all.

I have already set up an account in my state. So I guess I'm all set.

Guess again. Have you selected the program that provides you with the best benefits? If not, you may be better off transferring your account to a different state's 529 plan. If transfer is not a viable option (because of the restrictions and penalties imposed by some 529 plans), you can leave your current account where it is and open a second account (or third account, etc.) with another state that offers a more attractive program.

My broker tells me I am better off using his recommended mutual funds to save for college costs. Is he right?

Your broker may be right, but it really depends on your particular situation. The question you might better ask is how much your broker or financial planner knows about 529 plans. Until recently there were few who did, but many felt threatened by the concept of a 529 plan and viewed it as a competitive product that did not pay commissions. That situation has largely changed, now that many states have approved commissions for 529 plans distributed through investment advisers. Financial professionals across the country, including commissioned-based advisers as well as fee-only planners, have begun embracing 529 plans as a potential solution for their college-bound clients, and are finding ways to effectively incorporate them into long-term financial plans. Knowledge level remains the key, however. If you rely on a broker or financial planner in making investment decisions, be sure the adviser is up to speed on the technical and comparative aspects of 529 plans.

My child is a senior in high school. Isn't it too late for me to start using a 529 plan?

Not necessarily. Take a look at your most recently-filed income tax return. Did you pay any tax on interest, dividends, or capital gains distributions? If you did, then a 529 plan represents an opportunity to convert taxable investment income into tax-free investment income. Even if the account has a life of only a few years—remember that it will usually take two to five years or even longer to earn a degree—you will be saving taxes. In fact, many parents facing college bills in the near future want to have their money in safe, interest-paying investments. This is the where the tax protection of a 529 plan provides the greatest advantage.

It gets even better if you live in a state that offers a tax deduction for your contributions to its 529 plan. Instead of paying the college bills out-of-pocket, you can reap the benefit of a state income tax deduction by first making a contribution to the 529 plan, and then using your account to pay the bills. Bottom line: college expenses become a write-off for state income tax purposes.

Section 529 plans sound too good to be true. Won't the IRS or Congress shut them down?

Not likely. These tax-favored savings plans are quickly gaining ground across the country and there is every indication that government officials want to see them become more popular, not less.

There must be some disadvantages to 529 plans. What are they?

There is no single investment, including any of the 529 plans, that is the perfect option for every investor. The comparative advantages and disadvantages of 529 plans are discussed throughout this book. The following is a summary of some of the most significant disadvantages.

✦ They are confusing. It is difficult to get a good grasp on all of the considerations and options relating to 529 plans. There are plenty of places where you can learn about IRAs, savings bonds, and the like. The rules for these other programs are fairly straightforward and one sponsor's IRA is not going to be much different from another. The same is not true for 529 plans. The rules surrounding 529 plans invite many questions and planning considerations. And rather than one basic model, there are several to choose from. Each 529 plan has unique features that make comparisons between different programs tricky. Many financial and legal advisers have not yet gained the knowledge needed to counsel their clients in this area. You can find some helpful articles in the financial press, and the program materials available from the states provide a great deal of useful information. But apart from this book and the information on our companion Web site at www.savingforcollege.com, there is currently little comprehensive literature available from independent sources.

✦ The lower tax rates on capital gains do not apply to gains in your 529 account. Of course, if things work out right your earnings will be entirely tax-free, but if any part of a withdrawal turns out to be taxable, it is taxable at ordinary income rates. There will also be a 10% penalty, unless an exception applies.

✦ If your account loses value, you cannot simply sell the investment and claim a capital loss on your tax return. Under certain circumstances you may be able to claim a miscellaneous itemized deduction in the year you completely liquidate a 529 account, but many taxpayers will find little or no tax benefit in doing this.

✦ Investment selection in a 529 savings program is limited (although less so than in the past), and your ability to change investments is somewhat restricted. The ultimate responsibility for your account rests with the state agency or other person acting as trustee under the program trust. They make the rules, and they can change the rules. To date, almost all program changes have been beneficial to the participant but that may not always be the case.

✦ You may decide to invest with a particular 529 plan based in part on the program's selection of a particular mutual fund company or financial services firm as program manager, only to find that the program manager is replaced in a later year with a different investment firm. The contracts between the state and the outside program manager have terms lasting anywhere from 2 to 15 years, and at the end of that term the state can decide to bring in someone new. If that happens, it is likely that your account will have new investments and different expenses.

✦ The fact that you retain ownership and control over the account may work against you in certain situations. For instance, an account owner applying for Medicaid in the future may find that the state Medicaid agency requires that the 529 account first be used to pay for medical and long term care expenses before Medicaid payments can begin. Another risk is that creditors attempt to reach your account for unpaid debts. State law will control in most cases, and some states do provide specific protections for participants in their 529 plans (advice from an attorney is suggested). Federal bankruptcy protection does not extend to 529 accounts although at the time this book went to press there were bills in both houses of Congress that would provide some level of bankruptcy protection to 529 accounts.[1]

✦ Your 529 account, and any distributions from it, can impact the student's eligibility for need-based financial aid. This particular

---

1. See Senate Bill S. 420. Generally, up to $5,000 in contributions made to a 529 plan between 365 days and 720 days prior to the filing of the bankruptcy petition, and any amount of contributions up to program limits for contributions before that time, would be excluded from the account owner's or contributor's bankruptcy estate and would therefore be protected from creditor claims. There are certain requirements as to the relationship of the debtor and the 529 account beneficiary.

issue is covered in detail in Chapter 4 and throughout the other chapters in this book.

I'm not sure I like the idea of the state holding my money. What's to prevent the state from appropriating the program funds for other purposes?

In most states, if not all, your contributions to a 529 plan, and all earnings thereon, are maintained in a separate legal trust that cannot be reached by the state for other purposes. If you have concerns about this, you should not hesitate to contact the program administrator in the state operating the program and obtain specific assurances.

I have heard that I cannot count on my withdrawals being tax-free when my child goes to college because the law will change in 2011. Is that right?

The changes made to section 529 by the Economic Growth and Tax Relief Reconciliation Act of 2001 are scheduled to expire at the end of the year 2010. Unless Congress acts to renew these rules before then, we automatically revert to pre–2002 section 529 treatment. This means that qualified withdrawals would no longer be tax-free (the earnings portion would be taxed to the beneficiary) and other provisions would change as well. While there are no guarantees, it is difficult to believe that Congress will fail to act to preserve section 529 benefits considering that millions of families will have a direct interest in these programs by the time 2011 rolls around.

My employer has recently started promoting a payroll deduction plan for college savings. Is this something I should consider?

Contributing to a 529 plan on a regular basis through payroll deduction can be a simple and relatively "painless" way to budget for college savings. Your employer may be interested in helping you learn more about the benefits of saving with a 529 plan and may even offer assistance in the enrollment process. Often the support and education is provided directly by a 529 program manager, or a financial adviser representing a 529 plan, under special arrangement with the employer. You will usually have the opportunity to attend special educational sessions, study program materials, and get your questions answered.

You should not assume that the particular 529 plan being promoted in the workplace is the best program for you. You will always have the option to establish an account on your own with your own state's program or with any of the 529 plans that do not have state residency requirements. Some employers will handle payroll deduction for two or more 529 plans so that you have some choice in selecting a program that is most appropriate to your own situation. Employers will generally disclaim any responsibility for determining your suitability for the investment.

Contributions to a 529 plan through payroll deduction are made on an after-tax basis. Unlike a 401(k), your contributions are not subtracted from your taxable earnings, and they generally do not involve any payroll taxes or discrimination testing on the part of the employer.

I see that 501(c)(3) exempt organizations can open accounts in many 529 plans, but why would they want to?

Charitable organizations that already operate a substantial scholarship program may have little reason to be interested in a 529 plan. They do not reap any benefit from the tax exemption under section 529 (these organizations do not pay tax on investment income anyway), and most have already established an investment policy controlling the investment of their scholarship funds. However, there are other organizations that do not currently have a scholarship program that might be interested in starting one, if there were a simple way to administer a new scholarship fund. A 529 savings program can fill this role by offering professional investment management and account administration at low cost. There are many 529 plans that should be eager to facilitate the objectives of the scholarship program, including the processing of scholarship withdrawals to the institutions attended by scholarship recipients. There might also be valuable cross-promotional opportunities between the charity and the 529 plan.

THREE

Section 529 Overview

In this chapter, the provisions of Code section 529 are described, including the tax benefits made available to the participant, the tax rules for withdrawals, and the various qualification requirements. This is a fairly technical chapter and includes information needed by the professional adviser who will be working closely with clients considering these investments.

Unfortunately, the amount of guidance coming from the Treasury Department and IRS discussing section 529 and other education tax provisions has not been sufficient to address all the questions that arise. Proposed regulations under section 529 were issued in August 1998, and these were helpful at the time, but they have become obsolete as a result of the Economic Growth and Tax Relief Reconciliation Act (EGTRRA) signed in June 2001. A set of final regulations is expected to appear sometime during 2002, but not before the Treasury Department completes another period of review and public comment.

The tax regulations are extremely important because they describe the rules that the programs, and individual taxpayers, must follow in order to be in compliance with section 529. The literal reading of the law must be coordinated with the practical demands placed on the programs and their participants. The Treasury Department faces some particularly difficult issues in developing regulations under section 529 due to the unique character of these programs.

In the meantime, we can look to other IRS documents for some help. Notices, rulings, publications, and the tax forms themselves (along with their instructions) provide direction, but even these resources do not provide a lot of detail. The best place for taxpayers to find official IRS guidance is Publication 970, *Tax Benefits for Higher Education*, available on the Web at www.irs.gov. However, even the 2001 version (published in late December 2001) contains only 3 pages devoted to 529 plans.

Several of the rules described below are scheduled to change in 2011 following the sunset of EGTRRA. Unless new laws are enacted before that time that would extend or modify the provisions of section 529, the treatment of 529 plans and their program participants will revert to pre–2002 laws. Because it appears somewhat likely that Congress and the President will agree to act on these provisions before that time, pre-EGTRRA section 529 provisions are not fully detailed in this chapter.

What is a 529 plan and who can participate?

A 529 plan is a program designed to help families prepare for the cost of post-secondary education that meets certain requirements contained in section 529 of the Internal Revenue Code for a "qualified tuition program" or "QTP". There are two basic purposes served by section 529.

First, section 529 grants tax-exempt status to qualified tuition programs. Without statutory protection, the undistributed investment income earned by some of these programs could be subject to income tax.[1] Section 529 also makes it clear that this investment income will not

---

1. Tax-exempt status is already provided to states and their political subdivisions under Code section 115. The central issue in *Michigan v. United States (6th Cir. 1994)* (discussed in Chapter 1) was whether the Michigan Education Trust was an instrumentality of the state and thus protected from imposition of tax. The IRS felt the MET was not a state instrumentality. Several other state programs could be challenged on similar grounds if not for Code section 529.

be considered debt-financed income (and subject to unrelated business tax) if the only liability of the program is the liability to program participants.

The second purpose served by section 529 is in describing the federal tax treatment for the program participants, both for income tax purposes and for estate, gift and generation-skipping transfer tax purposes. In some ways, the treatment prescribed by section 529 as they relate to participants are in direct contradiction to the "normal" rules under other provisions of the tax law.

There are only two groups that can offer a 529 plan. The first group includes any state or state agency or instrumentality ("state"). The second group includes any eligible educational institution. An institutional or "private" program could not be qualified under section 529 prior to the 2001 tax law changes (EGTRRA), and in order to qualify now it must meet additional requirements and provide certain protections as discussed below.

A state-sponsored 529 plan is one that permits a person to either (1) purchase tuition credits or certificates on behalf of a designated beneficiary which entitle the beneficiary to the waiver or payment of his or her qualified higher education expenses, or (2) make contributions to an account which is established for the purpose of meeting the qualified higher education expenses of the designated beneficiary of the account.

The first type of program described in the preceding paragraph is commonly referred to as a prepaid tuition program ("prepaid program"), while the second type is commonly referred to as a college savings program or college investment program ("savings program"). A savings program can be viewed as a kind of state-sponsored mutual fund—a participant's contributions to the program are invested and the value of the participant's account is determined by the investment performance of the underlying securities. It is not uncommon for the media to describe 529 plans as only referring to the savings programs.

Prepaid programs are different from savings programs in that a participant's "return" is not linked directly to investment securities. Prepaid programs can operate like a futures contract, where the participant purchases a contract that obligates the program to deliver a certain bundle of tuition or other benefits in the future, or like an index fund, where the participant purchases redeemable "units" or "credits" whose value is pegged to average in-state public tuition or to some other tuition inflation index. In some significant ways, the unit-type prepaid programs have more in common with the savings programs than they have in common with the contract-type prepaid programs, and a couple of states have even relabeled their unit programs, replacing the word "prepaid" with the term "guaranteed savings".

An eligible educational institution that desires its own 529 plan is limited to offering a program that falls only into the first category, i.e. prepaid programs. In addition, it must hold its program assets in a "qualified trust", which is one that meets certain standards normally applicable to individual retirement accounts.

When you establish an account in a 529 plan, you are required to name one living individual as designated beneficiary of the account. Typically, this is your child or grandchild, but it is not necessary that the beneficiary be related to you in any way. If you want to have accounts for more than one beneficiary, you will have to establish more than one account. It is also acceptable in most, but not all, 529 plans for you to name yourself as beneficiary of the account you establish.

Accounts established by a state or local government (or agency or instrumentality thereof) or by a 501(c)(3) exempt organization as part of a scholarship program are not required to name a designated beneficiary. Beneficiaries can be selected at the time of distribution, and one account can presumably be used to assist multiple students in paying for college costs.

There are few restrictions as to who can participate in a 529 plan. There are no income or age limitations on either the account owner, the contributor (if different), or the designated beneficiary. There is no requirement that the participant reside in the sponsoring state or that the beneficiary attend a school located in that state. The 529 plan can establish its own restrictions, however, and so it is important to distinguish the flexibility permitted under federal law from the rules of the program itself.

What other requirements must a 529 plan meet?

There are several other requirements that all programs must meet in order to qualify under section 529. These are described below.

(Note that a state-sponsored 529 plan is not required to apply for a ruling or determination from the IRS as to its qualified status, although several states have requested, and some have received, such a ruling. An institution-sponsored program, however, is required to apply for and receive a determination from the IRS that it meets the requirements for qualification as a prepaid program under section 529. At the time this book was published, no institution-sponsored program had yet received such determination from the IRS. It is generally anticipated that the non-profit organization Tuition Plan, which represents a consortium of nearly 300 private colleges located through the U.S., will be the first to do so.)

1) The program can only accept contributions in cash. Cash includes payments made by check, money order, and credit card. Many 529 plans also permit electronic funds transfer from a bank or investment account. Contributions may not be made with investment securities or other types of property. If you wish to transfer other investments into a 529 plan you will need to liquidate those investments first, possibly triggering taxable income or capital gains. Under certain conditions, you may be able to transfer funds from an existing Coverdell education savings account or qualified U.S. savings bonds without triggering tax. These rules are explained more fully in later chapters.

2) The program must provide a separate accounting for each designated beneficiary. Separate accounting does not mean separate investing, and contributions are typically commingled in the program trust for investment purposes.

3) The program may not permit you or your designated beneficiary to direct the investment of your account. By statute, investment direction must be left to the sponsoring state. Although this somewhat paternalistic provision appears to be very limiting, a savings program can in fact provide substantial investment choice and flexibility to the account owner. Many of the programs now offer a menu

of investment options to the account owner. A contribution can be directed to one of these options, or in some 529 plans can be spread among the options (others might require that separate accounts be established if you want to invest in more than one investment option). Further, as a result of Notice 2001–55 issued by the IRS in September 2001, a 529 plan that "allows participants to select only from among broad-based investment strategies designed exclusively by the program" may now permit an account owner to change investment strategies once per calendar year.[2] Although it is not entirely clear yet what the IRS means by "broad-based investment strategy", the Notice seems to suggest that you will be allowed to reallocate your account among available investment options, subject to program approval. There are other ways to exercise some degree of investment control. A 529 plan may allow you to switch investments in the program any time you change the beneficiary of the account. You can also roll over your account to another state's program that has different investment offerings, subject to the rules for qualifying rollovers (discussed below).

4) The program may not allow accounts to be pledged by the account owner or designated beneficiary as security for a loan.

5) The program must provide adequate safeguards to prevent contributions on behalf of a designated beneficiary in excess of those necessary to provide for the qualified higher education expenses of the beneficiary. Almost all 529 plans currently place a specific dollar limit on contributions, expressed as either a cumulative contribution cap or as an account balance limit. An account balance limit means that new contributions will not be accepted once the account value reaches a specific level, although it will not prevent the account from growing beyond that limit based on investment performance.

The 1998 proposed regulations provide a safe harbor to programs that limit contributions on behalf of a designated beneficiary to an

---

2. Notice 2001–55, 2001–39 IRB (Sept. 24, 2001).

amount determined by actuarial estimates necessary to pay tuition, required fees, and room and board expenses of the designated beneficiary for five years of undergraduate enrollment at the highest cost institution allowed by the program. Programs relying on the safe harbor generally have contribution caps below $200,000 per beneficiary. Many programs have abandoned the safe harbor and include graduate school costs and other qualified expenses in the computation of their contribution limits, presumably with assurances from the IRS or legal counsel that they will not be jeopardizing qualification under section 529. You will find some 529 plans with account balance limits as high as $260,000 or even higher.

Notice that the limitation on contributions is imposed by the 529 plan on a per-beneficiary basis. If there is more than one donor to the account, or if there is more than one account in the program for a particular beneficiary, the accounts must be combined for purposes of determining total contributions. The proposed regulations do not, however, prohibit a designated beneficiary from having accounts in different states and contributing a combined amount that exceeds the individual program limits. Congress presumably did not intend that the "stacking" of accounts be used as a way to circumvent the safeguards imposed by any one program, and so it would be reasonable to anticipate that final regulations will impose additional requirements. Some states have started to require a representation from the donor that accounts in multiple programs are not being used as a way to make contributions beyond the level that can be reasonably supported as appropriate for the beneficiary's future higher education needs.

I see some mutual fund companies advertising their own 529 plans. Can any investment firm offer a 529 plan?

No. The reason you see advertisements for 529 plans from mutual fund companies, broker-dealers, or banks is because many of the state-sponsored 529 plans have outsourced program management and marketing to these firms. Tax law requires that the state or institution "establish and maintain" the program but does not prohibit the sponsor from hiring a vendor to assume the investment and operational duties. These vendors also have a direct interest in the success of the programs, as their fees are typically based on the level of assets under management in the program. Under the proposed regulations, in order to meet its duty, a state must set all the terms and conditions of the program and be actively involved on an ongoing basis in the administration of the program, including supervising all decisions relating to the investment of assets contributed to the program.

What are the federal income tax rules for 529 plan participants?

There is no upfront federal income tax deduction for your contributions to a 529 plan, but your account in the program grows tax-deferred. The only time you need to be concerned about federal income taxes is in a year during which you withdraw funds from the account or receive education benefits on behalf of the beneficiary. If you satisfy certain conditions, some or all of your account earnings will remain free from tax when distributed. These rules are described below.

In any year during which a distribution is made from your 529 account, the program administrator must calculate and report to you the "earnings portion" of the distribution. Shortly after year-end, the administrator will mail to you or your beneficiary a Form 1099-Q that reports two figures: total distributions from the program during the year and the earnings portion. These are the two figures you will need when you file your federal Form 1040. It will be up to you to figure how much of the earnings portion, if any, is subject to tax. (The portion of your distribution that represents contributions is never taxable for federal purposes, because your contributions to the account were not deductible.)

If the account beneficiary has incurred qualified higher education expenses or "QHEE" (defined later) that in total are equal to, or greater than, the total distributions from all 529 accounts as reported on Forms 1099-Q, the distributions are excluded from taxable income in their entirety. If, however, total QHEE are less than total distributions, only a portion of the distributed earnings is excluded from income. The remainder is taxable as ordinary income, as expressed by the following formula:

$$\frac{QHEE}{Total\ Distributions} \quad X \quad Earnings\ Portions \quad = \quad Ordinary\ Income$$

If withdrawals are taken from a Coverdell education savings account for the same beneficiary during the year, QHEE must be allocated between the 529 distributions and the Coverdell account withdrawals. That is because withdrawals from a Coverdell account follow the same general taxation rules as distributions from a 529 plan. It is not yet clear whether the IRS will require a pro rata allocation of expenses or if the beneficiary has the discretion to allocate expenses in any manner he or she chooses. Coverdell accounts are discussed in Chapter 9.

Another question that does not appear to be fully resolved is whether your payments for QHEE must match up in the same taxable year with the distributions from your 529 account. While this will not be a concern when the program makes qualifying payments directly to the school or third party vendor, it can become an issue if you make the payments yourself and request withdrawals from the 529 plan as "reimbursement". For example, let us assume you pay the tuition bill yourself on December 20 and immediately request a withdrawal from your 529 account. If it takes the program administrator two weeks to process your request and issue the distribution check, you risk having insufficient QHEE in the year of the withdrawal. Until further guidance is issued by the IRS, you should assume that QHEE and distributions will be accounted for on a cash basis and that it is important for you to receive the 529 account withdrawal in the same year you pay the qualifying expenses.

Beginning in 2002, any earnings that are subject to tax will also be subject to a 10% federal additional tax. This tax, which represents the penalty for the non-qualified use of a 529 account, is computed on Form 5329 and paid with the recipient's federal income tax return. Before 2002, the law required that a 529 plan itself impose a "more than de minimis" penalty on non-qualified distributions, and 10%-of-earnings was the standard penalty among savings programs. This requirement is now lifted, and the states may now eliminate their own penalties. Most are expected to do so although the transition has not yet occurred in some programs.

There are exceptions to the 10% additional tax in the following situations:

+ The distribution is attributable to the designated beneficiary being disabled. Disability means being unable to engage in any substantial gainful activity by reason of a physical or mental impairment of indefinite duration or that can be expected to result in death.

+ The distribution is made on account of a tax-free scholarship or allowance, to the extent the distribution does not exceed the amount of the scholarship or allowance.

+ The distribution is made after the death of the designated beneficiary to the beneficiary's estate or to a new beneficiary. Unfortunately, there appears to be a technical problem with this exception. Although it works fine for a Coverdell education savings account under section 530, which is where the tax code contains the penalty language, section 529 requires a *living* individual as beneficiary on every account (except for accounts established by state or local governments or 501(c)(3) organizations). An argument can be made that a 529 plan is required to liquidate the account and distribute it to the account owner upon the beneficiary's death, and this would constitute a non-qualified distribution that does not escape the 10% penalty. The IRS will have to clarify the rules surrounding this particular exception and tell us if the account owner may change the beneficiary, or treat the estate of the beneficiary as the account beneficiary, following the death of the previously named beneficiary.

+ The distribution is made in the 2002 or 2003 tax year and is includable in income although it is used for the qualified higher education expenses of the beneficiary. This exception was apparently designed for distributions from an institutional prepaid program since qualified distributions from an institutional program are not excludable until 2004. It is not clear at this time whether this exception can be applied to excess distributions caused by a taxpayer claiming the Hope or Lifetime Learning credit (see below).

How does the 529 plan administrator calculate the earnings portion of a distribution?

For each distribution, the administrator subtracts the "principal portion" from the amount of the distribution, leaving the earnings portion.[3] In a 529 savings program, the principal portion is determined by multiplying the distribution by a fraction—your investment in the account ("basis") divided by the value of your account at the time of distribution. Basis generally refers to the total contributions into the account less prior distributions of principal.

The calculation is slightly different in a 529 prepaid program. The total amount of distribution is based on the current value of the tuition and other education benefits your beneficiary receives during the year. The principal portion is calculated based on the number of tuition credits used or redeemed during the year as a percentage of total credits purchased. For example, if you originally purchased eight semesters of tuition and you use the program to pay for two semesters in a year, the principal portion is two-eighths or 25% of the amount you paid for the prepayment contract. Some of the "unit-type" prepaid programs deviate from this approach and use a "first-in-first-out" approach in assigning basis to redeemed units.

For purposes of this pro rata calculation, all accounts you have in the program for the same designated beneficiary must be treated as one account. Accounts in a state's prepaid program do not have to be aggregated with accounts in the same state's savings program.

Before 2002, distributions from all accounts in the state with the same beneficiary were required to be aggregated even where there were different account owners or they came from different types of 529 plans. Furthermore, in calculating the earnings portion of distributions the program administrator was required to pretend that all distributions were made on the last day of the year. These rules caused unforeseen difficulties and were loosened with the 2001 tax law changes and IRS Notice 2001–81.[4] The calculation should now be performed as of the

---

3. Section 529 applies the provisions of section 72 to the extent the distribution is not excludable under any other section of the Code (e.g. section 117 scholarship exclusion).
4. Notice 2001–81; 2001–52 IRB (Dec. 7, 2001)

date of distribution, although 529 plans will not be required to change to the new methodology for non-rollover distributions until 2003 (and in some cases until 2004).

A 529 plan administrator will need to keep track of your basis in order to satisfy these reporting requirements. Rollover contributions from another 529 plan, and tax-free transfers from Coverdell accounts and qualifying U.S. savings bonds, pose a special challenge to 529 plans because these transfers consist of both portions: amounts representing basis and amounts representing untaxed earnings. (These types of transfers are discussed in further detail below and in later chapters.) The basis of contributions associated with these transfers must be adjusted for their untaxed earnings. IRS Notice 2001–81 prescribes the procedures a 529 plan must now employ to ensure that this information is properly recorded.

The decision of the government to place responsibility for determining the earnings portion of a distribution with the program administrator and not the taxpayer lifts some of the paperwork burden from your shoulders. It also distinguishes the 529 plan from the Coverdell education savings account and similar investment vehicles that ask relatively little of the trustee or custodian beyond reporting gross distributions, but require that the taxpayer maintain basis records.

Reporting 529 distributions on your tax return in 2002 and later years will be anything but simple, however, because of the changes made to section 529 by EGTRRA. All you had to do before was provide evidence to the 529 plan administrator that distributions were being used for qualified higher education expenses, and if you couldn't do so, the program would assess a penalty. Because the requirement for a program-imposed penalty is now removed, the 529 plan administrator will no longer be required to verify the use of distributions unless those procedures remain part of state law or program rules[5]. Now it will be up to you, the program participant, to account for qualified higher education expenses with your

---

5. Some states, however, may continue to require that the use of distributions for qualified higher education expenses be verified by the program administrator. For example, a program might impose a penalty, additional fee, or recapture tax on non-qualified withdrawals only.

federal income tax return, and provide proof of these expenses in the event your return is examined by the IRS.

Who receives the Form 1099-Q, the account owner or the beneficiary?

This is an important question if distributions from a 529 plan are not fully excluded from income. If you are treated as the recipient, the earnings portion of the non-qualified distribution will be taxable to you at your marginal tax bracket. If your beneficiary is treated as the recipient, the earnings portion of the distribution will be taxable to him or her at a possibly lower tax bracket. The IRS says that distributions paid directly to the eligible educational institution are to be reported to the beneficiary as recipient. For any cash withdrawals, the Form 1099-Q will be sent to the person who received the funds as determined under the rules of the 529 plan.

> *Example*: Mr. Brown establishes an account with a 529 plan for his daughter Kelly and makes a one-time contribution of $10,000. Five years later, once Kelly has started college and the account has grown to $15,000, Mr. Brown requests a $9,000 withdrawal from the account made payable to Kelly. Kelly will receive a Form 1099-Q after the end of the year showing $9,000 in total distributions and $3,000 as the earning portion. The earnings portion is one-third of total distributions, based on the ratio of account growth at the time of distribution ($5,000) to total account value ($15,000). If Kelly can show that she incurred at least $9,000 of qualified higher education expenses during the year, the entire distribution is federally tax-free. If Kelly can only show $5,000 of QHEE, then 5/9ths of the $3,000 earnings portion will be tax-free and 4/9ths, or $1,333, will be subject to tax on Kelly's federal income tax return as ordinary income. She will also incur a 10% additional tax ($133).

What about state taxes?

State income tax laws are not uniform in their treatment of participants in 529 plans. Here, generally speaking, is the way it should work for most:

✦ You and your beneficiary will not be required to file an income tax return and pay taxes to another state merely because you decide to open an account in that state's 529 plan.

✦ You or your beneficiary will be required to pay income tax on the distributed earnings in your state of residency, assuming it imposes an income tax, unless your state grants a specific exemption or follows federal law that excludes qualified distributions.

✦ State treatment will follow federal treatment regarding the amount and timing of income, and in determining who reports the income (you or the beneficiary).

How might the states deviate from this approach? One concern is that the state sponsoring the 529 plan may decide that it can collect taxes from non-resident participants in that plan. This is rather unlikely, however, because income from intangible investment assets is generally sourced in the state where the taxpayer resides and not the state that offers the investment.

Another concern could arise for residents in a state that does not conform its rules to the federal computation of adjusted gross income (AGI). Most states use federal AGI or taxable income as a starting point for state taxable income, but some start with their own definition of "gross income." These states include Alabama, New Hampshire, Mississippi, Pennsylvania, and Tennessee. The risk in any non-conforming state is that the state will not recognize the section 529 income tax rules, i.e., deferral of income and exclusion of income on qualified withdrawals.

Some states will conform to the federal computation of AGI as of a specific date, but any changes to the federal tax laws after that date are not automatically incorporated into the state tax calculation. You should attempt to find out how your state intends to handle 529 accounts, and whether accounts in out-of-state programs are treated differently than accounts in the state's own 529 plan. Residents of states with their own definition of income—including Alabama, New Hampshire, Mississippi, Pennsylvania, and Tennessee—may find it especially important to solicit the advice of a tax professional.

State tax consequences of a 529 distribution can also be uncertain in a year in which you or your beneficiary moves between states.

What are qualified higher education expenses?

The definition of "qualified higher education expenses" or "QHEE" is critical in determining the tax consequences of a distribution from a 529 plan. As discussed above, distributions are fully exempt from federal income tax only if the beneficiary incurs an equal or greater amount of QHEE.

QHEE means tuition, fees, books, supplies, and equipment required for enrollment or attendance on a full-time or part-time basis at an eligible educational institution, plus, in the case of a "special needs beneficiary", any "special needs services"[6]. In addition, QHEE includes room and board expense (both on-campus and off-campus) for students enrolled in certain college programs on at least a half-time basis.[7] The student's qualifying expenses must be reduced by any tax-free scholarships or payments, and by educational assistance allowances provided under certain federal programs.

QHEE under current law does not include the cost of transportation or personal expenses, although they may be considered part of the "cost of attendance" for federal financial aid purposes. Repayment of student loans also does not qualify.

---

6. A "special needs beneficiary" is to be defined by Treasury Department regulations, which have not yet been issued.

7. The amount paid for room and board as QHEE cannot exceed (i) the allowance applicable to the beneficiary for room and board included in the "cost of attendance", as defined in section 472 of the Higher Education Act as in effect on June 7, 2001, as determined by the eligible educational institution for that period, or (ii) if greater, the actual invoice amount the beneficiary residing in housing owned or operated by the eligible educational institution is charged for room and board costs for that period. The room and board costs must be incurred during an academic period during which the student is enrolled or accepted for enrollment in a degree, certificate or other program (including a program of study abroad approved for credit by the eligible educational institution) that leads to a recognized educational credential awarded by an eligible educational institution. A student will be considered to be enrolled at least half-time if the student is enrolled for at least half the full-time academic workload for the course of study the student is pursuing as determined under the standards of the institution where the student is enrolled. The institution's standard for a full-time workload must equal or exceed a standard established by the Department of Education under the Higher Education Act.

Eligible educational institutions are defined by reference to Section 481 of the Higher Education Act of 1965 and will include any accredited post-secondary educational institutions offering credit toward a bachelor's degree, an associate's degree, a graduate or professional degree, or another recognized post-secondary credential. Certain proprietary institutions and post-secondary vocational institutions also are eligible institutions. The institution must be eligible to participate in Title IV U.S. federal financial aid programs. To determine if a particular institution has been assigned a federal school code by the Department of Education, and presumably eligible under section 529 as meeting these requirements, you may enter the name of an institution at the Department of Education's Web site at www.ed.gov/offices/OSFAP/Students/apply/search.html. You will find many foreign universities on the list. Some of the states have requested that the IRS provide an official listing of eligible educational institutions, but so far none has been published.

Can I claim the Hope or Lifetime Learning credit in the same year that I withdraw from my 529 account to pay for college?

Yes, the Hope or Lifetime Learning credit (see box below) can be claimed regardless of whether funds used for qualified tuition and related expenses come from a 529 account. However, in order to prevent "double-dipping", section 529 requires that QHEE incurred by the beneficiary be reduced by any of that beneficiary's expenses that were used to determine the Hope or Lifetime Learning credit. Unless you incur an amount of QHEE out of pocket (viz. not funded by 529 account distributions) that is at least equal to the amount of tuition and related expenses used in determining the Hope or Lifetime Learning credit, some portion of your 529 distribution will no longer be qualified and will become subject to income tax and the 10% penalty tax. (There may be a limited exception to the 10% penalty in these circumstances for the years 2002 and 2003 only, but the new law is not clear on this point.)

> *Example:* Eric is a second-year student in college who has his own 529 account. He withdraws $20,000 from the account during the

year to pay for all of his QHEE, including $8,000 in tuition. The entire $20,000 withdrawal would be tax-free, except that Eric claims the maximum $1,500 Hope credit against $2,000 of his tuition. He must reduce his $20,000 QHEE by $2,000, leaving $18,000. This means that $2,000 (or one-tenth) of his 529 withdrawal is no longer qualified. If we assume the earnings portion of the withdrawal is $5,000, then one-tenth of $5,000, or $500, is taxable to Eric as ordinary income and subject to a 10% additional tax. If Eric's marginal federal tax bracket is 15%, this amounts to $125 (including the penalty tax).

You may elect to waive the Hope and Lifetime Learning credit if you decide that the negative impact it has on 529 distributions is greater than the amount of credit. This will occur in a relatively small number of cases as the benefit of the credit will nearly always outweigh the tax and penalty on that portion of your 529 distributions.

Note that similar coordination rules apply to withdrawals from a Coverdell education savings account. Furthermore, if withdrawals are taken from both a Coverdell account and a 529 account in the same year for the same beneficiary, the QHEE must be divided between them for purposes of determining the amount of tax exclusion on the withdrawals from each type of account. See Chapter 9 for more information.

How about the new above-the-line deduction for qualified tuition and related expenses? Can I claim the deduction for expenses I pay using funds from my 529 account?

If you are eligible to claim the above-the-line deduction ("section 222 deduction") for up to $3,000 of qualified tuition and related expenses in 2002 and 2003—the maximum deduction increases to $4,000 in 2004 and 2005 before expiring—the use of your 529 account may affect the amount of deduction you can claim. The earnings portion of a 529 distribution used to pay qualified tuition and related expenses will reduce the amount that can be considered for the deduction. The IRS has not yet described how to allocate your 529 distributions between qualified tuition and related expenses, which reduce the total section 222 deductible amount, and other qualified higher education expenses such as books and room and board that are counted for section 529 purposes but not for section 222 purposes.

Note that a withdrawal from a Coverdell education savings account (see Chapter 9) works in the same way with respect to the section 222 deduction, except that the entire withdrawal used to pay for qualified tuition and related expenses, not just the earnings portion, reduces the section 222 deductible amount.

The Credits and Deduction for Tuition Payments

The 1997 tax law changes gave birth to two new credits, the Hope Scholarship credit and the Lifetime Learning credit, available to taxpayers with incomes below a certain level who incur qualified tuition and related expenses. The credits are nonrefundable and so the amount you claim cannot be greater than your tax liability excluding the credits. You may elect to claim the credits by attaching Form 8863 to your original or an amended federal income tax return. The 2001 tax law changes created an above-the-line deduction, the section 222 deduction, for the same category of expenses. The deduction is available to eligible taxpayers only for the years 2002 through 2005, but may not be claimed in any year you elect to claim the Hope or Lifetime Learning credit. The rules surrounding the Hope and Lifetime Learning credits were already complex; the introduction of a new and competing deduction will make tax planning and return preparation all the more difficult.

Hope Scholarship credit

The Hope credit is an amount equal to 100% of the first $1,000 of qualified tuition and related expenses paid by a taxpayer during the taxable year for the qualified educational expenses of a student during any academic period beginning in each taxable year, plus 50% of such expenses over $1,000, but the maximum credit is limited to $1,500 per year per student. This credit may be used only during two taxable years. It is not available for any taxable year if the student has completed two years of post-secondary education before the start of the taxable year. A student must be at least a half-time student for the Hope credit to be available with respect to a taxable year.

For purposes of this credit, the term "qualified tuition and related expenses" means tuition and fees required for the enrollment or attendance of (1) the taxpayer, (2) the taxpayer's spouse, or (3) any dependent of the taxpayer, at an eligible educational institution. Qualified expenses are reduced by tax-free scholarships and allowances.

Lifetime Learning credit

The Lifetime Learning credit for any taxpayer for any taxable year is an amount equal to 20% of up to $5,000 of the qualified tuition and related expenses paid by the taxpayer during the taxable year for education furnished during any academic period beginning in the taxable year. The $5,000 is increased to $10,000 for years beginning on or after January 1, 2003, increasing the maximum credit from $1,000 to $2,000. Qualified tuition and related expenses under the Lifetime Learning credit include expenses with respect to any course of instruction at an eligible educational institution to acquire or improve job skills of the individual. There is no limit to the number of years in which the Lifetime Learning credit can be claimed.

The same expenses cannot be used for both a Hope credit and a Lifetime Learning credit. Any expenses used in determining a Hope or Lifetime Learning credit will reduce total qualified higher education expenses used in calculating the tax exclusion for distributions from a 529 plan or Coverdell education savings account. Proper coordination and planning will maximize the benefits of these credits and exclusions over the course of a family's college years.

The Hope and Lifetime Learning credits are not available to taxpayers whose modified adjusted gross income (MAGI) exceeds specified levels. For single taxpayers, the credits are lost at $51,000 of MAGI in 2002, and for married taxpayers filing joint returns the credits are lost at $102,000. For single taxpayers with MAGI between $41,000 and $51,000, and for married taxpayers filing a joint return with MAGI between $82,000 and $102,000, a partial credit is available.

If you claim your child as a dependent, only you may claim the Hope credit or the Lifetime Learning credit with respect to your child's qualifying educational expenses. Your child may claim the credit if you do not claim the child as a dependent on your tax return. (An otherwise dependent child cannot claim a personal exemption, however, no matter what the parent decides to do about claiming the dependency exemption.)

Your ability to decide whether to claim your child as a dependent provides significant latitude. If your income falls above the limits, and your child has income below the limits, the child may derive a tax benefit from the credits when you cannot. You will lose the benefit of the dependency exemption, but some high-income parents are unable to derive full benefit from the dependency exemption anyway, due to the income phase-out of the exemption. In that case, you would make the easy decision to forego claiming your child as a dependent, and thereby allow her to apply the education credit against her tax liability.

The section 222 tuition deduction

Beginning in 2002, an eligible taxpayer may claim an above-the-line deduction for a limited amount of qualified tuition and related expenses. These are the same expenses that qualify for the Hope and Lifetime Learning credits. However, the benefits are mutually exclusive. You may not claim the deduction for yourself or your dependent student in any year in which you or that student claim the Hope or Lifetime Learning credit.

To be eligible for the deduction, you must not be a married individual filing separately or the dependent of another individual, and your MAGI must be below a certain level. If your MAGI is $65,000 or less ($130,000 or less on a joint return), you may deduct up to $3,000 in qualified tuition and related expenses in 2002 and 2003, and up to $4,000 in 2004 and 2005. If your MAGI exceeds $65,000/$130,000 but does not exceed $80,000 ($160,000 on a joint return), you may deduct up to $2,000 in qualified tuition and related expenses in 2004 and 2005 only.

Your total qualified tuition and related expenses must be reduced by the earnings portion of distributions from a 529 plan, and the entire withdrawals from a Coverdell education savings account, that are used to pay for such expenses. They are also reduced by any expenses used for the education savings bond exclusion (see Chapter 10).

What are the federal gift and estate tax rules under section 529?

Section 529 prescribes that the contribution to a 529 plan account is a completed gift for estate and gift tax purposes. The gift is from the individual contributor to the designated beneficiary (assuming the contributor and beneficiary are not the same person). This rule applies despite the fact that the account owner retains ownership rights which would otherwise cause the assets to remain in his or her estate. A further advantage is that the funding of the account is treated as the gift of a present interest qualifying for the annual $11,000 gift tax exclusion. Finally, section 529 provides that the contributor may elect to treat the gift as occurring ratably over a five-year period, so that the $11,000 exclusion can be leveraged to as much as $55,000 in a year. Chapter 8 describes these rules in more detail.

Can I change the beneficiary of my 529 account?

Section 529 allows the account owner to replace the current designated beneficiary with a new beneficiary who is a "member of the family" (see box below). All 529 plans accommodate a change in beneficiary without imposing a penalty, although some may have age or residency restrictions, and some may charge a fee. There are no federal income tax consequences of a beneficiary change; however, there can be gift tax consequences when the new beneficiary is at least one generation below the old beneficiary, as discussed in Chapter 8.

Can I transfer my account from one state's 529 plan to another state's 529 plan?

A qualifying rollover will not be treated as a distribution for purposes of federal income tax. A transfer of assets from an account for a particular beneficiary in one state's 529 plan to an account in another state's 529 plan for the same beneficiary is a qualifying rollover, but only if no such rollover had taken place during the previous 12 months. There is no limit on the frequency of rollovers, however, where the beneficiary is replaced with a qualifying member of the family. A rollover can be transacted either through a direct "trustee-to-trustee" transfer (program permitting), or by a withdrawal of funds followed by the contribution of equivalent funds within 60 days to a different 529 plan. Be sure to find out how the 529 plan you are investigating handles rollover requests, as there may be restrictions imposed by the program. Many prepaid programs will treat such a request as a cancellation of the contract.

Member of the Family

For purposes of changing beneficiaries, or transferring assets to an account for a new beneficiary, "member of the family" means an individual who has one of the following relationships to the current beneficiary:

+ A son or daughter (natural or legally adopted), or a descendant of either;
+ A stepson or stepdaughter;
+ A brother or sister (by whole or halfblood), or step-brother or stepsister;
+ The father or mother, or an ancestor of either;
+ A stepfather or stepmother;
+ A niece or nephew;
+ An aunt or uncle;
+ A son-in-law, daughter-in-law, father-in-law, mother-in-law, brother-in-law, or sister-in-law; or
+ The spouse of the designated beneficiary (who must be a member of the same household and have the same principal place of abode) or the spouse of any of the relatives listed above (who must be a member of the same household and have the same principal place of abode).
+ A first cousin (added by EGTRRA)

Can a corporation or trust be the owner of a 529 account?

Yes, section 529 refers to a "person", defined under section 7701 of the Code as an individual, a trust, estate, partnership, association, company or corporation. Many 529 plans do permit legal entities to establish accounts, although some do not. There will be special tax considerations whenever a non-individual taxpayer is account owner, and some of the issues surrounding entity ownership have not been fully explored or tested. For corporations, the compensation rules (Code section 83) must be considered, and perhaps also the anti-tax shelter provisions. For certain trusts, the effect of 529 plan distributions on "distributable net income" has to be determined. Your attorney and accountant should be consulted in these matters.

Can I transfer the ownership of my account to someone else?

There is nothing contained within section 529 prohibiting or regulating a transfer of account ownership. It is up to the individual 529 plan to provide rules concerning transfer of account ownership. Some programs will accommodate a request to transfer account ownership while others expressly prohibit such transfers prior to the owner's death or legal incapacity. The mere transfer of ownership appears to have no federal income, gift, or estate tax consequences. However, a new account owner will generally have all rights associated with original ownership including the power to revoke the account.

What happens to my account if I die?

The death of the account owner does not cause a 529 account to terminate. Instead, all rights of ownership and control over the account are passed to a successor account owner. The identity of the successor owner depends on the rules of the program and state law. Most 529 plans now permit you to name a successor owner on the account application or upon later submission to the program administrator. The program rules may specify the account owner in other situations, i.e. you fail to name a successor account owner, or the person you name as successor declines the appointment or predeceases you. For example, the rules of the 529 plan may specify that, in the absence of a named successor, the beneficiary of the 529 account will become account owner unless the beneficiary is a minor, in which case the beneficiary's living parent or guardian will become account owner. In any situation where there is no clear successor under the terms of your account or the rules of the program, ownership will pass according to your will or your state's laws of intestacy. If you live in a state with a community property law, you should consult with your attorney regarding the treatment of your 529 account.

FOUR

Financial Aid Considerations

Before going any further, we turn our attention to one of the most significant concerns that many parents will face in their consideration of 529 plans. This concern relates to the financial aid process and the impact of a 529 account on financial aid awards. Although the rules in this area remain somewhat uncertain, recent guidance from the U.S. Department of Education helps define how college financial aid administrators should be treating 529 plans in the federal financial aid application process.

In short, saving for college with a 529 plan will impact a student's financial aid eligibility, although the precise effect will depend on the type of 529 plan and the policies of the institution. Of course, saving for college through other means can have a negative impact as well, in many cases worse than a 529 plan. This process is explained below.

The authorization for federal financial aid comes from Title IV of the Higher Education Act of 1965, as amended (HEA). Most educational institutions will attempt to meet a student's financial need with a financial aid package that may combine grants, work-study, and loans. A student's financial need is determined by the institution as the difference between that particular institution's cost of attendance (COA)[1] and the student's expected family contribution (EFC). The expected family contribution represents the amount the family can be expected to contribute towards a student's college costs based on its particular financial situation.

The EFC is calculated based on data submitted to the Education Department on a form known as the Free Application for Federal Student Aid (FAFSA). The FAFSA is filed by high school seniors after January 1 in their final year of high school. In subsequent college years, the student files an abbreviated Renewal FAFSA. Under the EFC formula, 50% of the student's income (less an income protection allowance of $2,330 and allowances for federal, state, and social security taxes), and 35% of the student's assets are assumed to be available to pay for college costs.

For dependent students the formula also assumes that between 22% and 47% of the parents' income and at most 5.6% of the parents' assets are available to pay for college costs. The parents' income is reduced for this purpose by tax allowances and a maximum $3,000 employment expense allowance. The formula also provides "protection allowances", one for parental income based on the household census, and one for assets based on whether there is one parent or two and on the age of the older parent. For example, the asset protection allowance for two parents with the oldest being 45 is $38,600, and this figure increases with age. The income protection allowance for the parents in a family with two dependent children, one of whom is in college, is $20,320.

Parental contribution to EFC is pro-rated to each member of the family attending college in the upcoming year. This pro-ration can have a dramatic effect and many families that would not qualify for financial aid if there were one student in college may find that they do qualify for aid when they have two children in college at the same time.

The FAFSA is based largely on income as reported on the student's and parents' tax returns for the year prior to the year in which the student enters college (e.g., 2001 tax return for students enrolling in Fall 2002),

---

1. COA includes tuition, fees, room and board, books, supplies, transportation, and personal expenses. Some institutions will choose not to include transportation and personal expenses in the COA figure.

along with asset values as of the date on which the form is filed. The EFC is automatically zero for a dependent student with parents who earn less than $13,000 and where the student and parents are eligible to file Form 1040A or 1040EZ, or where they are not required to file any income tax return.

There is a separate formula for independent students without dependents, and another for independent students with dependents. A student is automatically considered independent if he or she is 23 years old, a veteran of the armed forces, a master's or doctoral candidate, married, or declared independent by a court, or if he or she has legal dependents other than a spouse. Parental assets and income are not considered in the need analysis for these students. The Department of Education maintains an extensive library of publications and other materials relating to federal financial aid on the Web at www.ed.gov.

Does all need-based aid come from the federal government?

No, most of the states also have need-based grant programs. Many of these programs use the federal methodology while others use state-developed criteria. In some states, the determination of student eligibility for state-funded programs does not count balances in the state's own 529 plan. This can be an attractive incentive.

There are also many institutions, primarily private colleges, providing substantial amounts of gift-aid out of their own endowments and other funds. A large number of these colleges utilize an alternative approach in determining need known as the "institutional methodology", developed by the College Board and administered by its affiliate College Scholarship Service (CSS). In order to apply for grants at colleges that use the institutional methodology, a student must complete an application called the PROFILE. The PROFILE is similar to the FAFSA in that it follows the same general approach and is used to compute the applicant's expected family contribution. But there are also many differences, some of which are significant. For example, the PROFILE application requires information about equity of the home and family farm, which are exempt assets under the federal methodology. It will also provide information to the financial aid administrator about any retirement accounts owned by the student. The rest of this chapter focuses primarily on the federal methodology, not the institutional methodology; as you read through it you should keep in mind that the treatment of 529 plans can differ. In fact, under recent changes, the PROFILE makes no distinction between 529 prepaid programs and 529 savings programs. Under the institutional methodology, both types are considered an asset of the parent in the calculation of EFC.

Does the federal methodology distinguish between section 529 prepaid tuition programs and savings programs?

Yes, despite the fact that both types of 529 plans receive the same federal income tax treatment, they are treated very differently for purposes of federal financial aid.

Presently there is significant concern regarding the treatment of prepaid programs because the HEA specifically provides that "prepaid tuition plans shall reduce the cost of attendance by the amount of pre-payment." This means that the value of a prepaid tuition contract is not included as an asset on FAFSA forms, but any payments made from a prepaid program for a student's tuition and other expenses are treated as an additional "resource", or as a reduction in the cost of attendance, in the same manner as a scholarship or a grandparent's direct payment of tuition. They reduce a student's financial need, and thus financial aid, on a dollar-for-dollar basis. Beneficiaries should inform the institution they wish to attend that they have prepaid tuition contracts and indicate the amount of the contract benefits to be paid out.[2] Even if not informed of the existence of a prepaid tuition contract, the institution will discover it when it receives payment from the program, and will make adjustments to the student's aid award.

Many financial planners will find fault with the programs offering prepaid tuition contracts for not warning the purchaser more fully about

---

2. Some administrators in prepaid plan states may interpret the federal rules as requiring that the total contract value (not just current year benefits) be counted as a resource. This would reduce the student's eligibility to an even greater extent.

the financial aid implications of such a contract. In many cases where the program enrollment materials fail to provide detailed explanation of this issue, the criticism appears justified. However, it should also be kept in mind that some financial aid programs may not be impacted. For instance, a prepaid tuition contract will not affect eligibility for a federal Pell grant or most state grants, and a federal subsidized Stafford loan (subject to certain limits) will be available to the extent the contract does not cover the "unmet" financial need of the student. But a prepaid tuition contract will reduce the chance of receiving work-study, a federal Perkins loan, or a Federal Supplemental Educational Opportunity Grant (FSEOG) (see definitions at the end of this chapter).

The federal financial aid treatment of assets in a 529 savings program works out much better for most families. The Education Department takes the position that the account is an asset of the account owner. If the account owner is the student's parent, the value of the account will be assessed at a maximum 5.6% rate, and if the account owner is the grandparent or some other relative it will not be assessed at all on the asset side of the EFC equation.

Note that assets are not considered at all if the family qualifies for the "simplified EFC formula." In order to qualify for this beneficial treatment, the dependent student and parents must have adjusted gross income less than $50,000 and meet all of the requirements to be eligible to file Form 1040A or 1040EZ (rather than Form 1040). For a family that might qualify, a 529 savings program may actually be a preferred type of investment for this purpose, since it will never result in the reporting of capital gains. If a student or parent were to invest in mutual funds or other securities, and then sell shares requiring Schedule D reporting, the family would automatically be disqualified from using the simplified EFC formula.

Aren't the distributions from a 529 plan included as "income" when calculating a student's financial aid eligibility?

That was certainly the case for qualified distributions from a savings program before 2002 when the earnings portion was included in the student's adjusted gross income, and so would count as student income. These earnings would be picked up on the following year's FAFSA and assessed at a rate of 50% if they exceeded certain allowances.

We have no word yet from the Education Department as to how tax-free distributions from a 529 savings program in 2002 and later years will be treated under the federal methodology. Some authorities have speculated that they will not figure at all in the determination of EFC. Others believe the entire amount withdrawal, including principal, will count as income. It seems more likely, however, that the Education Department will require an adjustment for the earning portion only, similar to the adjustment for tax-exempt municipal bond interest.

The earnings portion of distributions from a prepaid program should be excluded from student income in computing EFC in any case, considering that the benefits already reduce aid eligibility on a dollar for dollar basis. Whether aid applicants, and financial aid administrators, actually know enough about the interaction of tax law and federal financial aid to make the appropriate adjustments may be a different issue.

Does it make sense that prepaid programs and savings programs are treated so differently?

One certainly has to wonder why the Education Department has made such a sharp distinction between prepaid programs and savings programs, and whether the distinction is workable. As mentioned earlier, institutions using the "institutional methodology" for purposes of awarding private aid no longer make this distinction. And the fact of the matter is that prepaid programs and savings programs are not all that different. In some states the 529 plan is actually a hybrid containing features of both.

For example, the tuition unit programs in Pennsylvania and Ohio that in the past were classified as prepaid programs are now labeled "guaranteed savings" programs. By changing its name, Pennsylvania program authorities expect that their participants will be entitled to favorable financial aid treatment. They appear to be justified in claiming savings-program status (and so might some other unit plans that have not yet adopted the "guaranteed savings" label). The units are redeemed in a manner similar to savings programs, except that the valuation is based on an index of average tuition prices rather than underlying stock and bond funds.

Obviously, a family with little in the way of financial resources may want to think twice before committing scarce dollars to a prepaid tuition contract. A 529 savings program may be preferable for this purpose (unless the applicant may be eligible for a Pell grant).

How does a 529 savings account compare to other investment alternatives?

A 529 savings program is also treated more favorably than some other college investment alternatives. Many families discover too late that the transfer of investment assets to a child's UTMA or UGMA account in an effort to save income taxes will have negative financial aid consequences since student assets are assessed much more heavily than parental assets. A family using the Coverdell education savings account will face the same problem. The Education Department has indicated that a Coverdell account is considered an asset belonging to the student and that withdrawals must be added to the student's income in the EFC calculation (See Chapter 9 for a discussion of the Coverdell account).

Even a traditional or Roth IRA may have negative financial aid consequences to the unsuspecting family. Qualified retirement accounts are excluded from the asset side of the EFC computation and, as discussed in Chapter 11, penalty-free withdrawals from an IRA may now be taken to pay for college. The problem is that, like the Coverdell, the entire withdrawal is added to the parents' income in the EFC calculation. Compare this to 529 plans in which currently only the earnings portion of withdrawals, not the principal, is added to the student's income.

Families that desire to save for college with 529 plans should also realize that they can undertake strategies that will reduce or eliminate any negative impact the investment might have on financial aid availability. The choice of designated beneficiary and the decision of when and how to take withdrawals (qualified or non-qualified) could make a significant difference. For further discussion of this, see Chapter 12, Managing The 529 Account.

Some institutions have indicated that accounts in 529 savings programs would be given added weight in the packaging of a student's financial aid award, despite the position of the Education Department. Institutions have significant latitude in this area because the Higher Education Act specifically prohibits the Education Department from prescribing regulations to carry out the need analysis provisions in the law.

The good news for interested parents is that the treatment of 529 plans in the federal financial aid formula may improve in the future. There is a significant effort on the part of the states to have the Higher Education Act amended to treat all 529 plan accounts, both prepaid programs and savings programs, in a favorable manner. As justification, they point to the fact that federal financial aid policies currently favor borrowing (your *future* income escapes assessment in determining EFC) over saving. Such a change was not made as part of the most recent reauthorization of the Higher Education Act that was signed by former President Clinton on October 7, 1998. However, Congress and the Education Department are constantly making changes and interpretations to the rules surrounding federal financial aid programs and the new political correctness bestowed on college savings programs may bring about even better treatment before too long.

Of course, many families will not expect to qualify for financial aid regardless of who is credited with the assets and income. For them, the financial aid implications of a 529 plan will be of little concern. Others who would qualify for financial aid may discover that only non-gift aid, such as loans and work-study, are affected by an investment in a 529 plan and are so their level of concern is reduced as well.

Federally-Funded Student Aid

Federal Pell Grants—Non-discretionary grants. Up to $3,750 per year given to applicants with an "expected family contribution" of less than $3,501 (2001–2002 award year).

Federal Supplemental Educational Opportunity Grants (FSEOG)—Up to $4,000 per year allocated by the institution to students with financial need.

Federal Stafford Loans—Low interest loans directly from the government (Federal Direct Loan Program), or guaranteed by the government (Federal Family Education Loan Program), available to all students for the cost of attendance. Limited interest subsidy is available to students determined to have financial need.

Federal PLUS Loans—Similar to Stafford, but made to creditworthy parents of students.

Federal Perkins Loans—Up to $4,000 per year ($6,000 for graduate study) of 5%-interest loans allocated by the institution on the basis of financial need.

Federal Work-Study (FWS)—Funds provided by government for institution's part-time employment of students with financial need.

FIVE

Prepaid vs. Savings

There are two general categories of 529 plans: prepaid programs and savings programs. Which category does the program in your state belong to? Although this seems like a basic question that should have an easy answer, in actuality it's not. A 529 plan can have features that are common to both prepaid and savings programs. It can act like a prepaid program under some conditions, and like a savings program under different conditions. It may even be paired with a program of a different type, but marketed to the public as a single program with different options.

What is a prepaid program?

A prepaid program is one involving the purchase of tuition credits or certificates that entitle the beneficiary to a waiver or payment of future qualifying college costs. In essence, future tuition is being purchased today, at today's prices.

There are two basic types of prepaid programs. The most prevalent is the "contract" program. In return for your upfront cash payment, or your commitment to a series of cash payments, you receive a promise from the program that it will pay a pre-determined amount of future tuition and mandatory fees at public colleges, universities, or community colleges located in the state. The contract may cover anywhere from one semester to five years, depending on what options are offered by the program and the amount of tuition you wish to purchase. If your beneficiary attends a private or out-of-state school, the program will determine the value of your contract under a pre-set formula and make payments in an amount not to exceed that value.

The other type of prepaid program is actually a prepaid/savings hybrid that is sometimes referred to as a "unit" plan. It typically involves the purchase of tuition units or credits that represent a fraction (e.g. 1%) of the average yearly tuition and fees at public institutions in the state. These units change in value each year as average tuition and fees increases. They are redeemed in the future to pay for tuition and fees, and in most cases, they can be redeemed for other qualified expenses as well (room and board, books, supplies, and equipment).

A contract-type prepaid program is like a futures contract; the unit-type prepaid program is like an index fund (the index being average tuition at selected schools). Both types rely on the program trust fund (made up of participant payments or contributions) to generate an investment return sufficient to cover the program's liability for future tuition payments and unit redemptions.

Which general category of 529 plan the unit-type prepaid program falls into—prepaid or savings—is a matter of debate. The reason it makes a difference is because prepaid programs and savings programs are treated differently in determining student eligibility for federal financial aid (see Chapter 4). Pennsylvania recently reconfigured its 529 plan, TAP, in an effort to secure more favorable financial aid treatment for its participants. Previously recognized as a unit-type prepaid program, TAP is now characterized as a "guaranteed savings" program. Similarly, Ohio has repositioned its unit-type prepaid program (the oldest such program in the country) as the Guaranteed Savings option alongside the more conventional investment options in its CollegeAdvantage Savings Plan. Colorado, Tennessee, and Washington have unit programs that have not yet adopted the "guaranteed savings" label, but perhaps should do so. Massachusetts has the U.Plan, a unit program with unique features (and the only program included in this book that does not qualify as a 529 plan).

What is a savings program?

A 529 savings program is a more familiar type of tax-deferred investment, in many ways similar to a variable annuity or an individual retirement account. Contributions are made to a trust fund that is invested in mutual funds and other financial instruments. The idea is that your account will grow in value over time to keep up with, or preferably surpass, the increasing price of a college education.

Before Congress enacted Internal Revenue Code section 529 in 1996, the only state with a pure savings program was Kentucky. Other states had designed their programs as prepaid (or hybrid). Since the 1996 law change, a majority of the new 529 plans are savings programs. There appear to be a couple of reasons for this phenomenon. One reason is that most of the savings programs offer the potential for higher investment returns than prepaid or guaranteed savings programs. Accounts are usually invested in equity and bond mutual funds that have historically outpaced the increases in college expenses.

Another reason is that savings programs are easier and cheaper for a state to administer, especially when the outside vendor that handles the investments also agrees to handle much of the program administration and marketing. Recently, several states have launched new or redesigned programs in which the program fund is charged a fee that is shared by the program manager and the state treasury, in effect making the program a source of revenue for the state.

What are the major differences between prepaid and savings programs?

The type of 529 plan being considered is important, because there are significant differences between them. Most people evaluating alternative 529 plans will, quite naturally, focus attention on the investment aspects of the programs being considered. After all, we all want our investments to do as well as possible. Historically, over long periods of time, stocks have out-performed other types of investments, and certain types of common stocks have done better than others. On the other hand, stocks generally carry more investment risk than most other types of investments.

Nearly all 529 plans, of either variety, employ professional invest-ment managers to maximize potential return within a certain level of risk. In a savings program, the investment management is applied directly to the assets in a participant's account. In a prepaid or guaranteed savings program, the investment management is applied to the program fund to ensure that the obligation of the 529 plan to pay for future tuition or unit redemptions is adequately covered. Because a participant will have no choice in the 529 plan's selection of an investment manager, the partici-pant must rely on the judgment of program officials.

While most savings programs have the advantage of unlimited upside investment potential, prepaid and guaranteed savings programs have the advantage of keeping up with inflation of college expenses, no matter how high those costs may go.[1] A risk-tolerant saver may be more attracted to the savings program while a risk-averse saver may be more attracted to the prepaid or guaranteed savings program.

Following is a list of some of the major differences:

1) Prepaid programs (with the possible exception of the unit-type or guaranteed savings programs) are currently at a disadvantage when applying for federal financial aid programs. The financial need of a family is reduced dollar-for-dollar by amounts being paid for through the pro-gram. With a savings program, under current rules, the account value is generally considered an asset of the parent (a maximum of 5.6% of the account value is deemed available to pay for the cost of attendance) or other account owner. See Chapter 4.

2) Many prepaid programs have a specified enrollment period each year. Prepayment contracts must be purchased during the enrollment period, and the price of a contract is adjusted each year when the new

---

1. However, inflation that outstrips the investment returns of the fund assets in the prepaid program may jeopardize its solvency.

enrollment period begins. The savings programs do not have restricted enrollment periods and accept new accounts and contributions at any time.

3) Almost all prepaid programs require that either the account owner or the beneficiary be a resident of the state sponsoring the program. The vast majority of savings programs, however, are open to residents of any state. Any family considering investing in a 529 plan should evaluate the program in the state where the donor lives, the state where the designated beneficiary lives, and any state with a 529 plan that does not have residency requirements.

4) Most prepayment contracts are of limited duration. For example, the program may specify that the contract will be terminated, and a refund made, if the benefits are not used within 10 years after the beneficiary's normal college matriculation date. Most savings programs, however, have no program-imposed limit on account duration, and can remain open indefinitely as long as there is a designated beneficiary on the account.

5) Most contract-type prepaid programs provide only for undergraduate tuition and fees, while savings programs and unit-type programs can generally be used for any costs that meet the definition of "qualified higher education expense" under the federal tax law, including graduate school. This can be a significant limitation for students at most public institutions where tuition and fees comprise less than 50% of the student's total cost of attendance.

6) All 529 plans allow withdrawals to pay for out-of-state colleges and universities. However, contract-type prepaid programs are tailored to the child who will eventually be enrolling at an in-state public institution. For the beneficiary of a prepayment contract who attends an in-state private school, or an out-of-state school, the contract benefits must be valued before payments can be made. A common approach used by these 529 plans is to use the weighted average of credit hour value of in-state public universities. However, there are some prepaid programs that compute a value by adding a low fixed rate of interest to the original contributions into the account. Also, most of these programs will limit the benefits paid to private and out-of-state institutions to the lesser of actual tuition and fees or the value of in-state tuition and fees. This

means that a participant who moves out-of-state and then attends a public university in the new state will not get a refund if the new state has lower in-state tuition than the old state. In this situation, the owner of the contract should evaluate if the best option is to simply cancel the contract and obtain a refund. The choice of college is not an issue in most savings and unit-type prepaid programs because beneficiaries receive the same return whether they attend an in-state public, in-state private, or out-of-state school.

7) Even if the beneficiary chooses to enroll in an in-state public institution, the investment return on a prepayment contract will often depend on which particular institution is attended and how many credit hours are taken. A student attending the most expensive public university in the state, and taking the maximum number of credit hours covered under the contract, receives a better deal than the student who attends the least expensive university or takes fewer credit hours than the contract will pay for. In some states, the range of public tuition can be very wide. The ultimate choice of school does not have an impact on the investment return in a savings or unit-type program.

8) Most prepaid programs will make payments directly to the institution after receiving the bills from the contract holder. The savings programs generally permit cash withdrawals by the account owner or beneficiary, although in many cases requiring documentation as to the use of funds for qualified higher education expenses.

9) Prepaid programs seem to have more transaction fees than most savings programs. Perhaps this is because prepaid programs are more difficult to administer, or because they are operated by state agencies that are accustomed to imposing fees. All 529 plans will list the fees charged to participants including fees for enrollment, annual maintenance, and change of beneficiary or account owner. The savings programs compete more directly with other investment alternatives available to the college saver, and seem more intent on keeping fees and transaction charges to a minimum.

10) Some prepaid programs will require a minimum purchase of at least one semester's worth of tuition, but will allow payments to be made over time. The installment payments include an interest component,

although the full payments are credited to the investment in the account and none of the extra payment is treated as interest expense for income tax purposes. Savings programs do not work this way and simply credit the account whenever a contribution is received.

11) Prepaid programs, including the unit-type and guaranteed savings programs, make educated guesses (otherwise known as actuarial assumptions) about the future performance of the program trust fund. Actuarial assumptions concerning the investment return on fund assets, the future benefits to be paid by the program, the number of refunds, and other relevant factors are used to calculate the liability for future payouts. The bull market of the 1990s enabled the older prepaid programs to build large fund surpluses. These surpluses are maintained as "reserves" against future investment shortfalls, although one has to wonder how large a surplus has to be before steps are taken to use it to subsidize the cost of prepaid tuition contracts, establish a scholarship program, make grants to the public university system, or for any other purpose. Some programs are permitted to allocate excess reserves to participant accounts, while others are prohibited from doing so. (Pennsylvania's TAP program made a $4.3 million allocation of surplus to participant accounts in 1998, and will do so again in the future if reserves grow beyond the amount necessary for program stability). On the other hand, newer prepaid programs have not had time to build up these reserves and could find themselves in financial difficulty in a sustained bear market and/or a period of spiraling public tuition.

12) Some prepaid programs and unit-type programs are backed by the full faith and credit of the state, providing a safety net for participants in the event that the program fund becomes insolvent due to low investment returns and/or rapidly increasing tuition levels. Some other programs do not have this guarantee, but require that the state legislature consider an appropriation to the program if it runs into financial difficulties. Still others have no backing or guarantees from the state whatsoever. Savings programs typically have no state guarantee, and should have no reason to need one. (New Jersey is unique with its "moral obligation" to participants in its savings program that they do not lose money through their participation in the program.)

It is reasonable to expect that over time we will see further blurring of the lines that distinguish prepaid and savings programs. We are already beginning to see savings programs offering some of the inflation-protection features normally associated with prepaid programs, including guaranteed investment options. At the same time, many prepaid programs are becoming more flexible and investment-oriented. It may be difficult to achieve, but there is no reason why the best features of each type of 529 plan cannot be successfully incorporated into a single program. In fact, the best defense the states have against the possible "federalization" of 529 plans is to do just that.

SIX

What to Look for in a 529 Plan: A Checklist

Beyond the basic characteristics of the two types of 529 plans described in the previous chapter, there are numerous differences in program design among the various 529 plans in operation today. The task of sorting through all the choices can be somewhat daunting. Just understanding how the 529 plan in your home state works is difficult enough—shopping among competing 529 plans becomes extremely confusing.

The analysis should not merely involve a comparison of the particular investments or tuition guarantees being offered by the programs. Many other aspects of the operation of each 529 plan need to be considered. Your own family circumstances, investment objectives, risk tolerance, and financial knowledge will all play a large part in selecting an appropriate 529 plan. The "best" 529 plan for one family is not necessarily the best one for another.

How do you go about this selection process? Reading through this book (and checking our web site at www.savingforcollege.com) is certainly a good first step. Then be sure to obtain the program materials for your own state's 529 plan. Finally, request packets from the other states that have programs of interest to you and that will allow you to participate as a nonresident.

Many individual investors rely on a professional financial planner or investment adviser in developing, implementing, and monitoring an investment plan. Before 2001, there were few financial professionals with the knowledge, experience, and interest in 529 plans to be of much help to you in this regard. This situation has changed dramatically in the last two years as professionals have awakened to the benefits of 529 plans for their clients, and many programs have been adapted for distribution through advisers.

Whether you choose to use an investment adviser, or conduct the search on your own, you should learn as much as you can about the programs you are interested in. Here are the primary information sources that may or may not be included in the materials provided to you:

State statute—every state with a 529 plan will have a law on the books authorizing the program. Sometimes there is more than one section of the law involved, e.g., when special state tax treatment is provided for participants in the 529 plan.

Program rules—usually there is a state agency or program board charged with the responsibility of implementing and overseeing the operation of the program and acting as trustee of the program trust fund. The agency will develop the official rules of the program as allowed by the statute. These rules are extremely important because they contain all of the operational details of the program. The rules are prone to frequent change, however, and so it is important to be sure that the rules you are reading are the most current version.

Program description—many programs will provide an extensive explanatory booklet that attempts to present the rules in a more understandable manner. The program description will also explain the tax treatment of 529 plan accounts and will contain appropriate disclaimers.

Investment prospectuses—if a 529 savings plan uses mutual funds, it may send you the prospectuses for those funds. These are the same SEC-registered prospectuses that any investor would receive and so are not particular to the 529 plan. Note that the 529 plan itself is not required to produce a prospectus because securities laws treat interests in a 529 plan as "municipal securities" exempt from SEC registration requirements.

Program booklet—typically an attractive, glossy marketing piece that contains a lot of pictures of cute children and summarizes the key advantages of the program. This is often presented in a helpful FAQ (frequently asked questions) format. An enrollment/application form will be provided with the program booklet.

Web site—every 529 plan has a Web site. The Internet has become an extremely important and useful way to convey information and is perfectly suited to these programs. The best Web sites will make available all the materials provided in the enrollment packet, plus links to other higher education information: financial aid programs, colleges & universities, and college cost calculators. Some programs will even allow you to enroll directly through the Internet.

The remainder of this chapter describes many of the ways in which 529 plans may differ from one another, and suggests an approach for comparing the various programs. This approach takes the form of a three-step process:

Step 1: Eliminate from consideration any 529 plans that clearly fall outside your criteria for acceptability, as well as those that will not accept you (due to eligibility restrictions).

Step 2: From the remaining 529 plans, select those with investment or tuition prepayment programs that appear to offer the greatest benefits to you. In each case, ask yourself the question "If I contribute a dollar to this program, what can I expect that dollar to produce by the time my beneficiary is ready for college?" Your own investment objectives, future college plans, and risk tolerance will play a part here. Be sure to take into consideration the level of fees and expenses, as well as any state tax benefits offered (or forfeited) or other "perks" offered by the plans.

Step 3: Make your final selection based on a comparison of the restrictive features in the programs. Some restrictions will be relevant to your decision, while others will not be relevant. That is up to you to determine. You should also note that at least to some degree, you can nullify a restriction through the use of multiple 529 plans, or through a future rollover to another 529 plan.

How much time will you need to complete this three-step process? It could be a lot, depending on how many possibilities you wish to explore. There are so many 529 plans to choose from and they differ in so many ways that your beneficiary could be graduated from college before you finally complete the exercise. That would not be a good thing. The tools available in this book—the checklist below and the program descriptions contained in Part II—along with the online tools and information available at www.savingforcollege.com, can help shortcut the process.

Before making any final decisions, however, you should read and understand the official program materials of the 529 plans you are most interested in. You should feel free to contact the program administrators to obtain further explanation and clarification. For some important items (e.g., legal and tax questions) you should also consider having a conversation with your attorney, accountant, or other professional adviser. The importance of a thorough due diligence process cannot be overstated because it can greatly reduce the chances of being surprised or disappointed later on.

The checklist below is presented in three sections. It is organized in this manner so that you may more easily identify the 529 plans that are in the best position to meet your needs. You may find it useful to revisit this checklist occasionally as 529 plans are constantly making changes (usually improvements) to their program rules and investment options.

The first section describes "conditional criteria"—eligibility or use requirements that either the program or the program-seeker may impose when determining program suitability. These criteria will not be shared by everyone.

Section 1: Conditional criteria

1) Are there any state residency requirements?
2) What are the other eligibility requirements?
3) Can the account owner and beneficiary be the same person?
4) How does the program handle funds coming from an existing UTMA or UGMA investment account?
5) Will the program accept a corporation or trust as account owner?

6) Are interests in the 529 plan being sold through brokers?

7) What is the minimum contribution?

8) Does the program accept contributions through payroll deduction and/or electronic funds transfer from your checking or savings account?

9) Will your use of the program create any state-level gift or inheritance tax concerns?

10) Does the program participate in Upromise or other affinity programs?

11) Does the program place any restrictions on your ownership rights or give any of these rights to the beneficiary?

12) Is an account in the program protected from the claims of creditors under state law?

13) Can a non-owner make contributions to an account in the program?

14) Does the program permit the account owner to designate a successor owner?

15) How complete and accurate are the program disclosures?

16) How does the program report account activity to its participants?

17) Has the program received a determination from the IRS that it qualifies under section 529 as a "qualified tuition program"?

18) What expenses are covered by the program?

19) How does the program deal with your desire to rollover to another state's 529 plan?

The second section describes "investment suitability criteria"—an evaluation of the investment characteristics of the program in order to determine which programs best meet your college savings objectives. Note that questions 39 through 43 pertain only to prepaid programs.

Section 2: Investment suitability criteria

20) Does the program offer a college savings strategy consistent with your own objectives and preferences?

21) Does the program provide a "guarantee" that your investment will keep up with the increasing costs of college?

22) Does the savings program offer an "age-based" asset allocation strategy, a menu of "static" portfolios, or both?

23) Does the program offer a principal-protected option?

24) What are the other characteristics of the underlying securities in the options available under the savings program?

25) Does the program permit contributions to be allocated among multiple options?

26) Does the program permit you to switch between investment options as described in IRS Notice 2001–55?

27) How quickly does the program invest your contribution?

28) How are earnings in the portfolio credited to your account?

29) Does the program charge an enrollment fee?

30) Does the program charge an annual account maintenance fee?

31) What is the program's expense ratio?

32) Are there charges for other transactions?

33) Can you claim a state income tax deduction for any or all of your contributions to the program?

34) Does the program offer any other financial incentives?

35) How will an account in the program affect the beneficiary's eligibility for need-based financial aid?

36) What is the term of the program manager?

37) How popular is the program?

38) Does the program rely on a state subsidy?

39) How much will your prepayment contract be worth at the college your beneficiary ends up attending?

40) How much will be refunded to you if you cancel your prepayment contract?

41) What is the cost of the prepayment contract?

42) Is the "tuition guarantee" backed by the full faith and credit of the state?

43) Will the program allocate investment surpluses to participant accounts?

The third section describes "manageable restrictions"—restrictions or hazards that may be evident in a program but are avoidable through a timely rollover to another 529 plan without those particular concerns. The wide availability of rollovers means an unacceptable provision in any particular program should not necessarily take it out of contention. You simply have to manage the account and make the rollover at the appropriate time.

Section 3: Manageable restrictions

44) Are there any penalties or fees for withdrawing your money from the program?

45) Are qualified withdrawals from the program exempt from your state's income tax?

46) Are there any time or age limits on the use of the account?
47) Is there a minimum time period before taking qualified or non-qualified withdrawals from your account in the program?
48) Are there any other withdrawal restrictions in the program that can be avoided by first rolling over to another 529 plan that does not have those restrictions?
49) Will the program approve a request to transfer ownership of the account?
50) How much can be contributed to an account in the program?

1) Are there any state residency requirements?

The majority of 529 savings plans have no requirement that you or the designated beneficiary be a resident of the sponsoring state, but a few do. On the flip side, most contract-type and unit-type prepaid programs restrict enrollment to persons who meet state residency requirements. Even here, however, there are exceptions. At least one contract-type prepaid program, Alabama's, is fully open to nonresidents. And Colorado's unit-type prepaid program is open as well.

Often, a 529 plan with restrictions will permit enrollment if either the account owner or beneficiary is a state resident at the time of enrollment. If you are establishing an account for a grandchild who lives in a different state, for example, you may wish to consider the program offered in the state where your grandchild is located.

Questions regarding residency can arise in certain situations. Is there a minimum period of residency? What happens if the eligible resident moves out-of-state after the account is opened? What happens if enrollment is conditioned on the state residency of the beneficiary, and you later change the beneficiary to someone who is not a state resident? How are the residency restrictions applied to military personnel stationed in the state, or those originally from the state but now stationed elsewhere?

Some 529 plans that impose residency restrictions will accept nonresidents who meet other conditions. For example, Pennsylvania will accept into its guaranteed savings plan any nonresident whose place of employment is within the Commonwealth. Kentucky accepts anyone with "Kentucky ties". Nevada's contract-type prepaid program will allow a nonresident alumnus of a Nevada post-secondary institution to enroll.

2) What are the other eligibility requirements?

Many 529 plans require that the individual account owner be of legal age (e.g. 18). In addition, the program may be restricted to account owners who are U.S. citizens or resident aliens. The program may require that the beneficiary have (or obtain within a certain period of time) a Social Security number or a taxpayer identification number.

Most prepaid programs require that the beneficiary be below a certain age or grade level at the time of enrollment, making them unsuitable for older individuals who may be planning to attend college in the future.

3) Can the account owner and beneficiary be the same person?

You may be considering establishing a 529 account for yourself. Although just about every 529 savings programs permits you to do this (the programs managed by Fidelity Investments in Delaware, Massachusetts, and New Hampshire recently changed their rules to allow it), this may not always be feasible in programs that have age or grade limits on beneficiaries being enrolled.

4) How does the program handle funds coming from an existing UTMA or UGMA investment account?

Many families have children with assets in a Uniform Transfers to Minors Act (UTMA) account or Uniform Gifts to Minors Act (UGMA) account. If you are the custodian of the account, and you wish to invest the child's assets with a 529 plan, you will need to determine if, and how, the program accommodates funds coming from UTMA/UGMA accounts. There are a few different ways this is being done.

+ The program (e.g. New York) will permit the minor child to establish an account in his or her own name. A parent or legal guardian must execute documents and authorize decisions with respect to the account until the minor reaches the age of majority.

+ The program will permit the account to be titled in the same way as any other account owned by the minor under the UTMA/UGMA. The custodian is to notify the program administrator at the time the custodianship is terminated upon the child reaching legal age so that the account can be re-titled in the child's own name. The program generally prohibits a change in beneficiary, or any withdrawal that is not for the benefit of the minor, until the custodianship terminates.

+ The program will title the account in the name of the adult who is custodian but provide a "check box" to indicate that the source of funds is an existing UTMA/UGMA account. The account will be restricted as to beneficiary changes and withdrawals until the custodianship terminates.

+ The program will title the account in the name of the adult who is custodian with no special restrictions. The program administrator in this instance adopts the position that it is up to the custodian to ensure that the account is handled in accordance to whatever the appropriate UTMA/UGMA requires.

5) Will the program accept a corporation or trust as account owner?

A corporate-owned 529 account can provide unique benefits as part of a non-qualified deferred compensation plan. A trust may also be attracted to the investment and tax advantages of a 529 plan and wish to establish an account with the beneficiary of the trust named as beneficiary of the 529 account. The ability to name a trust as successor owner can be particularly important to an individual who establishes an account and wants to be sure that in the event of death the account is used in accordance with their wishes. Passing ownership directly to an individual successor owner may be viewed as too risky since control of those funds rest entirely on the shoulders of the new owner.

It is particularly important that anyone who wishes to establish a non-natural entity as owner or successor owner seek professional advice from an attorney and accountant. There are many legal and tax complications that can arise in this situation.

6) Are interests in the 529 plan being sold through brokers?

If you rely on a broker or financial planner who earns commissions from the sale of investment products, chances are that the number of different 529 plans offered to you by that adviser will be limited to the number of 529 plans that will pay a commission. This isn't necessarily bad. The broker-sold programs tend to be well-structured programs with flexible features. They have passed the scrutiny of your adviser's broker-dealer, who typically provides a substantial amount of education and technical and administrative support to the adviser.

On the other hand, if you wish to conduct all the research and analysis on your own, or if you use a financial planner who charges you a fee rather than earning commissions from the program, you will probably be more inclined to look for non-broker (i.e. direct-sold) 529 plans. You will generally incur lower program expenses in direct-sold plans and your choice of programs will not be restricted to those that pay a commission. In some cases a fee-only financial planner will be allowed to acquire shares in a broker-sold program at net asset value, which means that you do not pay the sales load that is normally charged.

Note that many direct-sold programs are prohibited by law from providing investment advice to you because they are not offered through licensed securities representatives or registered investment advisers.

Several states make direct-sold programs available to residents but require that nonresidents go through a broker or pay the higher cost associated with broker-sold shares. Rhode Island and Ohio are examples.

7) What is the minimum contribution?

The issue here is your ability to make at least the minimum required contribution to the 529 plan. Some programs have no minimum contributions while others have minimum contributions of $1,000 or more. Many savings programs waive the initial lump sum minimum contribution if you commit to an automatic investment plan. Prepaid programs generally offer different tuition packages at different prices. Many of these programs permit payments to be made on a monthly payment plan, albeit at a higher total cost.

8) Does the program accept contributions through payroll deduction and/or electronic funds transfer from your checking or savings account?

If you desire to make your contributions in this way, you will need to be sure that the program you select will accommodate it. Even if a program accepts contributions through payroll deduction, your employer must be able to meet the requirements of the program in establishing the payroll deduction process.

A small number of programs will now permit online enrollment and contributions under the new "electronic signature" rules. This can be a welcome convenience that will likely spread among other 529 plans in the future.

9) Will your use of the program create any state-level gift or inheritance tax concerns?

There are only a handful of states that have a gift tax, but if you live in one of them you need to consider whether your contributions to a 529 plan give rise to a taxable gift. States do not necessarily follow the federal gift tax rules and they may treat contributions to the in-state program differently from contributions to an out-of-state program. For example, Tennessee apparently will treat contributions by Tennessee residents to an out-of-state 529 plan as a gift qualifying for the annual exclusion, but may not recognize the five-year averaging election that is available for federal purposes. (Proposed Tennessee legislation may alleviate this concern.)

Your participation in a state's 529 plan should not subject your estate to inheritance tax or probate in that state, but there may be exceptions to that rule. The disclosure statement for the North Carolina 529 savings programs cautions that accounts owned by nonresidents may be subject to North Carolina inheritance tax. You should consult with your attorney on this matter.

10) Does the program participate in Upromise or other affinity programs?

Upromise is a privately-owned company offering a consumer rewards program that directs your purchase rebates from participating vendors into a 529 account. Membership is free (www.upromise.com). At the time this book went to print, Upromise had partnered with savings programs managed by Salomon Smith Barney (Colorado and Illinois) and Fidelity Investments (Delaware, Massachusetts, and New Hampshire). If you join Upromise, you should consider opening a 529 account in one of those programs. There are other 529 affinity programs (e.g. BabyMint at www.babymint.com) that have different options.

11) Does the program place any restrictions on your ownership rights or give any of these rights to the beneficiary?

The vast majority of 529 plans permit you as account owner or "participant" to change the designated beneficiary, determine when and for what purpose distributions are made, and revoke the account assets. Some programs do not. For example, Tennessee's BEST Savings Program has special UTMA-like provisions granting important ownership rights to the beneficiary. Michigan's prepaid tuition program, the Michigan Education Trust, is irrevocable and generally prohibits any refunds until after the beneficiary reaches age 18. Ohio also has a restriction in its CollegeAdvantage program against withdrawals before the beneficiary reaches age 18, but only in the Tuition Option. You should be aware of the possible implications of restrictions such as these. In certain situations they may be viewed as attractive features. The placement of ownership rights may affect other aspects of participation in a 529 plan—financial aid treatment, creditor concerns, and treatment of the account in applying for Medicaid.

12) Is an account in the program protected from the claims of creditors under state law?

A program offering special asset protection for participant accounts under state law may appeal to individuals with creditor concerns. There are several programs that offer this protection, although the degree of protection may vary. For instance, an account in New York's College Savings Program is entirely exempt if the account owner is also the beneficiary and a minor, but a maximum $10,000 is exempt if the account owner is anyone else. If you are participating in a 529 plan outside your own state, you should discuss with an attorney how the asset protection provided by that state applies to creditor actions in your own state.

13) Can a non-owner make contributions to an account in the program?

If you wish to establish an account that other persons, including your relatives, can contribute to without opening their own accounts, you will want to determine if the program you are considering will accommodate non-owner contributions. Some 529 plans indicate they will not, although anecdotal evidence suggests that these programs may not be very strict in applying that rule.

14) Does the program permit the account owner to designate a successor owner?

If you as account owner of a 529 plan were to die, your 529 account does not terminate. Instead, account ownership passes to a survivor. Many programs make it easy for you to designate a successor owner at the time of enrollment, and permit you to submit a change in your designation at any time. If you do not designate an owner, the program will either automatically install a new owner at the time of your death, or pass ownership to your estate. If passed automatically, the chain of possible successors might start with the program beneficiary or your spouse depending on the rules of the program.

15) How complete and accurate are the program disclosures?

The quality and quantity of program disclosures can vary widely among different 529 plans. Interests in a 529 savings program are "municipal fund securities" exempt from federal regulation; however, they must conform to the rules of the Municipal Securities Rulemaking Board, a self-regulatory organization responsible to the SEC. You may find that some programs have very extensive disclosures that will answer most questions, while others are not nearly as complete. Some areas to check are the following: investment policies, historical investment results of underlying funds; processing of contributions, withdrawal requests, and account change requests; description of resident state tax rules; and fees and expenses. Prepaid programs can have a longer list of items due to the manner in which they function. Check to see how current the program disclosures are and whether updated information is available on the official program Web site. You may also want to judge how knowledgeable and responsive the program call center is when you ask questions by telephone. If you are relying on a financial adviser, you should be comfortable that the adviser is willing and able to obtain education and technical support from the program manager and/or distributor.

16) How does the program report account activity to its participants?

Every 529 plan will send you a statement of your account at least annually, and many will send it more frequently. Perhaps you want to have online access to your account. Only some programs provide that. If you establish your account through a broker, it is unlikely that the 529 plan will appear along with other investment accounts on your monthly or quarterly statements. However, this may start happening more frequently in the future as financial advisers and individual investors begin demanding it. You should also read and understand a program's privacy policy. This is usually not a concern and your account information should be exempt from any state "open document" laws (but ask if you are not sure).

There can be a privacy concern stemming from the requirement that all accounts with the same beneficiary be aggregated when applying the program's contribution limit. You may become privy to what other family members or friends are contributing when you all have accounts for the same beneficiary (and vice versa). Some programs will even print the unused contribution limit on monthly or quarterly account statements. (Most families will not be too concerned about this issue and will probably appreciate staying informed about the remaining allowance.)

17) Has the program received a determination from the IRS that it qualifies under section 529 as a "qualified tuition program"?

A formal determination, although not required as a condition for a state to offer a 529 plan, can provide added comfort that the program is structured in compliance with section 529 of the Code. Several programs have already applied for and received favorable determinations. Others have applied and are still waiting. Some programs do not currently intend to apply for IRS determination and are willing to rely on the legal opinions of their attorneys.

18) What expenses are covered by the program?

Here we are talking primarily about the contract-type prepaid programs because this type of 529 plan will specifically describe the costs that will be covered under the contract. If you wish to use a 529 plan to save for all the qualifying costs of college and the prepaid program you are considering will cover only tuition and fees, you will need to add a savings, unit-type prepaid, or guaranteed savings program to your list of possibilities.

Some contract-type prepaid programs can be used to pay for other expenses besides tuition and fees in certain circumstances, e.g. the beneficiary receives a scholarship that pays for some or all the tuition.

Following the 2001 tax law changes, it is no longer up to the 529 program administrator to determine which expenses meet the definition of "qualified higher education expenses". It will be up to you to do that based on the statute and IRS pronouncements.

19) How does the program deal with a request to rollover to another state's 529 plan?

This last item in section 1 of this checklist may be one of the most important. Although federal tax law permits you to rollover your account without federal tax or penalty under certain conditions, the program itself is not required to accommodate this transaction. Section 3 below alerts you to restrictions and other concerns that may exist in a program but that are avoidable when you have the ability to easily, without cost or penalty, and at any time, transfer any amount from that program to a different one (assuming you meet the federal conditions for a rollover). To the extent that your current program does not do this, the red flags that may pop up from your review of the items in section 3 take on greater weight.

Most often it is matter of expense, as some programs charge a small fee or penalty on an outbound rollover. In prepaid programs, your decision to transfer to another program may require a full or partial cancellation of your contract and the financial consequences may be more significant. A small number of 529 plans may even restrict your ability to request a refund of any type unless your beneficiary has reached a certain age or you can convince the program administrator of your need for the funds.

A direct trustee-to-trustee rollover is the easiest to accomplish but not all 529 plans will do this for you. If not, then it becomes a matter of withdrawing funds from your existing 529 account and re-contributing those funds within 60 days to a new 529 plan. In either case, you must comply with the rollover restrictions concerning a change of beneficiary to another family member, or the limits on same-beneficiary rollovers (see Chapter 3).

20) Does the program offer a college savings strategy consistent with your own objectives and preferences?

This is the essential issue for most investors. What do I get for the money I contribute? How will my investment perform? How much risk am I accepting? How does it compare to other 529 plans, and to other types of investments? You will need to carefully consider what happens to your money after it is contributed to the program, and make the decision to join only after you become comfortable with its investment approach.

21) Does the program provide a "guarantee" that your investment will keep up with the increasing costs of college?

A "yes" answer is the hallmark of a prepaid program or guaranteed savings program, while a "no" answer indicates a savings program. Special considerations relating to prepaid programs and guaranteed savings programs are grouped below in questions 39 through 43. A savings program will not make any promises that your account is going to keep pace with any measure of increasing college costs (with very limited exceptions, such as Alaska's program that offers an option guaranteeing a minimum return equivalent to tuition increases at the University of Alaska, but only for beneficiaries who end up attending UA). You have the potential to do better than the college cost inflation rate; you also have the risk of seeing your account lag behind college costs.

22) Does the savings program offer an "age-based" asset allocation strategy, a menu of "static" portfolios, or both?

An age-based strategy is one in which your account is automatically moved to a more conservative asset allocation over time. Typically, the age of your beneficiary will determine the portfolio in the program into which your contributions are initially placed, although it is now common that a program will base the initial portfolio on the expected number of years to enrollment rather than age, or will simply allow you to choose your starting point among any of the age-based portfolios contained within the program.

The idea of an age-based asset allocation strategy is that you will want to be more aggressively invested when your investment time horizon is long (e.g. for a young child), and so your account will be invested primarily in equity funds. Over time, your account will gradually be shifted out of stock funds and into fixed income and/or money market funds; it finally comes to rest in the most conservative age-based portfolio until withdrawn.

There are two different mechanisms by which a savings program can manipulate asset allocations. One is by establishing a series of portfolios where each portfolio has a target asset allocation among equity, bond, and money market funds that generally does not change over time. Your account is transferred ("migrated") from one portfolio to the next at scheduled intervals. The second approach is to assign your account to a portfolio targeted to a particular year of use. Instead of moving your account from one portfolio to the next, the manager adjusts the underlying investments of the portfolio to achieve new asset allocation targets over time. Only when the target year of use is reached is the account transferred to a final "resting" portfolio.

Is one approach better than the other? Not necessarily. The first approach, in which your account is transferred among increasingly conservative portfolios, is more mechanistic yet more disciplined. You will know going in how your account is to be allocated among stocks, bonds, and money market funds at any point in the future. The second approach is less mechanistic and gives the portfolio investment manager a greater amount of discretion in adjusting the asset allocation for changing market conditions.

A "static" option in a savings program is one in which the targeted asset allocation of the portfolio you select does not change over time. It can be a 100% equity option, a 100% fixed income option, or a pre-determined blend of different asset classes. Most 529 plans with static options currently design each portfolio as a "fund of funds" using a mix of underlying mutual funds. An increasing number of programs, primarily broker-sold, are starting to offer single mutual funds in place of a blend of funds. Theoretically, there is no limit to the number of static options that a 529 plan can offer to participants.

23) Does the program offer a principal-protected option?

If you have no tolerance for downside risk with the principal portion of your account, you may desire an interest-bearing investment option within the savings program that protects your principal. In fact, the poor performance of the stock market over the last couple of years has caused many states to re-evaluate their program investments and add a "safe" option if none existed previously.

The amount of interest you earn may or may not match increasing college costs. A money market fund consists of short-term securities and is designed to maintain a level unit price, although its dividend/interest payout can swing dramatically over a short period of time. Some programs (including most of the programs managed by TIAA-CREF) are now offering "guaranteed" options that guarantee not only principal but a minimum level of interest as well (e.g. 3%). They declare an interest crediting rate on a periodic basis and are backed by a "funding agreement" with a life insurance company. Another variation being introduced into the 529 marketplace is the "stable value" fund. This is a product that seeks to combine the stable share pricing of a money market fund with the higher returns of a bond fund. By leveling the yields of its underlying fixed income securities, it also produces less variability in overall yield.

New Jersey is unique in offering blended stock/bond portfolios backed by the "moral obligation" of the state that your account will not lose value. The program may seek an appropriation from the state in the event that program resources are not sufficient to make good on this obligation.

Some of the "prepaid tuition" programs can also be viewed as guaranteed principal-plus-interest investments, except that their yield is pegged to tuition increases. For example, the College Savings Bank makes its FDIC-insured CollegeSure CD available through the Arizona and Montana programs. The interest rate is based each year on the increase in a national index of private college costs, with a minimum annual rate of 4%. The Colorado Prepaid Tuition Fund offers tuition units that inflate at the rate of increase of tuition at Colorado's public universities, and promises a minimum average annual return of 4%. Several of the contract-type prepaid programs permit you to cancel your contract and receive your payments back along with some amount of interest.

24) What are the other characteristics of the underlying securities in the options available under the savings program?

The purpose of this book is not to provide a technical analysis of investments. However, you should attempt to determine the investment fundamentals of portfolios in a 529 plan (or rely on a professional who can) and see that it fits well with your other investments (retirement accounts, etc.). How is the portfolio allocated among stocks, bonds, and money market funds? How much of the portfolio is invested in international stocks . . . junk bonds . . . large cap, medium cap, and small cap stocks? Who manages the underlying mutual funds? What are the track records of those funds? Does the program require that you develop your own "portfolio" by allocating your contributions among single mutual funds (or permit you to do so)?

You will find that some 529 plans utilize mutual funds from one particular fund family (typically an affiliate of the 529 program manager), while others are "multi-manager", incorporating the mutual funds from two or more separate fund families. Under either model, the investment history of most 529 plans has not been long enough to make conclusive comparisons, although a detailed analysis of the composition of various portfolios can yield useful information. Actual investment results for many of the programs can be found at www.savingforcollege.com.

25) Does the program permit contributions to be allocated among multiple options?

If the answer is "no", you will have to open separate accounts for the same beneficiary if you wish to utilize more than one investment option. Most 529 plans that permit you to allocate your contribution among multiple options will also allow you to change the allocation of future contributions.

26) Does the program permit you to switch between investment options as described in IRS Notice 2001–55?

Notice 2001–55 was issued by the IRS in September 2001 announcing that a 529 plan would not be violating the prohibition against participant investment direction if it permitted a participant to switch from one broad-based investment strategy available under the program to another, as long as the program had procedures to ensure that the switch was not done more than once in a calendar year or whenever a change of beneficiary occurred. Prior to Notice 2001–55 the IRS had taken the position that such a change would violate the restriction against investment direction and cause the program to risk disqualification.

It is up to each 529 plan to decide whether and how to implement the new flexibility permitted under Notice 2001–55. Most savings programs appear willing to go this route recognizing that programs updating their procedures will be viewed more positively by many investors. The timetable for making the necessary changes to program rules and documents may vary from one state to another, however.

27) How quickly does the program invest your contribution?

Not all 529 plans have the administrative capabilities to ensure that your contribution is invested within a day or two of when your check is received. This can be of particular concern at certain times during the year, most notably late December when a large inflow of contributions can overwhelm processing capacities. The day on which your contribution is processed can also depend on the method you use in making your contribution. For example, it may take longer to process an initial contribution using an electronic funds transfer from your bank account than one made by check.

A delay means that you will not have the benefit (or possible detriment) of market activity during that time. A program that is not managed by a outside investment firm may lack the administrative resources needed to process investments on a constant basis. For example, the Virginia College Savings Program places contributions into portfolios twice each month. The program uses the earnings from the 14 to 28 day "float" of your investment to help offset program expenses.

28) How are earnings in the portfolio credited to your account?

The vast majority of savings programs use daily valuation. You own "shares" of the program trust fund and the price of those shares will move on a daily basis to reflect the share prices of the underlying funds, along with any investment earnings and program expenses posted to the trust fund. A small number of programs utilize balance forward accounting instead of daily valuation. For example, in the Utah 529 plan, the net earnings of the program trust are allocated to participant accounts at the end of each quarter based on average account balances of all accounts in the trust fund. Your account in this program would be less affected by daily swings in the stock market.

29) Does the program charge an enrollment fee?

Enrollment fees are charged by some 529 plans and not by others. Sometimes the enrollment fee is waived, or the amount reduced, in particular circumstances, e.g. for state residents or during special promotions. If you open multiple accounts for the same beneficiary, or for beneficiaries in the same family, the program may offer a discount off normal enrollment fees. Because it is a fixed charge, the effect of any enrollment fee on your overall return will depend on how much money you invest in the program.

   If you are enrolling in a 529 plan through a broker or other financial adviser accepting commissions, there may a sales charge or "load" depending on which "class" of shares you choose to acquire. The upfront load may be as little as 1% or as much as 5.75% of your contribution.

30) Does the program charge an annual account maintenance fee?

An account maintenance fee is also a fixed dollar amount that is charged against your account on a quarterly, semi-annual, or annual basis. These fees can vary anywhere from $5 to $50 per year in those programs that have this expense. In some programs, the account maintenance fee is waived if you enroll in an automatic investment plan using electronic funds transfer from your bank account or through payroll deduction.

31) What is the program's expense ratio?

The expense ratio of a savings program typically consists of two pieces. The first piece is the total of any asset-based fees charged against the value of the program fund by the outside program manager and/or state agency in charge of administering the 529 plan. The second piece consists of the expenses of the underlying mutual funds that are indirectly incurred by you which can range from very low-cost index funds to relatively high-cost international equity or other specialized sector funds. In some savings programs there is a third source of expense—certain administrative costs charged to the program fund such as the cost of an annual audit—although these expenses tend to be a fairly small amount.

Some program managers include or "wrap" the underlying fund expenses in the fee they charge to the 529 plan. One advantage to this approach is that it presents a simple and easy-to-understand fee structure, and there is no incentive for the program manager to select mutual funds with high underlying fees. A possible disadvantage is that the investor with a conservative asset allocation will be paying the same expense as the investor with an aggressive asset allocation, despite the fact that bond and money market funds generally have much lower expense ratios than stock funds.

Asset-based expenses in savings programs not sold through a broker range from as little as 0.50% to as much as 2.00% Considering the valuable tax benefits available with a 529 plan, and the special effort required to design, market, and administer a plan, the total fixed-dollar and asset-based expenses associated with most programs will be seen as very reasonable.

Programs that are distributed through financial advisers will charge additional asset-based fees used to compensate the broker. An example of this would be a program that charges an extra 0.25% annual fee for "A shares" (along with a 3.5% sales load), an extra 0.90% annual fee for "B shares" that convert to lower-cost A shares after 6 years and do not incur a sales load, and an extra 0.60% annual fee for "C shares" that do not convert and do not incur a sales load.

32) Are there charges for other transactions?

Some programs may impose a charge on beneficiary changes, account owner changes, rollovers, and certain other requests.

33) Can you claim a state income tax deduction for any or all of your contributions to the program?

Over twenty states that impose an individual income tax will allow you to claim a deduction for some or all of your contributions to the state's own 529 plan. Depending on your state income tax bracket and any limits placed on the deduction, this can be a very powerful incentive for choosing your own state's program.

Be sure you understand how the tax deduction in your state, if any, is regulated. There are many important questions:

+ If the contributor is not the same as the account owner, which person claims the deduction?
+ Is the amount of deduction capped? If so, is the maximum deduction computed per contributor, per tax return, per beneficiary, or per account?
+ Do contributions in excess of the annual deduction limit get carried forward to future tax years?
+ Can you get a deduction for an account you establish for yourself? Or does the beneficiary have to be your dependent?

If you live in a state that offers a state income tax deduction, you may want to determine the circumstances under which you may be required to "recapture" the tax deduction in a future year. Most states require that you recapture prior deductions if you take a non-qualified withdrawal, and some states will apply the recapture to qualifying rollovers as well. If you are able to claim a deduction for only a portion of your contributions, you may want to understand the ordering rules for recapture if only a portion of your account is withdrawn for non-qualified purposes. You may find, however, that your state has not yet fully explained how recapture applies in all situations.

34) Does the program offer any other financial incentives?

In lieu of a state income tax deduction, Minnesota offers a partial match for contributions made by low and middle income residents into its savings plan. Louisiana and Michigan offer both—a limited state income tax deduction for contributions along with a partial match. New Jersey provides a first-year scholarship of as much as $1,500 to beneficiaries in its 529 plan that attend a New Jersey public or private university. Utah has a separate endowment fund with earnings that are credited to the accounts of participants in its "Option 1". Kentucky guarantees that beneficiaries of accounts that have been open for a sufficient period of years can claim resident status for Kentucky public school tuition pricing no matter where they end up residing. Pennsylvania has an agreement with SAGE Scholars, a private company that arranges tuition discounts at certain private colleges at no cost to the program participant. Several states disregard balances in their own 529 plans when determining student eligibility for state-funded financial aid programs.

These are all examples of how states are working to make their programs as attractive as possible.

35) How will an account in the program affect the beneficiary's eligibility for need-based financial aid?

As things now stand, there can be a significant difference in the student's eligibility for need-based financial aid depending on which type of 529 plan—prepaid or savings—is being used. See Chapters 4 and 5 for a discussion of this issue.

36) What is the term of the program manager?

The fact that a particular financial services firm has been selected to manage a 529 plan does not mean that the program will forever be using that manager. Management contracts are subject to terms of anywhere from 2 to 15 years. At the end of the initial program term, the contract may be extended or under certain circumstances the manager can be replaced. Naturally, in the event the manager is replaced, the program will probably look much different under the new manager. There are a few instances where this has occurred in the past.

Besides manager changes, many other aspects of a program are subject to change at any time. Thus far, nearly all changes we have witnessed are to the benefit of participants, but there is no guarantee that it will always be that way.

37) How popular is the program?

As a general rule, you want to join a 529 plan that has proven to be popular with others, or at least one that has the prospect of becoming popular. Level of assets in the program can be a proxy for popularity, although you need to consider several factors: how long the program has been around in its current form; restrictions on participation such as state residency, age, etc.; population of the sponsoring state; and whether the program is being distributed on a nationwide basis through brokers and financial planners.

It is important that programs attract a sufficient level of assets in order to generate the revenues needed to pay for administration, investment management, and oversight. If the program is unable to achieve critical size, it becomes more likely that changes will be made, and these changes can be dramatic. While a replacement or addition of a program manager, or changes to the investment offerings, can be a good thing, there are other alterations a stagnant program may make that are not so good, such as an increase in fees and expenses to cover the costs of operation. The worst result is where the state, or the firm hired as program manager, loses its enthusiasm for the program and scales back its resources or the amount of attention devoted to the program.

Although it is impossible to establish a strict standard, any program that is at least two years old and has not yet attracted $50 million in contributions can be considered small. A very large 529 plan would be one with over $500 million in assets at the beginning of 2002. The largest program in the country is Florida's prepaid program with approximately $3 billion.

At this point in the evolution of 529 savings programs, size does not correlate with investment performance. As mentioned above, the investment history of savings programs is still too short to make meaningful comparisons.

There are exceptions to the general rule concerning program size. For example, College Savings Bank offers a unique tuition-indexed certificate of deposit through the programs it manages for Arizona and Montana. Although the programs are relatively small due to the specialized characteristics of the investment, they are well-managed.

Another way to gauge program popularity is to search for articles in the local and regional press. Often, the media are able to pick up on developments or concerns by keeping tabs with state and program officials. Sometimes the state's 529 plan becomes fodder in the political wrangling that characterizes many state legislatures and official offices.

38) Does the program rely on a state subsidy?

State budgets can be difficult. A state subsidy to the program for operating costs can help keep the costs down for the participant but also raise the prospect of budget cuts in the future that may have a direct impact on the costs charged to your 529 account.

39) How much will your prepayment contract be worth at the college your beneficiary ends up attending?

With the typical prepayment contract, the program will pay the bills for tuition and fees at any in-state public institution for the number of credit hours, semesters, or academic years that you purchase. Your investment "return" is determined in large part by the rate of future tuition increases at state schools. In many states, tuition levels are more sensitive to budgetary and political considerations than they are to increases in the cost of delivering education. In some states, there is a statutory cap on annual tuition increases.

Average in-state tuition levels are not the only factor, however. You will derive greater value from the contract if your beneficiary attends an expensive in-state public school than if he or she attends a less expensive school. In some states the range of costs can be wide. In some instances, if your beneficiary were to attend one of the least expensive state schools you end up better off canceling the contract and receive a refund.

You will also want to find out how the prepaid program will calculate benefits payable to a private or out-of-state school, in the event that your beneficiary does not attend a state school. The typical prepaid program will limit the amount paid to weighted average in-state tuition and fees.

40) How much will be refunded to you if you cancel your prepayment contract?

Will you receive the current tuition value of the contract, your payments along with interest, or only your payments without any interest? Is there a separate cancellation fee? In many states offering a prepaid program, the amount of refund will depend on the reason for cancellation. You are likely to receive more if the reason is because your beneficiary has died, become disabled, or received a scholarship. An "at-will" cancellation will result in the least amount of refund.

When will the refund be paid? A cancellation of the contract may result in an immediate refund, or payments in installments, depending on the provisions of the contract.

41) What is the price of the prepayment contract?

Compare the price of tuition/fees under the program to the current tuition/fees at the institution your beneficiary is likely to attend. Is it the same, higher, or lower? Some prepaid programs and guaranteed savings programs, particularly the newer ones, are likely to charge more than the amount you would pay if your beneficiary were attending college this year. The premium is necessary for the program to cover administrative costs as well as to help build a "reserve" for shortfalls in the trust fund. A shortfall can occur if the program's obligation for future payments increases faster than the investment earnings in the trust. Any amount of premium reduces the overall return of your "investment" in the prepayment contract.

Older prepaid and guaranteed savings programs that were able to build up their reserves during the 1990s are less likely to build an "actuarial premium" into their pricing. They are usually able to price their tuition packages very close to current levels, if not below.

The price may vary based on the age of your beneficiary. Prepaid programs with this feature have determined that they can offer a discount to younger beneficiaries because they provide the opportunity for higher and more certain investment returns in the program trust fund.

Most prepaid programs permit you to pay for your contract in installments, which will allow you to fit the monthly payments into your budget. However, total payments under an installment payment plan will be higher than the amount you would pay in a lump sum. Check to see what your rate of "interest" is on the installment plan. Unless tuition prices increase more rapidly than the interest factor (often in the 6% to 9% range) built into the installment contract, you are losing ground on each installment payment. Once you enter into an installment payment contract, you may be required to pay the total amount of installments even if you later decide to prepay with a lump sum payment. Be sure to check how flexible the program is in this regard. Also investigate the consequences of missing a scheduled payment.

You should also check to see when your lump-sum payment or first installment payment is due. In some prepaid programs the payment deadline is several months after you enroll. If you decide to back out before the payment is due you will probably lose any enrollment fee paid.

42) Is the "tuition guarantee" backed by the full faith and credit of the state?

A full and faith credit guarantee means that the state is legally obligated to pay for the benefits promised by the prepaid program in the event the program itself becomes insolvent. Such a guarantee can provide welcome assurances to the participant. If a program is not backed by the state's full faith and credit guarantee, you run the risk that the program finds itself insolvent and provides less than full contract benefits to you or your beneficiary. Some prepaid programs do not have full faith and credit backing, but do have a legislative guarantee that requires the state legislature to consider legislation that would appropriate funds for the program in the event the trust fund becomes insolvent.

The size of the reserve built up by the program fund can be an important factor for prepaid programs because that represents the "cushion" against future shortfalls caused when tuition increases outstrip investment earnings in the program trust fund. You can obtain this information from the annual financial statements made available by the program, although the financial position of the program may have changed substantially by the time the annual report is issued. The financial statements will also describe the types of investments being made by the trust, and the actuarial assumptions used in determining the obligation of the program to provide future benefits to participants. Many of the older prepaid programs were able to accumulate substantial reserves during the bull market of the 1990s; that is not the case for most of the newer prepaid programs.

43) Will the program allocate investment surpluses to participant accounts?

If a prepaid program manages to build up a large reserve through positive investment performance matched with modest tuition increases, will any of the surplus be used to increase benefits or reduce the cost for program participants? Some programs may indicate "yes", while others are prohibited from doing so by state law. The Pennsylvania TAP program actually allocated several millions of dollars of additional benefits to participant accounts at one point in its history. In the current general and higher education economic climates, the chances of any program distributing this type of dividend in the near future may be slim.

44) Are there any penalties or fees for withdrawing your money from the program?

Until the 2001 EGTRRA changed the rules effective January 1, 2002, a 529 plan was required to impose a more-than-de minimis penalty on non-qualified withdrawals. Although no longer required to do so, some programs have not yet eliminated their penalties (typically 10% of the earnings portion) because their legislatures have not made the necessary changes to their enabling statutes. Until they do so, a non-qualified withdrawal may incur a penalty of 20% of earnings (including the new federal 10% penalty) or even more. Some programs, in eliminating their penalties, have added a fixed dollar charge (e.g. $50) on non-qualified withdrawals. Certain broker-sold interests may incur a "contingent deferred sales charge" on non-qualified withdrawals within a specified period of time.

45) Are qualified withdrawals from the program exempt from your state's income tax?

Before this year, several states provided an exemption from state income tax for qualified withdrawals from their own 529 plans; in only a few states was the exemption extended to withdrawals from other states' 529 plans as well. Beginning in 2002, however, withdrawals qualifying for federal tax exemption will also be exempt in many states, regardless of prior treatment. That is because the majority of states automatically conform to federal tax law changes.

Tax conformity is not across the board, however, and a state may enact new laws to restrict exemption to withdrawals from its own 529 plan. If that is the case in your state, you may still have the opportunity to take advantage of state income tax exemption if you rollover your balances in other 529 plans to your own state's program prior to withdrawal.

46) Are there any time or age limits on the use of the account?

If the 529 plan requires that the account be used by the time the beneficiary reaches age 30, for example, simply rollover the account to another state's program prior to reaching that point.

47) Is there a minimum time period before taking qualified or non-qualified withdrawals from your account in the program?

New York's 529 plan, for example, currently has a rule that says your account must be open 36 months before you can take qualified withdrawals, but there is no minimum time period for rollover distributions. If you wish to participate in New York's program, but plan to take qualified withdrawals within 36 months, you can avoid a penalty by rolling over your account to another state's program that has no such restrictions before withdrawing funds.

48) Are there any other withdrawal restrictions in the program that can be avoided by first rolling over to another 529 plan that does not have those restrictions?

Here are some examples:
+ your program has cumbersome substantiation requirements that other 529 plans may not have.
+ your program requires that the account owner be treated as the recipient of any undocumented withdrawals while other 529 plans give you the option of directing the withdrawal to your beneficiary (thereby shifting the income to a lower tax bracket).
+ your program has a minimum withdrawal amount or limit on frequency of withdrawals that other programs do not have.

49) Will the program approve a request to transfer ownership of the account?

There are a number of reasons why you may decide you want to transfer ownership of your 529 account to someone else. One possibility is that an account owned by you may be subject to the claims of your creditors. Another possibility is that you do not want your account considered a countable asset for Medicaid purposes if you were to enter a nursing home in the future. Finally, you may at some point decide that just do not want to be responsible for the management of the 529 account and would like someone else to handle it. The last two possibilities are particularly relevant for grandparents.

Some 529 plans do not approve requests for a transfer of ownership other than following your death or incapacity, or when ordered by a court in a divorce or other legal proceeding. To accomplish such a change, you would need to first rollover your account to another 529 plan that does permit owner transfers.

50) How much can be contributed to an account in the program?

One of the requirements for qualification under section 529 is that the program establish procedures so that participants do not contribute more than needed for the beneficiary's future qualified higher education expenses. These maximum contribution limits can vary significantly among 529 plans, with some savings programs as low as $100,000 per beneficiary and others as high as $260,000 or even higher.

If you plan on making very large contributions, you should be sure to understand how the contribution limits are applied. In some savings programs the limit refers to cumulative lifetime contributions. In others it refers to the account balance which, when reached, triggers a stop on further contributions. Often the limit for your own account will be reduced once you begin taking qualified withdrawals. In no event will a contribution limit prevent your account from growing in value beyond that limit.

The IRS requires that all accounts in a state's programs with the same beneficiary be aggregated when applying the limit, without regard to the fact that there may be different account owners.

Many 529 plans will increase their contribution limits on a periodic basis as the cost of college attendance rises. But what do you do if the 529 plan you are interested in does not permit you to contribute as much as you think you should invest for your beneficiary's future higher education costs? The answer would be to open accounts in more than one 529 plan. The IRS does not require that a 529 plan consider balances in other states' program when applying their limits. Although this may seem like an easy way to get around the individual state limits, caution should be exercised.

You are looking for trouble if you open accounts in multiple programs simply as a way to shelter more assets than you can reasonably anticipate as the amount your beneficiary will need for college and graduate school. A state that determines that you are doing this will likely terminate your account and possibly charge extra penalties. The IRS may also look to challenge you.

SEVEN

Income Tax Planning with 529 Plans

At first glance, the federal income tax rules associated with a 529 plan may appear fairly straightforward. The three major income tax benefits—tax deferred growth; the tax exclusion for earnings withdrawn for qualified purposes; and the possible shifting of earnings to a low income tax bracket when withdrawn for non-qualified purposes—are explained in detail in Chapter 3. Once these basic federal income tax benefits of 529 plans are understood, the next step is to explore income tax planning opportunities associated with 529 plans. This chapter will help you do that. What you will find below is a discussion of several income tax planning considerations related to 529 plans.

In which years should I take withdrawals from my 529 account?

Naturally, you should look to take withdrawals in years when the exclusion is available and avoid taking withdrawals that generate taxable income. This is not as easy as it sounds. A lot will depend on when the beneficiary is attending college, the expenses that will be incurred, the amount of money in your 529 account, the amount of untaxed earnings in the account, your tax brackets, and the other tax benefits that may be available to you and your beneficiary. Fitting all the pieces together in one plan for an optimal tax result can be very challenging. Be sure to consider the following:

1) Hope and Lifetime Learning credits

Avoid using your 529 account to pay for 100% of qualifying college costs in a year when you or your beneficiary will be claiming one of these credits. As explained in Chapter 3, claiming the credit will cause some portion of your 529 distribution to be subject to income tax and probably to the 10% penalty tax as well. Instead, consider using other non–529 resources to pay for some of the expenses and spreading your 529 distributions between years to effectively capture qualified expenses that are over and above the amount of expenses that go towards the credit. It is important to realize that the type of credit you claim can make a significant difference. The Hope credit "consumes" up to $2,000 of tuition and related expenses in 2002, while the Lifetime Learning credit consumes up to $5,000 of these expenses. The difference is even more dramatic after 2002 when the limit on expenses that can be used for the Lifetime Learning credit is increased to $10,000.

2) Section 222 above-the-line deduction

The coordination rules here are different, but the result is similar. If you plan on claiming this deduction in any of the years 2002 through 2005 (it expires after 2005), you should realize that the pool of deductible expenses is reduced by the earnings portion of distributions from a 529 account attributable to tuition and related expenses. Some taxpayers will not be affected by this adjustment because they will incur enough in tuition to claim the maximum deduction ($2,000 in 2002 and 2003, $4,000 in 2004 and 2005) even after reduction for the distributed 529 earnings.

3) Sunset of 2001 tax law changes in 2010

Unless the provisions of the 2001 Economic Growth and Tax Relief Rec-onciliation Act are extended or modified, the exclusion for qualified dis-tributions from a 529 plan is repealed effective January 1, 2011. The timing of distributions before or after that date will obviously make a dif-ference. However, it may not make much of a difference, since distributed earnings after 2010 will be taxable to the student and many students will be in a zero or very low tax bracket. In addition, the Hope or Lifetime Learning credits will be available to the eligible parent or student to offset or eliminate any tax caused by distributed 529 earnings. It is conceivable that post–2010 tax rules will produce an even better result, because the adjustment to total qualified expenses that can trigger a 10% additional penalty tax under current rules will go away.

4) Financial aid eligibility

As discussed in Chapter 4 and elsewhere, you can reasonably expect that the earnings portion of 529 distributions will be figured into the "expected family contribution" whether or not those earnings are excluded for federal income tax purposes. It is up to the U.S. Department of Education to make appropriate adjustments to the federal financial aid application forms that will reflect the changes on Form 1040 caused by the 2001 tax law. Any withdrawals from a 529 savings program in the stu-dent's senior year of college will presumably have no impact on financial aid eligibility. If you think your child may qualify for financial aid, it may make sense to target your 529 plan funding first to the senior year of col-lege, and then work backwards to the freshman year.

How can I time the distributions from my 529 account when that will be my only source of funds for paying for college?

You should attempt to anticipate this situation when deciding how much to contribute to 529 plans. You may want to invest in a different vehicle (such as tax-efficient mutual funds) for the expenses that will eventually go towards the Hope or Lifetime Learning credits. Another option you will have is to take out loans. Your ability to borrow funds in one year and repay in a later year offers the opportunity to time your 529 distributions for greatest effectiveness. Be aware, however, that the repayment of student loans is not included in the list of section 529 qualified higher education expense and so your use of the account for this purpose could result in additional tax and penalty.

How do distributions from a 529 plan affect the status of my child as a dependent for tax purposes?

The use of a 529 plan may affect your ability to claim the beneficiary as a dependent on your tax return. In order for you to claim anyone as a dependent, and take advantage of a $3,000 (in 2002) dependency exemption, certain tests must be met. One of these tests is the support test.[1]

Under the support test, a dependency exemption may be claimed by you only if you furnish more than one-half of the dependent's support during the year. It is not absolutely clear that withdrawals from a 529 plan account owned by you and used to pay for your child's college expenses will count as part of your support. If it does not count as your support, then the use of the 529 plan may cause you to fail the support test and prevent you from claiming the student as a dependent.

In many cases, failure of the dependency tests will be advantageous, especially if you have high taxable income. The student will be able to claim a personal exemption for himself that may save more in taxes on the student's return than you give up in lost tax savings on your return. This occurs because the dependency exemption is phased out for high income taxpayers. For 2002, the phase-out begins for married taxpayers filing jointly at an adjusted gross income of $206,000 and the exemption

---

1. The other tests are the relationship/household test, the citizenship test, the joint return test, and the gross income test. Usually the income from a 529 plan will not impact these tests if the dependent is your child under age 19, or between ages 19 and 23 and a full-time student for some part of each of five months during the year.

is phased out completely at an adjusted gross income of $328,500. The phase-out range for a single taxpayer is $137,300 to $259,800.

How will use of a 529 plan affect my state income taxes?

State tax planning can be important in getting the most tax benefits from a 529 plan. Several states provide an income tax deduction for all or a portion of your contributions to their 529 plans. If state deductions are available but are subject to a maximum annual amount, you may wish to consider spreading out your contributions over two or more years rather than contributing one amount that is in excess of the deduction limit. If you desire to contribute more than the amount allowed as a deduction, and the program allows for it, you might consider first transferring the non-deductible portion of your contribution to other close relatives and asking them to make the contribution into an account for your child. At least someone may get a tax break that would otherwise go unclaimed.

Some states that provide a deduction for contributions will require recapture of those deductions if non-qualified withdrawals are taken in later years. This recapture will be in addition to the earnings portion of the non-qualified withdrawal reportable on the state return. Be sure to understand how the recapture rules work for the 529 plan in your state. For example, some states may require that a pro-rata amount of your deduction be recaptured anytime a non-qualified withdrawal is made, while others will recapture your deduction only after total non-qualified withdrawals exceed any non-deductible contributions into the 529 plan. At least a couple of states provide a deduction for contributions and have no recapture rules. These states present the opportunity for pure tax savings even if the decision is made later to terminate the account and withdraw the balance. Of course, it is likely that any state which discovers it has overlooked the need for a recapture provision will eventually take the necessary steps to enact one.

Depending on where you live, tax benefits may be available to you for investing in your own state's 529 plan. Many states specifically provide that qualified distributions from its 529 plan are exempt from income taxes imposed on its taxpayers. Arizona, Colorado and New Jersey are notable for extending this exemption to earnings from other states' 529 plans (despite any harm this may cause to the marketing efforts of the 529 plans in these particular states).

In a state with an income tax that does not specifically exempt qualified distributions, the issue of taxability may depend on the degree to which the state conforms to federal tax law. Conformity means that the computation of state taxable income begins with federal adjusted gross income or federal taxable income. Many states will automatically conform to the 2001 federal changes that provide tax exclusion for qualified 529 distributions. Other states do not automatically conform but can be expected to pass a conformity law within several months after federal tax changes. Then there are those states that make no effort to conform to federal tax law, or those with only partial conformity.

There is no fully accurate survey of the states describing their treatment of distributions from out-of-state 529 plans. The best approach is to seek advice from your own tax professional.

Are there any tax benefits in opening multiple accounts for my child?

Establishing multiple 529 accounts can provide you with an opportunity to control the amount and timing of distributed earnings. Of course, if all distributions are tax-free anyway, there is no strategic value in maintaining separate accounts. It is when a distribution produces taxable income (i.e. a non-qualified distribution), or when the earnings make a difference in the financial aid application, that this becomes important.

The reason for this is because each 529 account will have a different earnings ratio depending on its investment history, making it possible to take withdrawals on a selective basis. This strategy is similar to selecting certain mutual fund shares to sell based on their unrealized gains or losses. A 529 savings account established 10 years prior to college is probably going to have a higher earnings ratio than an account established one year prior to college.

In years with sufficient qualified expenses, you would normally decide to withdraw from the account with the highest earnings ratio because the earnings will be excluded from taxable income. Withdrawals from the account with the lowest earnings ratio should be targeted for any years in which you decide to take a non-qualified withdrawal.

It may be possible to achieve this positioning by placing different types of investment into different accounts. For example, if you seek to diversify your college savings with a 50/50 blend of stocks and bonds, you can consider opening one 529 account with a 100% stock portfolio and a second 529 account with a 100% bond portfolio. Rather than dealing with just one earnings ratio for any distributions, you will have a choice in deciding which 529 account to take distributions from, and that decision may be based on their respective earnings ratios.

Note that this strategy will not work for multiple accounts you maintain for the same beneficiary in the same program. The IRS, under authority specifically provided by section 529, requires that these accounts be aggregated in determining the earnings ratio (see Chapter 3). The rule is confined to accounts with the same owner and beneficiary within one state's 529 plan, however, and so the use of multiple states will still provide this opportunity, at least for now.

Should I borrow money now and invest it in a 529 plan?

It may actually make sense to increase a college savings fund by borrowing money and contributing this money to a 529 plan. The reason for this is that the interest paid on the debt may produce an income tax deduction for you at a high tax bracket, while the earnings may escape taxation altogether.

The tax law contains a prohibition against deducting interest on debt used to produce tax-exempt income. If you go out and borrow money to invest in tax-free municipal bonds, for example, the interest expense on the loan would not be deductible.[2] One question that becomes critical in the wake of the 2001 tax changes is whether the exclusion of

---

2. Internal Revenue Code section 265(a)(2)

qualified distributions from a 529 plan invokes the prohibition against deducting interest on borrowings. The answer appears to be "no", simply because the distributions are not per-se exempt. Unless certain hurdles are cleared the distributed earnings become taxable (and are scheduled to become taxable in any event for distributions after 2010). Caution is urged however; the IRS has not yet ruled on this specific issue, nor has it ruled on the analogous issue of interest deductibility on a loan used to fund contributions to a Roth IRA.

Another question to be explored in considering whether to borrow is the character of the interest expense on the loan. If the interest is considered investment interest expense, it would be deductible as an itemized deduction, but only to the extent that you have investment income. Any excess investment interest expense is carried forward indefinitely and deducted against investment income in future years.

It is somewhat doubtful that the use of debt to fund a 529 contribution could be considered a use for investment purposes, despite the fact that the debt proceeds are being deposited into an investment account with the 529 plan. The IRS might take the position that the debt was incurred for personal purposes, and not for investment purposes, because the contribution into the 529 plan is treated as a gift, and gifts are personal in nature. If this were the correct answer, then the interest on the debt would be classified as nondeductible personal interest.

In order to avoid the characterization problem, the best way to borrow for 529 plan funding purposes would be with a home equity loan. Interest on qualifying home equity indebtedness of up to $100,000 is deductible on Schedule A of Form 1040, no matter what use is made of the borrowed funds. The home equity loan must be on a first or second home. The interest on home equity indebtedness used for this purpose would not be deductible for purposes of the alternative minimum tax (AMT), and so you should be careful in determining the possible impact of the AMT.

Once you are comfortable that a deduction for interest expense is available, you should compute the after-tax interest rate on the loan by applying your tax bracket to the deduction. This after-tax interest rate can then be compared to the expected gross return on your investment in the 529 plan (assuming you can count on distributions being tax-free).

Of course, there may be many other considerations to think about before borrowing for this purpose. Cash flow impact is one. The loan will need to be paid back over time, while your investment presumably stays in the 529 plan. Impact on your borrowing ability for other purposes could be another consideration. And finally, there is the risk that the college savings account may not perform as well as originally anticipated, and the leveraging strategy could result in a net loss.

What can I do if the beneficiary of my 529 account graduates from college and I still have money left in the account?

You can either withdraw the money, with the earnings portion of any withdrawal subject to federal income tax and 10% penalty, or you can leave it in the account, program-permitting, to continue growing tax-deferred. If you leave it in, you can keep the same beneficiary on the account (despite having graduated) or you can change the beneficiary to a qualifying family member.

Let's say that you no longer want to maintain the 529 account and would like the excess funds distributed to the account beneficiary. In this case, you will want to be sure that the withdrawn earnings are reported to the beneficiary (assuming the beneficiary is in a lower income tax bracket). Before taking a non-qualified withdrawal from a 529 plan that does not permit you to direct a non-qualified withdrawal to the account beneficiary, you may first want to rollover your account to a different 529 plan that does permit it.

Regardless of who is the recipient of a non-qualified withdrawal, the 10% federal additional tax will be owed on the earnings portion of the withdrawal unless one of the penalty exceptions can be applied. Before the tax law changes made by EGTRRA, there appeared to be a way to avoid the 10% penalty imposed by the states on non-qualified withdrawals: first replacing the original beneficiary with a dying family member, and then withdrawing the funds after the new beneficiary had died. This somewhat macabre technique will apparently no longer succeed since the penalty exception for death is now presented differently in the law. (Interestingly, the substitution of a beneficiary with a disabled relative still appears to fit within the penalty exception).

Does it have to be for college?

The obvious attraction of tax-deferred earnings may cause some investors to consider putting money into a 529 savings plan account without actually intending to use the account to pay for higher education expenses. After all, if the account is later withdrawn, the added penalty is only 10% applied against the earnings portion of the withdrawal, and a few financial calculations will demonstrate that the tax deferral benefits can overcome the penalty after just a few years. The investor contemplating this action can either set up the account and name himself as beneficiary no matter what his age (which many 529 plans permit), or he can name his child or other individual as beneficiary of the account but simply plan to revoke it in the future.

Naturally, this strategy would be viewed by many as an abuse of the tax laws. However, section 529 does not appear to contain any language that would put the individual investor at risk. Rather, the statute seems to place the burden on the state by defining a 529 savings plan as one "under which a person may make contributions to an account which is established for the purpose of meeting the qualified higher education expenses of the designated beneficiary of the account." If investors establish accounts for a different purpose, namely the deferral of income, the tax-qualified status of the program is in jeopardy. Some states, but certainly not all, have developed program rules that permit the program administrator to reject contributions or terminate accounts if it is determined that the purpose of the account is for a purpose other than the payment of the named beneficiary's qualified higher education expenses.

In any event, it would be difficult and perhaps unfair for a 529 program administrator to make this call. Many individuals are returning to school at a later age, even into their retirement years. And those who now have only a vague interest in returning to school may later decide to act on it once they have funds tucked away in a 529 plan account.

EIGHT

Estate Planning
with 529 Plans

The estate and gift tax rules surrounding 529 plans are unique and the planning considerations are anything but straightforward. In fact, the gift tax provisions contained in Section 529 create a result that flies in the face of the general gift tax rules contained elsewhere in the Internal Revenue Code.

The law provides that a contribution into a 529 plan made after August 5, 1997 is treated as a completed gift from the donor to the designated beneficiary of the account. Further, the gift is considered a gift of a present interest that qualifies for the $11,000 annual gift tax exclusion,[1] despite the fact that the designated beneficiary is generally precluded from receiving distributions until such future time as qualified higher education expenses are incurred. The portion of the contribution covered by the $11,000 annual gift tax exclusion is also excluded for purposes of the generation-skipping transfer tax.

---

1. The annual gift exclusion amount is adjusted for cost of living increases, in increments of $1,000. Prior to 2002 the annual gift exclusion amount was $10,000.

Section 529 goes one step further and provides an election that allows the donor to treat a contribution of more than the $11,000 annual exclusion as occurring ratably over five years for gift tax purposes. This means that you can contribute as much as $55,000 to the account of one designated beneficiary in a single year without creating a taxable gift, assuming that no other gifts are made by you to that beneficiary during that five-year period. Although not contained in the statute, the IRS takes the position that if a contribution of more than $55,000 is made to a 529 plan, the averaging election applies only to the first $55,000 and the remainder is treated as a gift in the year of contribution. The five-year averaging election is made on the federal gift tax return, Form 709.

The value of the 529 account is excluded from your gross estate, with one possible exception. If you make the five-year election but then die before the first day of the fifth calendar year, a special rule applies. The portion of the contribution allocated to calendar years beginning after your death is included in your estate.

Besides the five-year averaging election, what is so unique about these rules?

The most startling aspect of the section 529 gift and estate rules is that you can continue to exercise nearly complete control over your accounts. In almost all 529 plans the account owner can change the designated beneficiary to another qualifying family member at will. Further, you will have the option to simply terminate the account and receive a refund of the account value, subject to income tax and a federal 10% additional tax on the earnings. While this rescission may defeat the purpose of removing value from an estate, it certainly provides the level of control and flexibility that many individuals seek when talking to advisers about gifting and other estate reduction programs.

If you replace the designated beneficiary with a new beneficiary who is a member of the family of the former beneficiary, then no further gift is involved, unless the new beneficiary is assigned to a lower generation than the former beneficiary.[2] If the new designation crosses the generation boundary, then the former beneficiary is treated as making a gift to the new beneficiary subject to all the normal gift tax rules. In this situation, the five-year averaging election can be made by the former beneficiary, if necessary, to minimize or avoid gift tax consequences.

Under usual estate and gift tax principles, the level of control enjoyed by the account owner would most assuredly cause the contribution to be treated as an incomplete gift and the value of the account to remain in his gross estate. In fact, this was precisely the treatment accorded contributions to a 529 plan from the time section 529 was signed into law on August 20, 1996 until August 5, 1997, when section 529 was amended by the Taxpayer Relief Act of 1997. During this time period, a contribution made to a 529 plan was not treated as a gift, and the subsequent withdrawal to pay for educational expenses was not treated as a gift either, because it was deemed to be a direct payment of tuition, and direct payments of tuition (and medical care) on behalf of another individual are excluded from the definition of a gift.[3]

How much can I remove from my estate by using a 529 plan?

Almost all 529 savings programs allow contributions of $200,000 or more to the account of a beneficiary. A few allow as much as $260,000 or even more to be contributed for your child, grandchild, or other beneficiary. Contributions of this magnitude are likely to exceed the annual gift tax exclusions, even with the five-year election, and will result in a taxable gift. Your available lifetime exemption for gifts, currently $1 million, can be employed to shelter such large contributions. Grandparents looking to make substantial contributions for grandchildren can also look to apply their lifetime exemptions against the generation-skipping transfer tax.

---

2. The rules for determining the assignment of generation to any particular individual are contained in Internal Revenue Code section 2651.

3. Internal Revenue Code section 2503(e) describes the exclusion for certain transfers of educational or medical expenses.

This exemption is $1,060,000 in 2002 and increases to $3.5 million by 2009.

Many donors, however, will attempt to stay within the amounts that can be contributed under the shelter of the $11,000 annual exclusion. This can still add up to a substantial sum. Consider the wealthy couple that has four children to someday inherit the remnants of their estates (after estate taxes). With each parent contributing $55,000 to the 529 plan account of each child, this couple can effectively remove $440,000 from their combined estates in one day without using up a single dollar of their lifetime exemptions. Not only is the value removed from their taxable estates, but it is invested in a fund that should appreciate nicely over time without the drag of income taxes (because earnings are tax-deferred). And so the estate tax savings will grow even more substantially. That's effective estate planning!

Why should I make contributions to a 529 plan when I can make direct payments of tuition to reduce my estate?

A parent or grandparent may be planning to make use of the unlimited gift tax exclusion under Internal Revenue Code section 2503(e) for the direct payment of tuition to an educational institution. (In some states the payment of higher education expenses by the parent would be considered a legal support obligation and not a gift anyway.) To the extent that tuition expenses are paid directly, the funds in a 529 plan may not be needed for college. Note, however, that exclusion for direct payment of education expenses applies only to tuition, while a 529 plan may allow funding for all qualified higher education expenses.

There are other reasons to consider funding a 529 plan now even if you intend to make direct payments of tuition in the future. One of these reasons is the risk that you may not live long enough to attend to the tuition payment in the future, and so the funds you intend to target for education funding become subject to tax in your estate. Despite a 1999 letter ruling that appears to offer you an opportunity to utilize the section 2503(e) exclusion by paying now for tuition due years down the road[4], you may still be better off by funding the 529 plan and removing mortality risk as a factor.

Furthermore, you may decide that there is little harm done by funding a 529 plan and later deciding to make direct payments of tuition instead of taking withdrawals from the 529 plan. An over-funded 529 plan account can be redirected to another beneficiary in the family, or simply refunded subject to income tax and the 10% penalty.

What happens if I am making other direct gifts to the beneficiary?

You must be sure to consider any other annual exclusion gifts you make during the year to the beneficiary of your 529 account. These gifts reduce the amount of annual exclusion that you can apply to 529 contributions. For example, if you normally make a cash gift of $2,000 each year to your grandchild, you will have only $9,000 left in your annual exclusion. You should limit your 529 contribution under five-year averaging to $45,000 unless you are willing to exceed the exclusion amount.

How do I make the five-year averaging election?

You will need to file Form 709 Gift (and Generation-Skipping Transfer) Tax Return in any year that you wish to make the five-year averaging election for your contributions to 529 plans. Make your election by checking Box B on Schedule A. Attach an explanation to the return describing the beneficiary's name, the total amount contributed by you for the beneficiary, and the amount for which the election is made.

You need only file Form 709 in the year of election. You will not have to file it for each subsequent year of the election period as long as

---

4. In PLR 199941013, the IRS ruled that a grandmother, who made a sizable tuition payment to a private school for her grandchildren while on her deathbed, could take advantage of the section 2503(e) exclusion, despite the fact that the tuition was for schooling in future years. A key factor seemed to be that the tuition payment was not refundable in the event that her grandchildren did not attend that school in the future.

you have no taxable gifts or generation-skipping transfers to report in those years.

If you and your spouse agree to split your gifts, then one-half of your 529 plan contributions will be considered made by each of you. The five-year election would have to be on separate Forms 709 if applicable. Gift splitting can help keep your 529 contributions under the $11,000 annual exclusion amount (or the $55,000 five-year averaging maximum) when you and your spouse do not make equal 529 contributions or other gifts to individual donees. See the Form 709 instructions for information on the gift splitting election.

If my child's grandparents make contributions to a 529 account where I am account owner, who has made the gift to my child, the grandparents or me?

The gift is from the contributor to the designated beneficiary of the account even if the contributor is not the account owner. The contributor will not retain any of the rights of ownership, however, and so may wish to establish his or her own account before making contributions. Some grandparents will prefer leaving the responsibility for the 529 account to the beneficiary's parents and so the ownership rights will not be a concern. In fact, it may help prevent any future problems if eligibility for Medicaid becomes a concern.

What happens if the designated beneficiary dies?

There is some debate on this issue. One interpretation, apparently adopted in a few states, is that section 529 requires the account to be terminated (as it now lacks a living individual as beneficiary) and the balance to be distributed to the account owner. There is no step-up in tax basis and the earnings portion of the distribution remains subject to income tax on the owner's Form 1040. The earnings are also be subject to the 10% federal additional tax, as the exception for death applies only when a distribution is made to the beneficiary or beneficiary's estate.

A differing interpretation is that upon the beneficiary's death the account owner can direct a distribution to the beneficiary's estate, or substitute a new qualifying family member for the deceased beneficiary and continue the account. If distributions are made to the beneficiary's estate, or to a substitute beneficiary, following the beneficiary's death, the earnings will be taxable to that recipient but will escape the 10% additional tax.

The instructions to the newly designed Form 1099-Q indicate that refunds may be made to a beneficiary's estate. It is possible that final regulations, or technical corrections to the tax law, will provide additional clarity.

In either case, the proposed regulations make it clear that the value of the account is included in the deceased beneficiary's gross estate, despite the fact that he never had any control or ownership of that asset. Most beneficiaries of 529 accounts are young family members with few assets and so the inclusion of the asset value in the estate would usually not cause a concern.

Other issues to be resolved

There remain a number of other questions regarding the section 529 gift and estate tax rules that will require answers from the IRS. One such question is whether the five-year election can be made more than once in a five-year period if the donor does not make the full $55,000 contribution in the first year. Although the statute and Form 709 appear to permit it, the proposed regulations provide no assurances. Until IRS guidance is provided (presumably in final regulations), a donor desiring to make a $55,000 contribution to a 529 plan might be advised to do it all in one year rather than spread it out over two or three years.

The proposed regulations also do not address what happens if both the donor and the designated beneficiary die within that five-year time period, or what happens if the donor dies after the initial designated beneficiary is changed to a lower generation beneficiary (giving rise to a second gift). These possibilities will have to be unraveled by the IRS in future regulations or rulings.

C H A P T E R

NINE

529 Plan vs. Coverdell Accounts

The Coverdell education savings account, known until mid–2001 as the Education IRA, is a creation of the same 1997 tax law that gave birth to the Roth IRA, the Hope and Lifetime Learning credits, and the deduction for student loan interest. The Coverdell ESA is a direct competitor to the 529 plan, which has been around in the tax law for a year longer, because both provide college-bound families with an opportunity for tax-free earnings.

The "old" Education IRA was difficult to recommend. The biggest problem was that the Education IRA before 2002 was not compatible with the Hope and Lifetime Learning credits. Families were required to forego tax exclusion of qualified withdrawals if they wanted to claim either of the credits. There were other problems, too. The Education IRA created a recordkeeping burden, exposed the child to potential excise taxes in any year contributions were made to a 529 plan and an Education IRA and could severely impact eligibility for federal financial aid. Considering the fact that annual aggregate contributions to all Education IRAs for the same child were limited to $500, the potential tax savings could not easily overcome these disadvantages.

The Education IRA has now been given renewed life. The 2001 tax law changes (EGTRRA) increase the annual contribution limit from $500 to $2,000 and permit coordination, rather than mutual exclusion, between the Education IRA, the 529 plan, and the Hope and Lifetime Learning credits. In addition, elementary and secondary school expenses have been added to the list of qualified education expenses. In the month following the signing of EGTRRA, Congress renamed the Education IRA in honor of the late Senator Paul Coverdell, a leading proponent of the K–12 provision.

What is a Coverdell education savings account?

A Coverdell education savings account is a trust or custodial account created exclusively for the purpose of paying the qualified higher education expenses of a named beneficiary. Many banks, savings and loan associations, brokerage firms and mutual fund companies now offer Coverdell accounts in addition to traditional IRAs and Roth IRAs. However, a Coverdell account does not require that the contributor have earned income, and does not impact your ability to contribute to a traditional or Roth IRA. Annual contributions to Coverdell accounts may not exceed $2,000 per designated beneficiary and, unless the child has "special needs" under IRS' definition, may not be made after the beneficiary reaches age 18. The $2,000 dollar contribution limit is applied on a calendar year basis across all Coverdell accounts for the same child. You have until April 15 to make contributions counted towards the previous year's $2,000 limit.

Any individual, including your child, can contribute to a Coverdell as long as the contributor's modified adjusted gross income (MAGI)[1] is less than $110,000 ($220,000 if filing a joint return). An individual's ability to contribute up to $2,000 for any child is reduced on a ratable basis as

---

1. MAGI means the adjusted gross income increased by certain exclusions relating to income earned abroad or received from certain American territories or possessions.

the contributor's modified AGI goes above $95,000 and is phased out completely at $110,000 (for joint filers the phase-out range is $190,000 to $220,000). If you are above the income limits, there is nothing to prevent you from making a gift to someone else—probably the child—who is within the limits, followed by a contribution of your gifted funds into the Coverdell account. A corporation that makes contributions to a Coverdell account is not subject to the income limits.

What is the federal income tax treatment of a Coverdell account?

Although your contributions to a Coverdell account are not tax-deductible, any withdrawals from the account are exempt from federal tax to the extent the beneficiary incurs qualified education expenses during the year. Qualified education expenses include qualified higher education expenses (QHEE) and qualified elementary and secondary education expenses (QHESEE). See Chapter 3 for the definition of QHEE. QHEE must be reduced by any other tax-free educational benefits, including scholarship and fellowship grants and employer-provided educational assistance.

There are three categories of elementary and secondary school expenses included in QHESEE. These are the following:

1) Expenses for tuition, fees, academic tutoring, special needs services in the case of a special needs beneficiary, books, supplies, and other equipment which are incurred in connection with the enrollment or attendance of the designated beneficiary;

2) Expenses for room and board, uniforms, transportation, and supplementary items and services (including extended day programs) which are required or provided by the school in connection with such enrollment or attendance; and

3) Expenses for the purchase of any computer technology or equipment or Internet access and related services, if such technology, equipment, or services are to be used by the beneficiary and the beneficiary's family during any of the years the beneficiary is in school.

If a withdrawal is taken from a Coverdell account in excess of the amount of qualified education expenses for the year, the earnings portion of the excess withdrawal is includable in the beneficiary's gross income, and an additional 10% tax is imposed on the earnings. The earnings portion is computed by the beneficiary in the same manner that a 529 plan administrator computes the earnings portion of a 529 account distribution (see Chapter 3). The additional tax is computed on Form 5329 and paid with the beneficiary's federal income tax return. The 10% penalty tax does not apply to withdrawals made on account of the beneficiary's death, disability, or receipt of a tax-free scholarship (to the extent of the scholarship value).

IRS Form 8606 is filed with the beneficiary's tax return to report withdrawals from a Coverdell account. Check with your state concerning the state tax treatment. A state is not required to follow the federal rules described above.

What is the federal gift and estate tax treatment of a Coverdell account?

Just like contributions to a 529 account, your contributions to a Coverdell account are considered completed gifts from you to the beneficiary and qualify for the annual $11,000 gift tax exclusion. However, five-year averaging is not available.

What happens if the account is not spent by the time the beneficiary graduates from college?

Any balance left in a Coverdell account when the beneficiary turns age 30 must be distributed within 30 days and the earnings portion will be subject to income tax and the 10% penalty tax. (There is no age limit for "special needs beneficiaries".) Subject to the policies of the financial institution serving as trustee or custodian of the Coverdell account, a change in designated beneficiary may be made before then without incurring tax or penalty, as long as the new beneficiary is a member of the family. The definition of "member of the family" follows the definition contained in section 529 (see Chapter 3). A new beneficiary must be under age 30. A rollover of a withdrawal from a Coverdell account within 60 days into another Coverdell account for the beneficiary or member of the beneficiary's family who under the age of 30 is permitted, but only once in a 12-month period.

A balance in Coverdell account may also be withdrawn tax-free and penalty-free in a year when equal or greater contributions are made to a 529 plan for the same beneficiary. This option provides you with a significant amount of flexibility if you start out investing with a Coverdell account and you later decide that you are better off in a 529 plan. It can also maintain the deferral of earnings beyond age 30.

Who makes the decisions as to the investments, withdrawals, and beneficiary changes?

These aspects are governed by the adoption agreement used by the Coverdell account trustee or custodian. The IRS has made available two "model" agreements for use by financial institutions, Form 5305-EA for custodial accounts and Form 5305-E for trust accounts. Since the Coverdell account is established for a minor, a "responsible individual" must be named to the account. Forms 5305-EA and 5305-E generally specify that the responsible individual must be the beneficiary's parent or legal guardian (presumably to guard against multiple account contributions that exceed the $2,000 annual limit). However, the custodian or trustee may establish policies that permit someone else to be the responsible person.

The contributor who opens the account makes the initial investment selection and names the responsible individual. The contributor will also indicate whether the responsible individual is permitted to change the designated beneficiary to another qualifying family member, and whether control of the account passes to the beneficiary when he or she reaches the legal age of majority. After the account is established, it is the responsible individual who makes decisions as to investments, withdrawals, and beneficiary changes.

Which is better—the 529 plan or the Coverdell education savings account?

For any family that wishes to save for a child's college education, a decision will need to be made as to whether the first $2,000 of savings goes into a 529 plan or to a Coverdell account. Beyond $2,000 in annual contributions, the Coverdell is not an option. For a parent or other relative who is not eligible to contribute to a Coverdell account because of the income limits, it still appears possible to arrange the contribution by first gifting the money to the child (or anyone else with income below the limits) and then arrange for the contribution by that individual. The factors to consider include the following:

+ **K through 12 expenses.** A Coverdell account can be withdrawn tax-free for qualifying elementary and secondary school expenses while a 529 account cannot be used for that purpose without incurring tax and a 10% penalty on the earnings. A family that plans to send their child to a private school may find this feature of the Coverdell to be very attractive. Even for children who will be attending public grade schools, the ability to use the Coverdell account for home computer purchases and certain other expenses may be seen as a significant advantage. Anyone who is home schooling their children must be careful; some states do not recognize this type of education as a "school". Legislation (S. 1622) is being considered in Congress that would specifically include home schools.

+ **Investment options.** The financial institution that serves as custodian or trustee of a Coverdell account can offer the same types of investments found in individual retirement accounts (IRA), including self-directed investment accounts. Contributions may not be invested in life insurance. The menu of investment options available through 529 plans is more limited.

+ **Fees and expenses.** Because Coverdell accounts generally require less effort to administer, you may find that expenses are lower than with an equivalent amount invested in a 529 plan. Fees can vary significantly from one sponsor to another, however.

+ **Account ownership.** With most 529 plans, you remain the owner of the account and can revoke it at any time. That is not the case with Coverdell accounts. Any distributions from a Coverdell account will be paid to the beneficiary, and may not revert to the contributor or responsible individual. If the beneficiary of a Coverdell account dies, the account must be paid out to the beneficiary's estate unless another qualifying family member is substituted as beneficiary.

✦ **Financial aid.** Because the Coverdell account is accessible only for the benefit of the student, the account is considered an asset of the student in determining eligibility for federal financial aid, and therefore is assessed at a 35% rate. This puts the 529 savings program at an advantage for many families, since the value of a parent-owned 529 account is assessed at a maximum 5.6% rate. The Coverdell account may impact aid eligibility even more in the year following the year of any withdrawals. The financial aid application (FAFSA) and instructions suggest that the entire amount of the withdrawals, including principal, is considered student income assessed in many cases at 50%.

✦ **State tax benefits.** Your state may offer you a state income tax deduction for some or even all of your contribution to its 529 plan. There do not appear to be any states that permit a deduction for contributions to a Coverdell account. If you live in a state that imposes an income tax or a tax on dividends and interest, you should find out how withdrawals from a Coverdell account are treated, and how the treatment compares to distributions from a 529 plan. Many states conform to federal tax treatment for both programs, but that is not necessarily the case in your state.

✦ **Deduction for higher education expenses.** For some reason, in enacting the new 2002 above-the-line deduction for qualified tuition and related expenses, Congress decided to reduce the amount of expenses that qualify for the deduction by the entire distribution from a Coverdell account, while only the earnings portion from a 529 plan distribution will reduce the amount of deduction.

✦ **Excise tax.** If contributions to all Coverdell accounts for a child exceed $2,000 in a year—or are made after the child reaches age

18 or by a taxpayer who is not eligible based on modified adjusted gross income—the excess contributions are subject to a 6% excise tax for each year until corrected. The excise tax is computed on Form 5329 and is either filed alone or with the child's Form 1040 if the child is required to file an income tax return. An excess contribution can be corrected for the year in which it arises by removing the contribution, along with all earnings attributable to the contribution, prior to the child's tax filing deadline for the year (including extensions). The earnings portion of a corrective withdrawal is subject to tax (but not the 10% penalty on non-qualified distributions) on the child's tax return for the taxable year for which the contribution was made. The excess contribution is automatically corrected in a subsequent year to the extent that contributions to the Coverdell account in the subsequent year are less than the maximum allowable contribution. There is no such thing as an excess contribution to a 529 plan because there is no such thing as an excess contribution for federal tax purposes. Rather, the programs themselves will establish and monitor contribution limits. Any contributions beyond those limits will not be accepted by the 529 plan or will be returned when discovered.

✦ **Tax reporting.** Before 2002, the tax reporting of distributions from a 529 plan was much easier than reporting Coverdell withdrawals. With a 529 account, you or the beneficiary would simply include in the "other income" line of Form 1040 the amount of earnings reported to you on Form 1099-G. There was no need to worry about paying a penalty with your tax return, because any non-qualified distribution penalty was withheld by the 529 plan. Starting in 2002, the reporting of 529 distributions and Coverdell withdrawals will be very similar, including your responsibility to pay the 10% penalty with your income tax return. The only major difference is that a 529 plan will keep track of your basis and compute the earnings portion of distributions. With a Coverdell account, you will need to keep track of basis yourself. The financial institution, in its capacity as

Coverdell account trustee or custodian, will simply report total withdrawals for the year.

✦ **Asset protection.** Assets in your child's Coverdell account may be better protected from your creditors than the assets you have in your 529 account. You should speak to your attorney about the laws in your state, and how any special protections enacted in the state that sponsors a 529 plan might apply to you.

✦ **Sunset of EGTRRA changes.** The provisions of the 2001 EGTRRA expire on December 31, 2010. If not extended or otherwise modified through future tax law changes we revert to pre–2002 treatment of 529 plans and Coverdell accounts on January 1, 2011. The risk associated with the sunset provision seems to favor the Coverdell over the 529 plan for an equivalent amount of contributions, because qualified withdrawals from a Coverdell account were tax free before 2002 while qualified withdrawals from a 529 plan were not tax free. Recall, however, that before 2002 a tax-free withdrawal from a Coverdell account eliminated the possibility of claiming a potentially more valuable Hope or Lifetime Learning credit for the student's expenses. Many families would elect to pay tax on the Coverdell withdrawals in order to claim the credit, placing Coverdell withdrawals in about the same position as 529 plan withdrawals.

✦ **Transfer of assets.** You can always transfer assets from a Coverdell account to a 529 account on a tax-free basis as long as there is room for contributions under the limits of the 529 plan. However, it does not work the other way around, i.e. from a 529 account to a Coverdell account. You may even decide to plan for future transfers from the outset. For example, in order to maximize state tax benefits in a state that offers a limited annual deduction for contributions to its 529 plan, you may decide to "park" your savings beyond the deductible amount in a Coverdell account until a later year when the transfer of those savings into the 529 plan will yield a tax deduction. Note that the untaxed earnings portion of the Coverdell withdrawal will be recorded as earnings in your 529 account and included as part of any future distributions from the

529 plan. You will be required to provide the 529 plan administrator with documentation that shows the earnings portion of the Coverdell withdrawal.

Can I regain direct ownership of the assets in my child's Coverdell account by transferring these assets to my 529 account, as long as I name my child the beneficiary of the 529 account?

Although you satisfy the literal requirements for a tax-free and penalty-free withdrawal, you may be violating state laws that would protect the ownership rights of your child in the Coverdell account. This situation is similar to assets that are owned by a minor through a custodial arrangement (UTMA or UGMA). You should seek the advice of your attorney in this situation as you may be required by law to establish the 529 account in such a way as to protect the minor's ownership rights.

TEN

529 Plan vs. Qualified Savings Bonds

Under certain conditions, an owner of U.S. savings bonds may redeem those bonds and exclude the interest from income if the proceeds are used for qualified higher education expenses. These rules are contained in section 135 of the Internal Revenue Code. Series EE bonds issued after 1989, including the new "Patriot Bonds", and all Series I bonds, that are purchased by an individual who is at least 24 years old before the bond's issue date, may qualify for the exclusion. These eligible bonds are sometimes referred to as education savings bonds.

Savings bonds are attractive to many savers because they are backed by the full faith and credit of the U.S. government, interest on the bonds is exempt from state and local income taxes, and the bonds are easy to purchase. Applications are available through most banks, and bonds can be purchased directly over the Internet with your credit card (www.savings-bonds.gov). They are issued in face values as low as $50.

A Series EE bond issued today will earn interest at the rate of 90% of the average yield on marketable Treasury securities with five-year maturities, adjusted every six months. They are issued at a 50% discount to face value so that the cost of a $50 bond is $25. Accrued interest is added to the value of the bond and it is guaranteed to reach face value no later than 17 years after issuance.

Series I bonds (known simply as I Bonds) were first issued in September 1998 and are sold at face value, not at a discount. Interest is comprised of a fixed rate of return plus a variable semiannual inflation rate. The 30-year fixed rate on I Bonds issued between November 1, 2001 and April 30, 2002 is 2.00%. These particular bonds had an initial composite earnings rate of 4.40%, to adjust on May 1, 2002 for a new inflation figure.

Series EE and I bonds earn interest for up to 30 years and are redeemable after six months, although you forfeit three months of interest if you redeem a bond within five years of its issuance.

In order to exclude any of the bond interest under the section 135 education exclusion, your income must be below a certain level in the year of redemption. In 2002, the exclusion is phased out for joint filers and surviving spouses with modified adjusted gross income between $86,400 and $116,400. The phase-out range for single taxpayers is $57,600 to $72,600. (Married taxpayers filing separate returns do not qualify for the exclusion.) These limitations are adjusted each year for inflation. For many taxpayers, it will be difficult to predict future income levels at the time of bond purchase, and so the bond owner may end up not being able to take a tax break that was anticipated at the time of purchase. The rule requiring that you be at least 24 years old is designed to prevent you from effectively avoiding the income limitation through issuance of bonds directly in your child's name.

The entire amount of bond redemption proceeds is compared to qualified higher education expenses in determining the amount of interest excluded from your gross income. If the redemption proceeds exceed qualifying expenses, the amount of excludable interest is reduced pro rata. The exclusion is figured on Form 8815, which is filed with your federal income tax return in the year you redeem the bonds.

The term "qualified higher educational expenses" is defined differently for purposes of the bond income exclusion than it is for purposes of 529 plans and the Coverdell education savings account. For purposes of the bond income exclusion, it includes only tuition and fees for the bond owner or the bond owner's spouse or dependent. Grandparents may not take advantage of the exclusion. Qualified expenses for this purpose exclude any costs for sports, games, or hobbies, unless they are incurred for courses as part of a degree program. Total qualified expenses are also reduced by the amount used in determining the Hope credit or Lifetime Learning credit; tax-exempt scholarships; 529 plan distributions; and withdrawals from a Coverdell account.

Qualified distributions from a 529 plan or Coverdell account can also impact your ability to take advantage of the education bond exclusion if the distributions cause your beneficiary to fail the support test for tax dependency. Chapter 7 discusses this issue with respect to 529 plans. (Coverdell withdrawals are clearly included in the student's self-support.) If your child no longer qualifies as a dependent, your redemption of savings bonds to pay for the child's college expenses will be taxable.

For the college saver who appreciates the investment characteristics of savings bonds, this set of rules makes planning interesting, to say the least. And to use the bonds in conjunction with an account in a 529 plan is particularly challenging. After reducing your child's total tuition and related expenses by your 529 distributions and Coverdell withdrawals, there will likely be little, if any, qualified expenses to use against bond redemption proceeds. Can the 529 plan distributions be used to cover non-tuition, section 529-qualified higher education expenses, such as room and board, leaving the tuition and fees for use against bond redemption proceeds? It appears the answer is no, as the relevant statute is not worded in a way that allows you to apply 529 plan distributions on a selective basis.

Which is better for college savings—savings bonds or a 529 plan?

If you had to choose between them, the 529 plan will be the preferred vehicle for many, although a number of variables have to be considered. Certainly, your anticipated future income level is an important factor because the tax break on savings bond redemptions is lost for higher income taxpayers. If you own savings bonds but never find a way to fit within the education exclusion, the interest will be taxed to you at your rate when you redeem the bonds. Your income level will not prevent you from taking advantage of the tax exclusion on 529 plan distributions. Even if qualified distributions after 2010 become subject to tax (because of the sunset of EGTRRA provisions), the tax will be figured at the student's tax rate, not yours. State and local income taxes can also make a difference; interest on savings bonds will always be exempt, which is not the case with qualifying distributions from 529 plans.

Another obvious consideration is the gross investment return available from a U.S. savings bond versus a 529 plan. Over a long investment horizon, a 529 savings account invested in a portfolio of equity and debt securities is likely to outperform a savings bond. But the level of market risk is higher, too, and so a conservative investor may be more attracted to savings bonds no matter how long the targeted investment horizon is.

A 529 prepaid program will outperform a savings bond if the value of benefits under the contract, based on future tuition increases, exceeds the interest earnings on the bond. Recent history has shown tuition inflation on average to be significantly higher than increases in the Consumer Price Index. Whether the interest premium on savings bonds (such as the 2.00% fixed rate on I Bonds purchased from November 2001 through April 2002) can close the tuition inflation gap is a question that has no certain answer.

Yet another variable is the amount of money you have available for investment. A 529 savings program can be used for certain educational expenses (such as room and board) that savings bonds cannot cover under the education exclusion.

I already have a significant investment in eligible U.S. savings bonds, but I am interested in 529 plans too. What are my options?

Since it is difficult to effectively combine the tax exclusion for savings bonds with other education tax incentives, you will probably need to decide whether to count on the bond education exclusion as being your best bet. Fortunately, you may not need to make this decision now. The tax law permits you to claim the exclusion for redemptions in any year to the extent that contributions are made to a 529 plan or Coverdell education savings account for the benefit of you, your spouse, or your dependent. In essence, the contribution to a 529 plan constitutes a qualifying expense for purposes of the education savings bond exclusion.

The ability to make this transfer out of savings bonds without triggering tax provides a wonderful degree of flexibility. In fact, you may decide to purchase qualifying savings bonds with the *intent* of making this transfer in a future year. It is important to remember, however, that you must satisfy the income requirements in the year of redemption in order to take advantage of the opportunity.

Here are some situations in which the transfer should be considered:

+ You currently own qualifying U.S. savings bonds and your income is within the limits this year. The problem is that the bonds are targeted for the college expenses of your child in a future year, and there is a chance that your income will be too high in that future year. By redeeming the bonds this year, and transferring the proceeds into a 529 plan or Coverdell account, you succeed in "locking in" the tax exclusion on bond interest no matter what your income level is in the future. Note, however, that the untaxed interest will cause a downward adjustment to the tax basis of your 529 or Coverdell account, and so any non-qualified withdrawal in the future will incur not only income tax but the 10% penalty as well. (You will be required to provide the 529 plan administrator with documentation that evidences the untaxed interest in any year that bond redemption proceeds are transferred to your 529 account.).

+ Rather than being unsure of your income in a future year, you may be unsure of your ability to claim your child as a dependent under the various dependency tests. You may decide to make the transfer from savings bonds to a 529 plan this year while your child is still a dependent. It will not matter for section 529 distribution purposes whether the beneficiary is a dependent or not.

+ Your dependent child is in college and you intend to use your qualifying savings bonds to pay for the cost. Despite the fact that your income is within the bond exclusion limits, you discover that you will not be able to take full advantage of the exclusion because you lack sufficient qualified expenses. This can easily occur, for instance, when the tuition is counted toward the Hope or Lifetime Learning credit, or when it is reduced by qualified distributions from a 529 or Coverdell account. You will save taxes by first directing the bond redemption proceeds to a 529 plan or Coverdell account and then taking distributions for college expenses. The reason for this may not be obvious, but it relates to the fact that 529/Coverdell withdrawals can be used to pay for certain expenses (i.e. room and board, books, supplies, and equipment) that are not considered qualified expenses under the section 135 education savings bond exclusion.

+ Now that Coverdell accounts can be used for certain elementary and secondary school expenses, the conversion of U.S. savings bonds for this purpose could also make sense.

+ You may be one of the relatively small number of bond-holding parents in position to claim the section 222 above-the-line deduction for qualified higher education expenses before it expires at the end of 2005 (see Chapter 3). The entire amount of expenses used to determine the bond exclusion will reduce the amount you can deduct under section 222. If you first transfer the bond proceeds to a 529 plan, and then take the distribution, only those expenses attributable to the earnings portion of the 529 distribution will reduce the amount you can claim as a deduction. You will possibly gain a deduction for the principal portion that would have gone unclaimed.

I am a grandparent who owns post–1989 savings bonds and I would like to use these bonds to pay for my grandchild's college costs. Can I take advantage of the education bond exclusion?

Unfortunately, unless your grandchild is also your dependent you do not qualify for the section 135 education savings bond exclusion. You will have to report the interest income on your tax return in the year you redeem the bonds even if you use the proceeds to fund a 529 plan for the grandchild. However, it looks like there may be a loophole. Program permitting, you can establish a 529 account and name yourself as beneficiary. You may now cash in your bonds tax-free by funding the 529 account. Later on, you can change the beneficiary of the 529 account to your grandchild. Be sure to discuss this strategy with your own tax professional before attempting it.

Why should I worry about qualifying for the education bond exclusion when I can avoid tax by purchasing the bonds in my child's name and reporting the accrued interest on her tax return each year?

That strategy can work well. Assuming your child can effectively shelter the annual bond interest accrual with her $750 standard deduction, choosing to report the interest each year can produce the best after-tax returns regardless of your circumstances in the year of redemption. Take care that this election, which applies to all future years unless you request permission from the IRS to change, does not backfire in the event your child is under the age of 14 and earns total investment income above the "kiddie tax" trigger (currently $1,500). For more information see IRS Publication 550, available online at www.irs.gov.

Also be sure to consider other aspects of placing investments in the name of your child, such as gift tax consequences and student financial aid impact.

Some parents who otherwise qualify for the education bond exclusion discover too late that the savings bonds were originally issued in the child's name, violating the requirement that the bonds be issued to an individual at least 24 years old. If they had not elected annual reporting of interest, the entire amount of accrued interest is taxable to the child upon redemption. It may be possible, however, to re-register the bonds in the name of the parent. Go to www.savingsbonds.gov for more information about correcting mistakes in the registration of your bonds.

ELEVEN

529 Plan vs. Other Investment Alternatives

There are many different strategies and financial products available to the family seeking to save for future college costs. Besides the tax-qualified programs discussed in previous chapters—the Coverdell education savings account and U.S. savings bonds—a number of other investment choices and forms of ownership have become popular over the years. While these investment alternatives may not be directly or exclusively geared to college savings, their features can make them adaptable to this purpose. This chapter will discuss several of these options in comparison to the 529 plan.

IRA Withdrawals Used for Higher Education Expenses

Before the Taxpayer Relief Act of 1997, a withdrawal from an individual retirement account taken before the owner turned 59 and one-half years of age and used to pay for education expenses would incur a 10% penalty on premature distributions. The changes made by Congress in the Taxpayer Relief Act of 1997 now allow a premature IRA withdrawal to be taken without penalty if used to pay qualified higher education expenses of the taxpayer or the taxpayer's spouse, child, or grandchild. (Qualified higher education expenses are reduced by the proceeds from the tax-free redemption of qualified U.S. savings bonds.)

This change can certainly be helpful. Many individuals have assets in individual retirement accounts and it is nice to know that those assets are accessible not only for retirement, but also in the event they are needed for college expenses. Note, however, that any earnings in a traditional IRA will still be taxable when withdrawn for college. (The principal portion of a withdrawal will also be taxable to the extent you claimed a deduction for contributions to the IRA.)

A Roth IRA can be more effective than a traditional IRA when tapped for college expenses. Like a traditional IRA, the earnings portion of a premature Roth IRA distribution for qualified higher education expenses will still be subject to income tax. With a Roth IRA, however, distributions are first considered a return of principal; earnings come out only after the principal is exhausted. A viable strategy is to withdraw principal for college expenses and leave the earnings to grow in the Roth IRA. Once you turn 59 ½ (and assuming the Roth IRA is at least five years old), you can withdraw earnings at any time and exclude the earnings from tax.

Which vehicle should I use—an IRA or a 529 plan?

The answer to this question for many people would be the IRA, and more specifically, the Roth IRA. The Roth IRA offers federal income tax benefits equivalent to the 529 plan (and perhaps even better after 2010 if the section 529 exclusion expires). In addition, the Roth IRA withdrawn in retirement can be used for any purpose without negative consequences, whereas the 529 plan is restricted to qualified higher education expenses. Consider also that for many people the objective of funding retirement has a higher priority than funding college. Borrowing is almost always an option for college expenses but that is not the case for retirees who have inadequate financial resources.

So why not forget about the 529 plan and just concentrate on using the Roth IRA? Perhaps you should, if you are not already contributing the maximum amount to a Roth IRA. But consider that your ability to contribute to a Roth IRA is subject to income limitations just like the Coverdell account. Furthermore, the annual contribution limit in 2002 is only $3,000. And beyond that, it requires that you have earned income of at least the amount of the contribution.

For federal financial aid purposes the use of an IRA or a Roth IRA is a mixed blessing. The IRA balance will not be counted as an asset in the computation of the expected family contribution. But if withdrawals are taken from an IRA during the year, the financial aid application requires that any untaxed principal be added to the student's or parents' income in the calculation. With 529 plan withdrawals, it appears that adjusted gross income will be adjusted only by the earnings portion.

You will probably find that the IRA is not the total solution to saving for your child's college expenses. Even if it were large enough to cover the cost, tapping it for college means it will not be there for your retirement. A 529 plan will probably still provide the best means to save for the largest portion of future college expenses.

How about my employer's 401(k) plan? Should I redirect any of the savings that come out of my pay to a 529 plan instead?

Unlike an IRA, a 401(k) cannot be tapped directly for college expenses before you retire. If the plan permits you to take a loan, you could use the loan proceeds to pay college expenses, but remember that you must repay the loan to the 401(k) plan.

You will need to make any decision regarding a 401(k) based on your own particular circumstances. As discussed above, the importance of saving for retirement may turn out to be your overriding concern and you will want to maximize any opportunity you have to contribute to qualified retirement plans. An analysis of your current and projected future tax situation can also help in your decision. With a 401(k) you are making "pre-tax" contributions—i.e. you receive an upfront tax break on your contributions—but you pay income tax down the road on the distributions. Contributions to a 529 plan are made with after-tax dollars, but the distributions may come out tax-free.

If your state offers you a tax deduction for contributions into its 529 plan, you may decide that is reason enough to direct some dollars into that program. However, in most cases it will be unwise to do so if it means you will be giving up any matching contributions by your employer to its 401(k) plan.

Tax-Exempt and Tax-Deferred Securities

Traditional investment planning for college-bound families will often include the transfer of income-producing assets from parent to child in order to take advantage of the child's low tax bracket. When the child is under age 14, this planning must consider ways to avoid the "kiddie tax." Assuming the child has no earned income, up to $1,500 (in 2002) of investment income can be received by the child at low cost ($750 is sheltered by the standard deduction and the next $750 is taxed at the 10% tax rate), while investment income above that level will be taxed at the parents' top marginal tax rate. One strategy often employed by families facing the kiddie tax will be to have the child under 14 invest in tax-exempt municipal bonds or tax-deferred U.S. savings bonds. The investment choices will broaden in the year the child turns 14 because income at that time will be taxed entirely at the child's tax rate. For children owning U.S. savings bonds, choosing to recognize interest income each year as it accrues may be beneficial if (1) the child is under 14 and does not have enough income to trigger the kiddie tax, or (2) if the child is 14 or older and can recognize the annual interest accrual at a lower tax rate than in the year the bonds are redeemed.

Of course, investment assets in the child's name may not be recommended if financial aid eligibility is a consideration because a child's assets are assessed at a higher rate than parents' assets in calculating the expected family contribution to college costs. Families in this position may consider investing in annuity contracts or life insurance because these assets are generally not assessable in the financial aid calculation.

Life insurance products can have attractive tax features including tax-deferred build-up of value and tax-free death benefits. Annuities are one type of insurance product often chided for their low investment return as affected by mortality and expense charges, as well as for the penalties charged on withdrawal or surrender in the first five to ten years. There is an additional problem for most college parents in that annuity payments received prior to the age of 59 and one-half will not only incur income tax but a 10% federal excise tax. A 529 plan will provide a better tax outcome when used for college expenses.

Universal life insurance policies will work better than annuities for college saving. In addition to the death benefit coverage and the favored tax treatment of life insurance, these policies are flexible and allow parents to adjust the level of premium payments, borrow against cash value, and make partial withdrawals. A related product, variable universal life, gives the policy owner an ability to select the underlying investments from a menu of mutual funds and provides more upside potential in the cash value build-up. If a cash-value policy is used as a college savings vehicle, it is important to start early in the child's life to allow time for the policy to build in value. A careful review of the prospectus is necessary to understand all costs and restrictions.

Treasury Inflation-Indexed Securities

The U.S. Treasury is promoting its 10-year inflation bonds (sometimes known as TIPS) as an appropriate investment for college savings. These bonds are sold in $1,000 denominations and the principal value is adjusted upwards each year for inflation as measured by the CPI. The redemption value of the bond after 10 years includes the annual inflation adjustments. The coupon rate paid on these bonds is lower than a comparable-term regular Treasury bond, but the rate is applied to the inflation-adjusted value and so the interest paid to the bondholder increases each year. Even if you are satisfied with the yield, the tax treatment of these bonds is a disadvantage. Investors must pay federal tax each year not only on the interest payments, but also on the value increase from the inflation adjustment.

The inflation protection offered by TIPS and the tax advantages of a 529 plan might seem like an attractive combination for the safety-conscious investor interested in hedging tuition inflation. In fact, 529 savings program in at least two states (North Carolina and South Dakota) offer an investment option partially invested in TIPS. This may become a feature in some other 529 plans as well.

Zero Coupon and College Savings Bonds

Zero coupon bonds are bonds that do not make payments of interest but are issued at a discount to face value. The size of the discount determines the effective interest rate on the bond if held to maturity. Zero coupon bonds can be useful for college saving because maturities can be matched to the college years, and holders do not have to deal with the reinvestment of interest (unlike interest-paying bonds). The price of a zero coupon bond sold prior to maturity is affected not only by the amount of unearned interest, but also by market conditions at the time of sale. In a period of rising interest rates, the relative value of the bond will decrease.

There are several types of zero coupon bonds, each with unique tax and investment characteristics. Zero Coupon Treasury bonds are U.S. Treasury bonds or notes that have been stripped of their coupons and sold on a discount basis. Corporations issue zero coupon bonds that provide a higher return on investment because they are subject to the risk of default (principal and earned discount could be lost). Banks may issue zero coupon certificates of deposit that are FDIC-insured (up to $100,000).

All of these zero coupon alternatives suffer a disadvantage in that they require that the discount earned each year be reported as interest and included in taxable income. Zero coupon municipal bonds do not present this problem because their interest is tax-exempt for federal and state purposes (except for the individual who has to pay state tax on an out-of-state bond).

Several states have issued bonds that are specifically targeted to families saving for college. These are essentially zero coupon municipal bonds although they are often given the name of college savings bonds, baccalaureate bonds, or something similar. The most significant disadvantage of this investment option is that municipal bonds generally yield less than taxable bonds and may not keep pace with rising college costs. States that have issued these types of bonds include Arkansas, Connecticut, Hawaii, Illinois, Massachusetts, Michigan, Minnesota, New Hampshire, Ohio, Rhode Island, Tennessee, Virginia, and Washington. There will likely be less activity in this area in the future due to the increasing use of 529 plans.

Private Prepaid Tuition Plans

At some point, you may run across a prepaid tuition program that is not a qualified 529 plan. This would most likely be an arrangement established and administered by a commercial enterprise, although it may involve a private educational institution. A program like this may purport to provide many of the same benefits as a 529 plan by accepting prepayment for future tuition at that institution. Be careful. These arrangements will not necessarily receive the same tax benefits as a program that qualifies under section 529. Do not rely entirely on the representations of the promoter of a private prepaid tuition plan. Anyone considering one of these arrangements should be sure to thoroughly investigate all aspects of the investment and seek professional advice. For example, consider what happens to your investment in the event that the educational institution wants to back out of the agreement, or the sponsor goes bankrupt?

The good news is that eligible educational institutions, including private colleges, are now able to establish their own 529 prepaid programs. In these programs, your funds must be held in a separate trust as added protection for you. Another requirement is that the program apply for and receive a favorable determination from the IRS. The non-profit Tuition Plan, a consortium of over 275 private colleges, hopes to launch its 529 prepaid program in 2002. Please note: section 529 tax exclusion for qualified distributions from private prepaid programs first becomes effective in 2004.

Mutual Funds

There are three main advantages commonly cited for the use of taxable mutual funds as a college savings vehicle as opposed to a 529 plan. They are (1) potential for superior investment performance, (2) ability to direct the investments, and (3) low capital gains taxes. Each of these factors is examined below.

The first supposed advantage, potential for superior investment performance, was more true in prior years when the prepaid program was the prevalent type of 529 plan. Prepaid programs are designed to protect the participant from increases in tuition, not to maximize long-term investment returns. The long running bull market of the 1990s had many investors flocking to equity mutual funds even for relatively short-term college savings. The stock market performance over the last two years has provided ample demonstration that equity funds can quickly turn the other way, however, and prepaid programs have enjoyed a resurgence of interest. Your tolerance for risk becomes an important consideration, and that tolerance can (and should) depend to a significant degree on the period of time you have before needing the funds for college.

Even assuming the stock market resumes an upward trend, the perceived investment superiority of a taxable mutual fund approach can no longer be cited as an advantage over 529 plans. The 529 savings programs provide the college saver with returns directly linked to the investments in the 529 plan portfolios, and these investments are often the same equity mutual funds that would be attractive to the non–529 college saver. In fact, they may be even better. Some taxable mutual funds are managed in a "tax-efficient" manner so as to reduce the investor's tax liability generated by the investment activity in the fund. This may restrict the fund manager from making investment decisions that would be made based on pure investment considerations. The manager of a 529 savings program has no reason to be concerned with the tax consequences of investment activity and can focus entirely on making the best investment decisions within its asset guidelines and investment policy.

The second noted advantage of taxable mutual funds, the ability to direct investments among different funds at the discretion of the owner, will never be totally matched by 529 plans absent a change to the law. By definition, a 529 plan may not allow the account owner to directly or indirectly direct the investments. In actuality, the increasing number of 529 savings programs, the ever expanding menu of investment options available, and the conditional ability to change your investment option or rollover your account to another state's program, together provide as much flexibility as most investors may ever want.

Several 529 savings programs have recently introduced, or have announced plans to introduce, a lineup of single mutual funds available to participants. An investor will be able to customize 529 portfolios using one or more of these mutual funds, if desired, and reallocate balances between the funds at least once every year.[1] This innovation injects a new dimension of self-direction to the 529 realm, and will enable the investor to concentrate his or her savings in sectors that are not widely available through the traditional portfolio options, such as small cap funds or international stock funds.

Perhaps more relevant, however, is the question of whether your ability to direct investments is an advantage or a disadvantage. The majority of 529 savings programs still utilize professional money managers and large financial services companies to determine the mix of investments

---

1. See Chapter 3 for a discussion of the investment flexibility now permitted under IRS Notice 2001–55.

that will produce the best balance of risk and return for any particular beneficiary's college savings. Is it likely that the self-directed account will perform better over the relevant time period? That is a question that investors are going to have to answer themselves (or with the help of their professional advisers).

Many experts who have studied this issue as it relates to self-directed 401(k) accounts would answer "no" to that question. The "age-based" portfolios available through many 529 plans may be an advantage because they prevent the novice investor from doing damage to his or her own savings. Of course, what this strategy does not do is select an asset allocation and investment approach that takes into account all the other components of your financial situation. A professional investment adviser or financial planner can provide valuable services even if you select an auto-pilot option, and should be able to incorporate the 529 investment into your total financial picture in an effective way.

The final perceived advantage of taxable mutual funds, lower capital gains rates, will not stand up to close scrutiny, particularly now that qualified distributions from a 529 plan are federally tax free. A recent study by the TIAA-CREF Institute compared after-tax investment returns of an investment in New York's College Savings Program (Managed Allocation option) to the after-tax return on a portfolio of equivalent investments in a taxable account.[2] Under one set of assumptions—using a 35% federal tax rate, a 6.85% state tax rate, and average annual returns on stocks, bonds, and short-term securities of 10%, 6.5%, and 5% respectively—the 529 account finished 8.9% ahead of the taxable portfolio if liquidated after six years, 17.8% ahead after 12 years, and 28.7% ahead after 18 years. The advantage of the 529 plan comes not only from tax exemption for qualified distributions, but also because the exchange of funds over time to achieve a more conservative asset allocation triggers capital gains in the taxable account.

There may be an advantage in using your existing mutual funds or individual stocks to save for a child's college education if those investments have significant unrealized gain from past appreciation. Transferring these

---

2. Keith R. Davenport, Douglas Fore, and Jennifer Ma. Miracle Growth. *Investment Advisor*, September 2001.

securities to your child can shift the ultimate capital gains burden to the child at the child's lower capital gains tax bracket. Stock, mutual funds, or other property cannot be contributed to a 529 plan. The contribution must be in cash. If appreciated securities must be liquidated in order to fund a 529 plan, there will be a tax cost to doing so.

Finally, consideration would have to be given to the ways in which assets are transferred to the child. An outright gift to your child may not be desirable due to the loss of control of the investment as well as possible state law restrictions on the ownership of property by a minor. An alternative method to transfer ownership would have to be carefully arranged. The basic options are discussed below and compared to an interest in a 529 plan.

Uniform Gifts or Transfers to Minors Act

The Uniform Gifts to Minors Act (UGMA), adopted in some form in all 50 states, allows assets to be transferred to a custodian for the benefit of a minor child. The child receives direct ownership of the assets upon reaching the age of majority (18 or 21) as determined under state law. The Uniform Transfers to Minors Act (UTMA) is a more recent alternative to the UGMA, available in many states, that works in essentially the same manner. The UTMA account is preferable in several respects, because it may stay open for a longer period of time (up to age 25 in some states), and because it can hold certain types of assets, such as real estate interests, that cannot be owned by a custodian for an UGMA account. UGMA/UTMA accounts do not provide the level of control available to the donor in a 529 plan where assets may be kept out of the hands of the beneficiary indefinitely.

Dividends, interest, or capital gains realized in an UGMA/UTMA account will be taxed to the minor beneficiary and are subject to the "kiddie tax" if the child is under age 14. However, the donor, not the child, will recognize the income from an UGMA/UTMA account if the income is used to satisfy the donor's legal obligation to support the minor. Payment of college expenses could in some instances constitute the legal obligation of the donor/parent, and so the income burden could shift back to the parent.

You also need to be careful about the estate tax treatment of UGMA/UTMA accounts. While a contribution to a 529 plan is removed from your gross estate (subject to partial add-back if you die in the five-year period after making the gift-tax averaging election), UGMA/UTMA transfers will be included in your gross estate if you die while serving as custodian. To avoid this risk, you should name someone else (perhaps your spouse) as custodian at the time the account is established and relinquish your control over its management.

Can I transfer my child's existing UTMA assets into a 529 plan?

Yes, if you are custodian and decide that a 529 plan is a better way to save, you can liquidate the current investments and reinvest the proceeds in a 529 plan. The sale of investments may generate a tax on capital gains. See Checklist Item #4 in Chapter 6 for a description of the different ways 529 plans accommodate contributions from an existing UGMA/UTMA account. Ultimately, it is your responsibility as custodian to comply with state law in handling UGMA/UTMA funds. Some parents will be disappointed to learn that a transfer of assets to a 529 plan will not result in a transfer of ownership rights from the minor to the parent. The minor will assume direct ownership of the 529 account at the age of majority or other age established under the law. For this reason, you may want to consider the possibility of spending down current UGMA/UTMA assets for the benefit of the minor, and replace those funds with your own money going into a 529 plan. If you do have a 529 account for a minor under UGMA/UTMA, you should establish a different account for any of your own funds.

Irrevocable Trust

A gift to an irrevocable trust allows you to maintain some level of control over the assets by dictating the terms of the trust agreement. The trust agreement could provide that your beneficiaries will receive trust corpus and income only under certain conditions. There are several problems with this approach, however. One problem is that any income retained in the trust is taxed not to you or to the trust beneficiary, but to the trust itself, at tax brackets that become very high very quickly. Another problem is that your transfer to the trust is considered a gift of a future interest, and a gift of a future interest does not qualify for the $11,000 annual gift tax exclusion.

It is possible to deal with the gift tax problem by providing the beneficiaries with "Crummey" withdrawal powers. These arrangements are known as "Crummey Trusts." A Crummey power provides the beneficiary with a right to withdraw the current year's contribution for a limited period of time (often 30 days). The beneficiary will not be expected to exercise this right. When properly drafted and executed, a gift to a Crummey trust will qualify for the $11,000 annual gift tax exclusion as a gift of a present interest, to the extent of the beneficiary's rights to withdraw the gift. Income generated by the trust may be taxed to the trust, to the beneficiary with Crummey withdrawal rights, or to the distributee of the income, depending on the circumstances.

A 529 plan offers the asset control that individuals establishing Crummey trusts are attempting to achieve, without all the complications. Crummey trusts work well with life insurance policies, however, which are not an option when dealing with 529 plans.

Section 2503(c) Minor's Trust

Another way to qualify the gift-in-trust for the $11,000 annual gift tax exclusion is to establish the trust under Code section 2503(c). This type of trust, called a minor's trust, must provide that the trustee has total discretion to expend trust corpus and income for the benefit of the minor before he turns 21, and that the beneficiary (or the beneficiary's estate) receive any remaining balance upon reaching age 21. The estate tax and income tax consequences are variable depending on a number of factors.

There would be little reason to use a section 2503(c) minor's trust to hold investment securities when the 529 plan is a better option.

Section 2503(b) Income Trust

This is a trust that requires all income to be distributed at least annually. The income interest will qualify for the $11,000 annual gift tax exclusion as a gift of a present interest, valued under IRS tables, while the remainder interest is a gift of a future interest. There is no requirement that the trust terminate when the beneficiary turns 21. Again, the 529 plan is superior to the 2503(b) trust in that income remains in the 529 plan until you decide to withdraw it, the earnings are tax-deferred and potentially tax free, and the entire contribution (not just the income interest) qualifies for the annual gift tax exclusion.

Family Partnership

A family partnership or family limited liability company can be formed to hold securities and other investments that may be targeted for college savings or any other purpose. This can be a very useful tool for transferring assets to the next generation and can provide a way to shift income, reduce a large estate, and even provide some level of creditor protection. For gift and estate tax purposes, an added benefit of the family investment partnership is the possibility that a valuation discount may be available for the fractional partnership interest gifted to the child. This may of course be challenged by the IRS, which wants to see a "business purpose" for the partnership and has a particular problem with family partnerships consisting only of marketable securities and no other business assets. In addition to all the potential tax advantages of a family partnership, there is an additional benefit in that you can maintain effective control of the portion of the assets that are gifted away by giving away limited partnership interests and retaining the general partnership interest. The general partner has the authority to make decisions for the partnership, including the timing and amount of distributions to the partners.

The disadvantage of family partnerships is that they must be carefully crafted and they require significant effort for annual recordkeeping and tax reporting. In addition, the Internal Revenue Code contains certain income tax provisions targeted directly at family partnerships that must be followed. A full explanation of the advantages and disadvantages of a family partnership is beyond the scope of this book and anyone interested in this option should consult an attorney who specializes in this area. Due to the expense of setting up and maintaining a family partnership, they are usually only recommended when a large amount of assets is at stake. A 529 plan, on the other hand, is a much simpler and much less expensive way to set up a college savings program for your family.

TWELVE

Managing Your 529 Account

A parent—let's call him John—decides to use 529 plans but wants to keep it all as simple as possible. John begins by establishing an investment account, or purchasing a prepayment contract, for each of his children in the program offered by his own state. As the years go by, he pays little attention to the 529 plan, comfortable in the knowledge that it will be there to help pay the costs at whatever college each of his children decides to attend. When the college bills finally roll in, John taps the entire value of each account or contract for that purpose.

For John, as well as for many others, this uncomplicated approach will produce the desired results, and even the most restrictive 529 plan can be an appropriate choice. Realize, however, that federal tax law offers a significant degree of flexibility to those utilizing 529 plans as a savings vehicle. From a planning perspective, this flexibility can be extremely attractive. It means that you are not locked into the decisions made when the account is first established. As circumstances change, either planned or unplanned, you can make adjustments to ensure that the benefits of your college savings accounts are maximized.

Most 529 plans will accommodate your desire to change some aspect of your account. As you will see, well-timed changes can save federal and state income taxes, estate taxes, and generation-skipping transfer taxes, and can enhance eligibility for federal financial aid as well. Even when you find no reason to make any account modifications, you will still have to make some decisions along the way in order to obtain the most benefits from your use of 529 plans.

It is important to point out that the flexibility allowed under federal tax law is not fully incorporated into many 529 plans. As demonstrated in Chapter 6, the rules for a particular state's program may significantly limit your maneuverability. These limitations should be understood before you begin making contributions. This factor could influence your choice of program.

Basic Account Management

Let's assume that you have made your decision as to which 529 plan to use in saving for the future higher education costs of your beneficiary. Your selection was based on a careful analysis using the checklist in Chapter 6; or perhaps you have relied on the guidance provided by your financial planner. Either way, you have read through the packet of official program materials and feel that you have a good understanding of how this particular program works. If it is a savings program that offers different investment options, you have selected the option, or combination of options, with which you feel most comfortable. What else do you need to think about? There are at least three questions you face between now and the time your child graduates from college.

1) When should you make your contributions?

It may not be a good idea to take every penny you can get your hands on and throw it all into your chosen 529 plan (or plans) at your very first opportunity. You should look to time your contributions to obtain the most benefit from your investment and save as much in taxes as possible. Here are some reasons why:

- **Capital gains tax.** If you are liquidating your other investments in order to fund your 529 account, you need to carefully consider the tax consequences. Properly timing the sale can make a difference in how much income tax you pay.

- **State tax benefits.** If your state offers a state income tax deduction for your contributions, or perhaps a matching grant, consider how the timing of your contributions can affect the amount of benefit you receive. For instance, if you live in a state like New York that offers a limited deduction for your contributions to its 529 plan, with no carryover of excess contributions, you may want to spread your contributions over more than one year to capture a greater tax benefit.

- **Gift tax.** If you have more than $11,000 to contribute for any one beneficiary, or if you are making other gifts to that individual, you should be careful to formulate a gifting strategy. One of your objectives may be to get as much money into the 529 plan as possible without exceeding the $11,000 annual gift tax exclusion. Careful use of the five-year averaging election will help you do this. If it is already late in the year, you should consider making your $11,000 contribution this year, and waiting until the beginning of next year before putting in another $55,000 under the five-year averaging election. This way you have funded your account with $66,000 in gift-tax-free contributions rather than $55,000 (you will have consumed your annual gift exclusions going into year 6 rather than year 5, however.)

- **Account expenses.** Consider how the timing of your contributions might affect the overall cost of the program to you. Some 529 savings programs will waive annual account maintenance fees if you sign up for automatic deposits from your checking or savings account. The fee might also be waived if you maintain a minimum account balance. With prepaid programs, the price of your contract can vary significantly based on the age of your child. It may be to your benefit to purchase a contract this year to get better pricing. In some cases, you may be better off waiting until next year if you can determine that the price will not increase by much and you can set the money aside in an interest-earning account in the meantime. In many prepaid programs, you will also need to decide whether to purchase a higher-priced contract under an installment payment plan (total payments will be more than the lump-sum cost of the contract), or purchase a lower-priced contract now with the intent to buy additional semesters or tuition units in future years.

✦ **Market risk.** Investing in a 529 savings program is similar to investing in mutual funds. Although the concepts of modern portfolio theory are beyond the scope of this book, some experts espouse "dollar cost averaging" as a way to manage the risk of a volatile stock market. This involves making contributions at regular intervals. Remember also that your college savings accounts are probably just one piece of your total investment "pie" and that you should be balancing your asset allocation across all your investments. If you do not feel comfortable managing your own investments, seek the help of an investment professional.

2) When should you take distributions to pay for college costs?

In a 529 prepaid program you may not have a great deal of flexibility in the timing of your benefits, because payout procedures are probably standardized. This does not mean that you should forget entirely about timing opportunities, however. The date that the program makes payments to your child's school will determine the year in which the expenses are considered paid under any other tax provisions including the Hope credit, the Lifetime Learning credit, and the above-the-line section 222 deduction for higher education expenses. A payment of second semester bills in January rather than December can make a significant difference in your tax liability.

With the 529 savings programs, and with most of the unit-type prepaid or guaranteed savings programs, you will have much more latitude in the timing of distributions. It is up to you to decide how to allocate your account between academic years, and when to request distributions. It appears under the recent tax law changes that you must carefully coordinate any cash withdrawals from your 529 savings account so as to fall within the same calendar year as your payment of qualifying expenses. In order to determine the tax consequences of your withdrawals, you will be required to compare the beneficiary's total qualified expenses to total 529 withdrawals. If you pay for college costs this year, but receive your 529 plan withdrawal next year, you may find that you have a tax problem. The IRS may develop rules that permit some crossover in matching expenses with cash withdrawals, but any such rules would add to your recordkeeping burdens.

Keep in mind that the various tax incentives for higher education requiring coordination can make the planning analysis very complex. As an example, consider that section 529 qualified higher education expenses are reduced by expenses used to determine a Hope or Lifetime Learning credit. Since a Hope credit is calculated on up to $2,000 in qualified expenses, but a Lifetime Learning credit is calculated on as much as $10,000 in qualified expenses (after 2002), you may find that it is better to target the 529 withdrawals to the Hope credit years rather than to the Lifetime Learning credit years. See Chapter 7 for a more extensive discussion of income tax planning considerations.

3) When should you take a non-qualified withdrawal?

Consider taking a non-qualified withdrawal in any year in which you determine that the tax and financial aid consequences will turn out better for you than the use of your account for qualified higher education expenses. Because you will be subject to income tax and a 10% penalty, this tactic is not often recommended, but here are some possible scenarios where a non-qualified withdrawal may be beneficial:

✦ In many prepaid programs, the value of the contract for beneficiaries attending college out-of-state is limited to actual tuition at the institution being attended. A beneficiary who is enrolled in the prepaid program but later moves and becomes a resident of another state may find that public university tuition in the new state is lower than tuition in the prior state of residence. In this situation, the value of the contract may be higher if it is canceled than if it is used to pay tuition at the lower rate.

✦ A refund of the account might make sense when its use for qualified expenses would severely impact a financial aid award. You will not necessarily know this until your child is close to college age and you assess the prospects for financial aid.

✦ If your account has lost value—the balance is less than cumulative net contributions—a termination and liquidation of the account may produce an income tax benefit. The loss may be deductible on your income tax return as a miscellaneous itemized deduction. You should be sure to discuss this with a tax professional before claiming such a deduction. Many taxpayers will be unable to gain any tax relief from miscellaneous itemized deductions because of the 2%-of-adjusted gross income floor, or because of the impact of alternative minimum tax.

If a qualified distribution produces an unwanted result, and you have no immediate need for the funds, you can consider leaving the account alone (if permitted under the rules of the 529 plan). An account in a 529 savings program will continue to grow tax-deferred until such time as you decide to take distributions, and that can be many years down the road.

Managing Multiple Accounts

There are several reasons why you may want to open multiple accounts for the same beneficiary:

1) *To gain state tax deductions.* A few states that place limits on the amount of contributions you can deduct each year, like Virginia and Maryland, allow multiple accounts to generate multiple deductions.

2) *To diversify your investments.* While some savings programs give you ample opportunity to diversify your investments within one

account by spreading your contribution among different investment options, others may require that you establish multiple accounts if you wish to use more than one of the available investment options. Further diversification can be achieved by establishing accounts in different 529 plans.

3) *To combine a prepaid program with a savings program.* Because prepaid programs typically cover tuition and fees only, it is becoming more common to combine prepaid and savings programs as a way to save for all qualified higher education expenses.

4) *To contribute more than the individual state contribution limit.* If the 529 plan you've chosen has a contribution cap of $100,000 and you have $150,000 to invest, you would have to open accounts in multiple states. You should not, however, attempt to use multiple states as a way to deposit more than you can reasonably justify as an amount needed for your beneficiary's higher education expenses.

5) *To take advantage of a limited benefit.* Some states provide a tax deduction, or a partial match, for your contribution, subject to a dollar limit. While the incentive may persuade you to direct your first dollars into that program, you may decide to use a different 529 plan for contributions beyond the amount that secures the maximum benefit.

6) *To start the clock running.* Even if a particular 529 plan is not your first choice, you may want to open a small account with it if there are any benefits that require a minimum period of participation. For example, a few 529 plans require that your account be open for a minimum period of time before taking qualified withdrawals. Or perhaps your state offers a 529 plan that allows your beneficiary to "vest" as a state resident for purposes of paying tuition at the state's public institutions. This can be a valuable benefit if your family moves out-of-state and sends a child back to a public university in that state.

7) *To reduce income taxes.* See Chapter 7 for a discussion of how multiple accounts can be used to your advantage by permitting selective withdrawals based on each account's "earnings ratio".

Multiple accounts can mean multiple fees, however, and also can mean that you may not be able to achieve the breakpoints in some 529 savings plans where your fees are reduced or eliminated. Multiple accounts will also result in more statements and other collateral material coming your way from the program (or programs).

Account Management Beyond the Basics

Advanced account management involves making changes to your account after you have established it. There are three basic categories of change, any one of which should be considered in the appropriate circumstances:

1) Changing the designated beneficiary—a beneficiary change can be made in most 529 plans simply by filling out a change form and submitting it to the plan administrator (sometimes a fee will be charged). To avoid termination of the original account, and the triggering of income tax and penalty, the new beneficiary must qualify under the section 529 definition of "member of the family" (see Chapter 3). As an alternative to a complete change of beneficiary, the owner may be able to accomplish a partial change by establishing another account for the new beneficiary and transferring some funds from the first account to the second through a rollover.

2) Changing the account owner—many 529 plans will allow the original donor to establish an account and later transfer ownership of the account to someone else. In programs that accommodate this change, there is usually no requirement that the new account owner be a member of the family or have any other specific relationship. Some 529 plans, however, do not provide a mechanism for changing the account owner prior to the original owner's death or incapacity, while others spell out procedures in limited circumstances, such as when the account owner and spouse are separated or divorced. It appears that for the most part a change in account ownership is a tax-neutral event. However, this is an area that invites IRS scrutiny and can create tax uncertainties, especially when questions surrounding the generation-skipping transfer tax arise, or where a non-individual account owner is involved (some states allow corporations, trusts, and other entities to be account owners).

3) Transferring balances between 529 plans—section 529 allows a tax-free rollover from one state's 529 plan to another state's 529 any time the beneficiary of the account is changed to a new beneficiary who is a member of the family of the old beneficiary. In addition, a same-beneficiary rollover can be transacted once in any 12-month period. (You should check to be sure that the no one else has completed a rollover involving the same beneficiary in the prior 12 months.) It is important that you understand a 529 plan's rollover rules before you make a contribution, because you will want to know whether you can move the account easily and inexpensively to another state if the original investment loses its appeal.

The following strategies exemplify the use of rollovers.

Change strategy #1: For the undecided investor

Assume that you are attracted to the tax advantages and investment approach of a 529 plan, but currently have no specific plans to use your savings for your own or someone else's education. The possibility certainly exists that you, your children, your grandchildren, or some other family member might have need for education funds in the future—you just do not want to irrevocably commit your savings to that purpose. You may establish an account and name yourself as beneficiary. If you later decide to use the account to fund a relative's college education, or graduate school, you can then change the beneficiary designation to that relative.

> *Example* 1: Joyce is a 50-year old grandmother and has $20,000 invested in bank certificates of deposit. She is already funding her 401(k) account and Roth IRA to the maximum extent allowable, and has substantial assets in those retirement plans. Joyce decides to open an account in a 529 savings plan using the $20,000 received when her CDs mature. She names herself as beneficiary of the account, with the notion of taking post-graduate classes in the future, although having no specific plans to do so. Joyce has successfully converted taxable CD interest income

into a tax-deferred savings vehicle. Ten years later, Joyce retires with substantial assets in her retirement accounts, and she decides to change her 529 account beneficiary designation from herself to her grandson, who is now 11 years old. She makes the five-year averaging election so that the value of the gift (now $55,000) does not consume any of her $1 million lifetime gift exemption. The account will continue to grow tax-deferred until the grandson uses the funds for college, and distributions at that time are either tax free (if used before 2011) or taxable to the student (if used after the 2010 repeal of the tax exclusion).

Alternatively, Joyce can name her grandson as initial beneficiary of the account even when she feels there is a chance she may need to use the account for her own personal needs in the future. She will always have the ability to request a non-qualified withdrawal from the account, subject to income tax and penalty. The advantage of this approach is that the value of the account is removed from her taxable estate now, along with any future earnings and appreciation. Of course, if she does in fact request a nonqualified withdrawal in the future, the amount of the withdrawal will come back into her estate.

With her substantial assets and a desire to shelter as much income from tax as possible, Joyce may want to establish two sizable accounts: one account for herself, and another for her grandson. She can, for example, contribute $55,000 in 2002 to a 529 plan for her grandson and make the five-year averaging election for gift tax purposes. Instead of waiting until 2007 to make an additional gift-tax-free contribution to that account, she establishes a second account with herself as beneficiary. Joyce's contributions to this account can now grow tax deferred and in 2007 she can simply change the beneficiary to her grandson and shelter another $55,000 (or more if the annual exclusion is increased by then) from gift tax.

It is possible that the administrator of the 529 plan will not accept Joyce's contributions, or will later terminate the account, if the administrator determines that Joyce does not intend to use the account to pay the higher education expenses of the named beneficiary (whether it is her grandson or herself).

Change strategy #2: For the family that may qualify for financial aid

Chapter 4 describes how an interest in a 529 plan may impact the student's eligibility for financial aid. As an example, let's say you have purchased a contract in your state's prepaid program and discover as your child prepares to enter college that the tuition benefits paid by the program will reduce a need-based grant on a dollar-for-dollar basis. As mentioned above, you may find you are better off by canceling the contract and receiving a refund.

An even better answer might be a rollover of your account from the prepaid program to a savings program. Under current federal aid methodology, the savings account may result in a better financial aid package. There are some states, like Virginia, that offer both a prepaid and a savings program and will facilitate the transfer of accounts between the programs.

Finally, if there are younger children in the family, you may want to consider changing the beneficiary designation on your 529 account to a younger child. Assuming you can finance the older child's college education from other resources, including the financial aid package, you at least are able to delay the consequences to a future year.

> *Example*: The Quigleys have 529 savings accounts for their four children. When the eldest child, Jackie, begins her senior year of high school, the parents investigate her eligibility for federal financial aid. Their investigation reveals that their "expected family contribution" (EFC) will probably be low enough to qualify for significant gift-aid, but they are told by the financial aid officer at the college Jackie plans to attend that the existence of the 529 account will reduce this aid on a dollar-for-dollar basis. The Quigleys change the designated beneficiary on Jackie's account to a younger child in the family. This exercise may be repeated for

each child as he or she enters the college years. After Jackie has completed her aid application for her senior year of college, her parents may decide to transfer 529 assets back to her to pay for the final year of college costs (as long as doing this will not cause an adjustment to her award).

A word of caution if you own 529 accounts for the student's siblings: it is not entirely clear that you can exclude the value of the accounts from parental assets in completing the federal aid application FAFSA. Although the U.S. Department of Education does not appear to require inclusion, some financial aid administrators will take these accounts into consideration when developing the aid package.

Change strategy #3: For those in states offering benefits to college savers

If you have more to invest than your state allows as an income tax deduction, and don't want to delay any contributions to a future year, consider parking the excess in another state's 529 plan. Roll over the assets to your home state program in a later year to claim additional state tax deductions. Your state shouldn't care that the assets are coming from another 529 plan.

You can also seek to avoid "wasting" the in-state benefits of a large contribution by gifting a portion of your contribution dollars to someone else on the understanding that the money will be contributed to an account for your designated beneficiaries. For example, you may be able to secure additional state tax deductions for your own parents by gifting cash to them for the purpose of establishing 529 accounts for your children. You run the risk that your parents, who now control the account, will use the money for something other than educating your children (unless they transfer account ownership back to you). The contributions may also be attributed to you for purposes of federal gift tax, and so you will need to consider the consequences if total contributions exceed your $11,000 annual gift exclusion.

There may be a way to invest with an out-of-state 529 plan and still take advantage of the tax deduction offered by your state. This involves a rollover to the out-of-state program after first establishing an in-state account (and claiming the deduction for your contributions to it). It is important that you check to see if your state requires "recapture" of your deduction on a rollover to anther state's program.

Besides maximizing any state benefits on your contributions, you should also look for state tax exemption on qualified distributions. Let's assume your state imposes income tax on the earnings distributed from out-of-state 529 plans, but provides an exemption for qualified distributions from its own 529 plan. You can consider a rollover from the out-of-state program to the in-state program anytime prior to using the account for qualified expenses.

Planning for state income tax savings can be an uncertain exercise, particularly where 529 plans are concerned. You should obtain the advice of a tax professional in your state.

Avoid Abusive Change Strategies in Estate Tax Planning

The estate and gift tax rules surrounding 529 plans offer unique opportunities to reduce the gross estate of someone attempting to shift assets to a lower generation. They also give rise to strategies that some individuals believe will allow for a large tax-free intergenerational transfer of wealth that cannot be accomplished through traditional gifting techniques. These strategies pose a challenge to the IRS as it attempts to regulate the use of section 529, and they pose a risk to taxpayers who use them without adequately considering the consequences of an IRS challenge. For example, consider the following "loophole":

> *Example:* John desires to make contributions of $220,000 to a 529 plan for his son Freddy but wants to avoid gift taxes. He can only make $55,000 of contributions this year for his son under the five-year averaging election without causing a taxable gift. However, John has three nieces and so he decides to establish accounts for them with a $55,000 contribution to each account. He makes

the five-year election for each of the contributions to avoid gift taxes. John figures that he can change the beneficiary designation on these accounts to his son whenever he wants without triggering any further gift tax consequences. The 2001 tax law changes amended the section 529 definition of "member of the family" to include first cousins, and so the change of beneficiary by John qualifies as a rollover. Because the cousins are within the same generation, there is no deemed gift from any of the nieces to Freddy (see Chapter 9).

This maneuver is an end run around the annual gift tax exclusion limits, and the IRS will probably not be happy if it finds out about it. But how can this apparent abuse be distinguished from a situation where John truly intends to help fund the future college expenses of his nieces, and only because of unforeseeable circumstances does he find it necessary to later change the beneficiary to his own son?

There are similar "opportunities" to leverage the annual exclusion through other family members. For instance, John conceivably could have established 529 accounts for his own five brothers and their wives using the available annual exclusions to place hundreds of thousands of dollars into tax-deferred investment accounts, removing these assets from his estate without incurring gift tax. The substitution of his son as designated beneficiary on these accounts would be a deemed gift from these extended family members to John's son due to the difference in generations, but annual gift exclusions could again be deployed to avoid gift tax consequences.

To carry this to its absurd conclusion, consider how you might try to create a tax problem for the relative that you dislike.

Example: Ed never forgave his brother Sean for taking, and then losing, his baseball card collection forty years ago and now sees an opportunity to make him pay for it. Ed makes a contribution to a 529 plan in the amount of $55,000, designating brother Sean as the account beneficiary, and electing five-year averaging to avoid any gift tax consequences. As owner of the account, Ed then changes the beneficiary from Sean to Ed's own son, Kyle. Sean is never aware of his brother's actions, which have the result of creating a gift from Sean to his nephew Kyle (Kyle belongs to a lower generation than Sean). Sean understandably fails to make the five-year averaging election, and so has unwittingly made a taxable gift that utilizes part of his $1 million lifetime exemption. Ed lets Sean know about this after it is too late to do anything about it, and Sean is made to realize that he has now lost some of his lifetime exemption, or even worse, has failed to report a taxable gift requiring payment of gift taxes, interest, and possible penalties.

Although the literal reading of the statute appears to demand this result, and donative intent is not required for the federal gift tax to apply, it seems unlikely that an unsuspecting donor could actually be assessed gift tax by the IRS. Perhaps the final regulations under section 529 should require that the original intended beneficiary must "accept" the designation before the gift of a contribution through a 529 plan can be considered "completed." Rules similar to the qualified disclaimer provisions of the Internal Revenue Code could accomplish this. In the above example, Sean would have had the opportunity to smell the trap and refuse the position of designated beneficiary.

Besides a change in beneficiaries, a change of account owner can also be an opportunity for abuse. Many 529 plans will grant approval for you to transfer your ownership of an account to someone else. The mere act of transferring ownership has no federal income tax or gift tax consequences. This follows the logic of section 529, provided the 529 account is ultimately expended for the beneficiary's qualified higher education expenses. But what happens if the new account owner revokes the account? Is there a gift tax consequence? If the answer is no, then the opportunity presents itself to transfer wealth without making a gift.

Example: Shirley is a wealthy grandmother making maximum annual exclusion gifts to her son Todd and her grandson Timmy. Todd is wealthy in his own right and making his own annual exclusion gifts to Timmy. To bypass Todd's generation and get more of the family wealth to her grandson, Shirley establishes a 529 account for Todd, using the money she normally gifts directly to him. Shirley then transfers ownership of the 529 account to Timmy so that now Timmy is the account owner with his father as beneficiary. Timmy simply revokes the account and receives the money without any gift tax (although generation-skipping transfer tax may still be a concern).

An often-heard phrase in tax planning is that "if it's too good to be true, then it probably isn't." Section 529 of the Internal Revenue Code challenges that notion, especially in the area of estate and gift taxes. There is no question that the law provides unique benefits that are counterintuitive to anyone familiar with the "normal" estate and gift tax rules. The best advice, however, is to stay within reasonable bounds and remember that 529 plans are intended to be a tax-advantaged college savings vehicle, not a tax shelter.

State by State Comparisons

This Appendix contains a brief description of each state's 529 plan as of the date this book went to press. **Although substantial effort has been made to be as accurate as possible in these descriptions, they are not a substitute for your thorough review of the materials available from the particular program being considered, including enrollment materials, the application form, and the master contract. These descriptions have not been approved or verified by program officials.**

Note that many states with existing programs are contemplating or in the process of making substantial changes to their 529 plans. Please visit the Web site at www.savingforcollege.com to find out about these changes.

STATE: **ALABAMA**

PROGRAM NAME:	Alabama's Prepaid Affordable College Tuition Program (PACT)
529 TYPE:	Prepaid contract
STATE AGENCY:	Board of Trustees of the Trust Fund, chaired by the State Treasurer
INITIAL YEAR OF OPERATION:	1990
TELEPHONE:	1-800-252-7228
INTERNET:	www.treasury.state.al.us

Who can purchase a contract? Individuals at least 19 years old or represented by a guardian or custodian and approved legal entities. There are no residency requirements.

Enrollment period: The most recent enrollment period was the month of September 2001. The next enrollment period is scheduled for September 2002.

Time or age limitations on beneficiary or on use of benefits: The beneficiary must be in the 9th grade or below at the time of enrollment. Contract benefits must generally be used within 10 years of the beneficiary's projected college entrance date.

Contract benefits: The contract pays undergraduate tuition and mandatory fees for up to 135 semester hours at any Alabama public college or university. The value derived from the contract will depend in part on the selection of institution and number of credit hours taken, because public institutions in Alabama have different tuition and fee levels. If the beneficiary decides to attend a private college in Alabama or an out-of-state college, PACT will pay an amount up to, but not more than, the weighted average tuition and mandatory fees paid at Alabama public four-year institutions. There is a $25 out-of-state school transfer fee charged each academic period. If the beneficiary receives a scholarship or grant, the amount that PACT pays to the institution can be applied to room and board, books, or supplies.

Contract options: A four-year (maximum 135 semester hours) contract is the only option.

Costs: There is a one-time $75 enrollment fee. For the September 2001 enrollment period, the lump-sum price for a student in the ninth grade was $14,484. Prices are discounted for younger beneficiaries to as low as $10,577 for an infant. The contract price may also be paid in 60 monthly installments or over an extended period through the year of projected enrollment. Monthly payments are computed to include an effective annual 8%-9% cost for making payments over time along with a small transaction fee.

Cancellation provisions: Cancellation of the contract results in the refund of contract payments (less a cancellation fee of $25), plus interest. The rate of interest applied will be the average passbook savings interest rate at Alabama banking institutions, but not greater than 5%, as computed for each year. The program may, at its discretion, pay the refund in installments, rather than in a lump sum. The cancellation fee is waived if the beneficiary has died or become disabled.

Contract changes: Accepts requests to change beneficiary ($55 fee, plus a possible additional payment if the new beneficiary is older), and transfer contract ownership ($20 fee). There are no special provisions concerning rollovers/transfers to another 529 plan (cancellation provisions would apply).

State backing: Contracts are not backed by the full faith and credit of the state of Alabama. The program trust fund carries a reserve to protect against any shortfall in fund investment performance.

Special considerations:

- Qualified distributions from this program are exempt from Alabama state income tax. Any withdrawals from other state 529 plans could subject an Alabama resident to state tax as Alabama does not appear to conform to federal tax exemption for qualified withdrawals.

STATE:	**ALABAMA**
PROGRAM NAME:	Alabama College Education Savings Program
529 TYPE:	Savings
STATE AGENCIES:	Board of Trustees and the State Treasurer

This program is being developed for launch during the first or second quarter of 2002. The Board of Directors has selected Van Kampen Investments to handle investments and management services for ACES.

STATE:	**ALASKA**
PROGRAM NAME:	University of Alaska College Savings Plan
529 TYPE:	Savings
STATE AGENCIES:	University of Alaska and the Alaska Trust
PROGRAM MANAGER:	T. Rowe Price Associates
INITIAL YEAR OF OPERATION:	2001
TELEPHONE:	1-800-478-0003
INTERNET:	www.uacollegesavings.com

Who can open an account? U.S. citizens or resident aliens, UTMA/UGMA custodians, and legal entities.

Time or age limitations on beneficiary or on use of account assets: None.

Age-based investment options: The Enrollment-Based Portfolios contain eight portfolios of underlying funds, ranging from 100% equity to 20% equity. Contributions are initially placed into the portfolio corresponding to the number of years to expected enrollment based on the age of the beneficiary or as selected by the account owner. Seven portfolios shift to a more conservative investment allocation over time, eventually transferring to the "college" portfolio.

Static investment options: Select among four portfolios: the Equity Portfolio, the Fixed Income Portfolio, the Balanced Portfolio (60% stocks and 40% fixed income), and the ACT portfolio (30% stocks and 70% fixed income and money market).

Underlying investments: Mutual funds from T. Rowe Price.

Fees and expenses: $30 annual account maintenance fee (waived for accounts with at least $25,000; for accounts with an investment in the ACT portfolio; or for accounts enrolled in an automatic investment or payroll deduction plan), 0.30% annualized program management fee charged against value of account (except for ACT), and underlying fund expenses of approximately 0.32% in the ACT portfolio and ranging from approximately 0.55% to 0.71% in the other portfolios. There is no enrollment fee.

Broker distribution: None.

Maximum contributions: Accepts contributions until all Alaska account balances for the same beneficiary reach $250,000.

Minimum initial contribution: $250 ($50 with automatic investment plan).

Account changes: Accepts requests to change beneficiary, transfer account ownership, name a successor owner, rollover/transfer assets within the program or to another 529 plan, and change investment option once per calendar year.

Special considerations:

- The ACT portfolio carries a guarantee by the Alaska Trust that the earnings rate will keep pace with tuition inflation at the University of Alaska to the extent that account assets are used to pay for tuition at the University of Alaska.
- Contributions can be made to the ACT Portfolio through the Alaska Permanent Fund Dividend without first completing an account agreement.
- There are no state income tax incentives because Alaska does not have a personal income tax.
- Under Alaska law, an account is exempt from a claim by the account owner's or the beneficiary's creditors and is not subject to involuntary transfer or alienation (with an exception relating to child support orders).

STATE: **ALASKA**

PROGRAM NAME:	T. Rowe Price College Savings Plan
529 TYPE:	Savings
STATE AGENCIES:	University of Alaska and the Alaska Trust
PROGRAM MANAGER:	T. Rowe Price Associates
INITIAL YEAR OF OPERATION:	2001
TELEPHONE:	1-800-369-3641
INTERNET:	www.troweprice.com/collegesavings

Who can open an account? U.S. citizens or resident aliens, UTMA/UGMA custodians, and legal entities.

Time or age limitations on beneficiary or on use of account assets: None.

Age-based investment options: The Enrollment-Based Portfolios contains eight portfolios of underlying funds, ranging from 100% equity to 20% equity. Contributions are initially placed into the portfolio corresponding to the number of years to expected enrollment based on the age of the beneficiary or as selected by the account owner. Seven portfolios shift to a more conservative investment allocation over time, eventually transferring to the "college" portfolio.

Static investment options: Select among three portfolios: the Equity Portfolio, the Fixed Income Portfolio, and the Balanced Portfolio (60% stocks and 40% fixed income).

Underlying investments: Mutual funds from T. Rowe Price.

Fees and expenses: $30 annual account maintenance fee (waived for accounts with at least $25,000 and for accounts enrolled in an automatic investment or payroll deduction plan), 0.30% annualized program management fee charged against value of account, and underlying fund expenses ranging from approximately 0.55% to 0.71%. There is no enrollment fee.

Broker distribution: None.

Maximum contributions: Accepts contributions until all Alaska account balances for the same beneficiary reach $250,000.

Minimum initial contribution: $250 ($50 with automatic investment plan).

Account changes: Accepts requests to change beneficiary, transfer account ownership, name a successor owner, rollover/transfer assets within the program or to another 529 plan, and change investment option once per calendar year.

Special considerations:

- Under Alaska law, an account is exempt from a claim by the account owner's or the beneficiary's creditors and is not subject to involuntary transfer or alienation (with an exception relating to child support orders).

STATE:	**ALASKA**
PROGRAM NAME:	Manulife College Savings
529 TYPE:	Savings
STATE AGENCIES:	University of Alaska and the Alaska Trust
PROGRAM MANAGER:	T. Rowe Price Associates
DISTRIBUTION PARTNER:	Manulife Financial
INITIAL YEAR OF OPERATION:	2001
TELEPHONE:	1-866-222-7498
INTERNET:	www.manulifecollegesavings.com

Who can open an account? U.S. citizens or resident aliens, UTMA/UGMA custodians, and legal entities.

Time or age limitations on beneficiary or on use of account assets: None.

Age-based investment options: The Enrollment-Based Portfolios contains six portfolios of underlying funds, ranging from 100% equity to 20% equity. Contributions are initially placed into the portfolio corresponding to the number of years to expected enrollment based on the age of the beneficiary or as selected by the account owner. Five portfolios shift to a more conservative investment allocation over time, eventually transferring to the "college" portfolio.

Static investment options: Select among four portfolios: the Future Trends Portfolio, the Equity Portfolio, the Fixed Income Portfolio, and the Short-Term Bond Portfolio.

Underlying investments: Mutual funds from T. Rowe Price, MFS, Davis, AIM, Franklin Templeton, Oppenheimer, and PIMCO.

Fees and expenses: $30 annual account maintenance fee (waived for accounts with at least $25,000 and for accounts enrolled in an automatic investment or payroll deduction plan) and underlying fund expenses ranging from approximately 0.45% to 1.38%. In addition, accounts are subject to one of two alternative expense structures that will determine any initial sales charge and additional asset-based fees.

Broker distribution: This program is designed for distribution through financial advisors.

Maximum contributions: Accepts contributions until all Alaska account balances for the same beneficiary reach $250,000.

Minimum initial contribution: $500 per portfolio ($50 with automatic investment).

Account changes: Accepts requests to change beneficiary, transfer account ownership, name a successor owner, rollover/transfer assets within the program or to another 529 plan, and change investment option once per calendar year.

Special considerations:
- Under Alaska law, an account is exempt from a claim by the account owner's or the beneficiary's creditors and is not subject to involuntary transfer or alienation (with an exception relating to child support orders).

STATE: **ARIZONA**

PROGRAM NAME:	Arizona Family College Savings Program (CSB)
529 TYPE:	Savings
STATE AGENCY:	The Arizona Commission for Postsecondary Education
PROGRAM MANAGER:	College Savings Bank
INITIAL YEAR OF OPERATION:	1999
TELEPHONE:	1-800-888-2723
INTERNET:	http://arizona.collegesavings.com

Who can open an account? U.S. citizens, UTMA/UGMA custodians, state/local governments, and 501(c)(3) organizations.

Time or age limitations on beneficiary or on use of account assets: Since the underlying investment is a certificate of deposit with maturities ranging from one to twenty-five years, CDs are timed to mature in the years the beneficiary attends college and/or graduate school. The CDs are subject to early redemption penalties of as much as 10% of principal for withdrawals prior to maturity.

Age-based investment options: None.

Static investment options: Funds are invested in CollegeSure® Certificates of Deposit (CDs).

Underlying investments: CollegeSure CDs earn interest at a rate tied to the year-to-year increase in average national private college costs. The interest rate adjusts each July 31. The minimum annual interest rate is 4%.

Fees and expenses: There are no enrollment or account maintenance fees.

Broker distribution: Accounts may be opened through intermediaries who receive a commission. The commission is paid by College Savings Bank and does not affect investment returns.

Maximum contributions: The maximum lifetime contribution limit is $177,000 per beneficiary. The limit is adjusted each year based on seven times the College Board's Independent College 500 Index.

Minimum initial contribution: $250 ($100 with the automatic investment plan and $50 with a payroll deduction plan).

Account changes: Accepts requests to change beneficiary (one change at no cost, then $50), transfer account ownership (but only to beneficiary, or to owner's spouse as part of a divorce proceeding), name a successor owner, and change investment option once per calendar year. The Commission has not ruled on whether a qualifying rollover to another state's 529 plan will be assessed a 10% penalty on earnings.

Special considerations:

- Principal and interest are backed by the full faith and credit of the U.S. Government up to $100,000 per depositor.
- Qualified withdrawals from this program and all other 529 plans are exempt from Arizona state income tax.
- The account is established as a revocable trust with spendthrift provisions, providing additional protection from creditors.

STATE:	**ARIZONA**
PROGRAM NAME:	Arizona Family College Savings Program (SMR)
529 TYPE:	Savings
STATE AGENCY:	The Arizona Commission for Postsecondary Education
PROGRAM MANAGER:	Securities Management and Research, Inc.
INITIAL YEAR OF OPERATION:	1999
TELEPHONE:	1-888-66-READY (1-888-667-3239)
INTERNET:	www.smrinvest.com

Who can open an account? U.S. citizens, UTMA/UGMA custodians, state/local governments, and 501(c)(3) organizations.

Time or age limitations on beneficiary or on use of account assets: None.

Age-based investment options: None.

Static investment options: There are ten SM&R mutual funds from which to select ranging from technology to money market.

Underlying investments: SM&R mutual funds, including SM&R Alger funds. The program fund purchases shares at net asset value (there is no initial sales charge).

Fees and expenses: The Arizona Commission for Postsecondary Education collects a one-time $10 fee for each account opened. The annual underlying expenses of the mutual funds range from 0.49% to 1.29% for the fixed income funds and from 1.30% to 2.10% for the equity funds.

Broker distribution: Accounts opened through a financial advisor will be subject to an initial sales charge and possibly additional asset-based fees.

Maximum contributions: The maximum lifetime contribution limit is $177,000 per beneficiary. The limit is adjusted each year based on seven times the College Board's Independent College 500 Index.

Minimum initial contribution: For the SM&R Alger funds, the minimum initial investment is $500 per fund ($50 per fund with the automatic contribution plan). For the SM&R Growth, Equity Income, Balanced, and Government Bond funds, the minimum initial investment is $100 per fund ($20 per fund for the automatic contribution plan). For the SM&R Primary and Money Market funds, the minimum initial and subsequent contribution is $100 per fund even under the automatic deposit plan.

Account changes: Accepts requests to change beneficiary, transfer account ownership, name a successor owner, rollover/transfer assets within the program or to another 529 plan, and change investment option once per calendar year.

Special considerations:

- Qualified withdrawals from this program and all other 529 plans are exempt from Arizona state income tax.

STATE:	**ARIZONA**
PROGRAM NAME:	Waddell & Reed InvestEd Plan
529 TYPE:	Savings
STATE AGENCY:	The Arizona Commission for Postsecondary Education
PROGRAM MANAGER:	Waddell & Reed, Inc.
INITIAL YEAR OF OPERATION:	2001
TELEPHONE:	1-888-WADDELL (1-888-923-3355)
INTERNET:	www.waddell.com

Who can open an account? U.S. citizens, UTMA/UGMA custodians, trusts, state/local governments, and 501(c)(3) organizations.

Time or age limitations on beneficiary or on use of account assets: None.

Age-based investment options: There are three portfolios: Growth (80% equity, ages 0-8), Balanced (60% equity, ages 9-15), and Conservative (20% equity, ages 16+). Each portfolio invests in six or seven underlying mutual funds. Contributions are initially placed into the portfolio corresponding to the beneficiary's age, and later reassigned to more conservative portfolios as the beneficiary reaches certain ages.

Static investment options: Invest directly in the Growth, Balanced, or Conservative portfolios. Accounts are not automatically moved between portfolios as the beneficiary ages.

Underlying investments: Mutual funds from the Waddell & Reed Advisors Fund family.

Fees and expenses: The Arizona Commission for Postsecondary Education collects a one-time $10 fee for each account opened. The expenses of the underlying mutual funds range from approximately 0.79% to 0.92% (portfolio weighted average). In addition, accounts are subject to one of three alternative expense structures that will determine any initial sales charge, contingent deferred sales charge, and/or additional asset-based fees.

Broker distribution: Accounts may be opened through any Waddell & Reed advisor or Legend advisor.

Maximum contributions: The maximum lifetime contribution limit is $177,000 per beneficiary. The limit is adjusted each year based on seven times the College Board's Independent College 500 Index.

Minimum initial contribution: $500 ($50 with an automatic contribution plan or $25 with payroll deduction).

Account changes: Accepts requests to change beneficiary, transfer account ownership (but only to beneficiary, or to owner's spouse as part of a divorce proceeding), name a successor owner, and change investment option once per calendar year. The Commission has not ruled on whether a qualifying rollover to another state's 529 plan will be assessed a 10% penalty on earnings.

Special considerations:

- Qualified withdrawals from this program and all other 529 plans are exempt from Arizona state income tax.

STATE: **ARKANSAS**

PROGRAM NAME:	GIFT College Investing Plan
529 TYPE:	Savings
STATE AGENCIES:	Arkansas Tax-Deferred Tuition Savings Program Investment Committee and the Executive Director of the Arkansas Teacher Retirement System
PROGRAM MANAGER:	Mercury Advisors
DISTRIBUTION PARTNER:	Franklin Templeton
INITIAL YEAR OF OPERATION:	1999
TELEPHONE:	1-877-442-6553
INTERNET:	www.thegiftplan.com

Who can open an account? Individuals, UGMA/UTMA custodians, and legal entities.

Time or age limitations on beneficiary or on use of account assets: None.

Age-based investment option: The Age-Tailored Active Allocation Portfolio contains nine portfolios of underlying mutual funds. Contributions are initially placed into the portfolio corresponding to the beneficiary's age or as selected by the account owner. Eight portfolios shift to a more conservative investment allocation over time, eventually transferring to the "college" portfolio.

Static investment options: Select among four portfolios: Growth (100% equity), Growth and Income (75% equity), Balanced (50% equity) and Fixed-Income.

Underlying investments: Mutual funds from Mercury Funds and Franklin Templeton Investments.

Fees and expenses: $25 annual account maintenance fee (waived for Arkansas residents and for accounts with a balance of at least $25,000), 0.60% annualized program management fee charged against value of account, and underlying fund expenses ranging from approximately 0.70% to 1.35% (portfolio weighted average).

Broker distribution: Accounts opened through a financial advisor are subject to an additional fee at an annual rate of 0.35%.

Maximum contributions: Accepts contributions until all account balances for the same beneficiary reach $245,000.

Minimum initial contribution: $250 for residents, and $1,000 for nonresidents and for accounts opened through a broker.

Account changes: Accepts requests to change beneficiary, transfer account ownership, name a successor owner, rollover/transfer assets within the program or to another 529 plan, and change investment option once per calendar year.

Special considerations:

- Qualified withdrawals are exempt from gross income for Arkansas income tax purposes. Any withdrawals from other state 529 plans could subject an Arkansas resident to state tax as Arkansas does not appear to conform to federal tax exemption for qualified withdrawals.

STATE:	**CALIFORNIA**
PROGRAM NAME:	Golden State ScholarShare College Savings Trust
529 TYPE:	Savings
STATE AGENCY:	ScholarShare Investment Board
PROGRAM MANAGER:	TIAA-CREF Tuition Financing, Inc.
INITIAL YEAR OF OPERATION:	1999
TELEPHONE:	1-877- SAV-4EDU (1-877-728-4338)
INTERNET:	www.scholarshare.com

Who can open an account? Individuals living in the U.S. who have reached the age of majority, emancipated minors, UTMA/UGMA custodians, and legal entities.

Time or age limitations on beneficiary or on use of account assets: None.

Age-based investment options: The program offers a choice between two schedules: the Age-Based Asset Allocation option and the Aggressive Age-Based Asset Allocation option. Contributions are placed into one of 15 portfolios corresponding to the selected schedule and the beneficiary's age. Each portfolio shifts to a more conservative investment allocation over time.

Static investment options: There are three supplemental investment options: the 100% Equity Option (80% domestic equity and 20% international equity), the 100% Social Choice Equity Option, and the Guaranteed Option. The Guaranteed Option is invested in a funding agreement that guarantees principal and a minimum 3% rate of interest (actual rate is declared quarterly).

Underlying investments: TIAA-CREF institutional mutual funds and TIAA-CREF Life Guaranteed Funding Agreement.

Fees and expenses: 0.70% annualized program management fee charged against value of account, including expenses of underlying mutual funds. The ScholarShare Investment Board also charges an administrative fee of up to 0.10% annually. There are no enrollment or annual account maintenance fees.

Broker distribution: None.

Maximum contributions: Accepts contributions until all account balances for the same beneficiary reach the maximum account value, which is anywhere from $124,799 to $174,648 depending on the age of the beneficiary.

Minimum initial contribution: $25 ($15 with automatic payroll deduction).

Account changes: Accepts requests to change beneficiary, transfer account ownership, name a successor owner, rollover/transfer assets within the program or to another 529 plan, and change investment option once per calendar year.

Special considerations:

- California does not provide specific state tax incentives for residents in this program. All withdrawals by a California resident from any 529 plan will be subject to tax unless California passes conformity legislation for the federal tax law changes.

STATE:	**COLORADO**
PROGRAM NAME:	CollegeInvest - Prepaid Tuition Fund
529 TYPE:	Prepaid unit
STATE AGENCIES:	Colorado Student Obligation Bond Authority (CSOBA) and State Treasurer
INITIAL YEAR OF OPERATION:	1997
TELEPHONE:	1-800-478-5651 (national), 1-888-SAVE NOW (Colorado residents)
INTERNET:	www.collegeinvest.org

Who can purchase a contract? Individuals with a social security number and legal entities.

Enrollment period: Open.

Time or age limitations on beneficiary or on use of benefits: Initial purchase of units must be before the beneficiary reaches 9th grade and at least three years prior to the "first payout date" (July 31 of the year benefits are intended for), and additional units purchased must be held at least 12 months before redemption. Units must be used within 10 years from the first payout date, unless an extension is approved.

Unit value: One tuition unit will be worth at least 1% of the average resident undergraduate tuition at Colorado four-year public colleges and universities and state community colleges. Any withdrawal within 12 months of the contract purchase will return only the original purchase price. A withdrawal after 12 months, but before the "first payout date" established at the time of purchase, returns average tuition per unit or the amount contributed to date, whichever is greater. When used for qualified higher education expenses after the first payout date, the program guarantees a minimum average annual increase in tuition unit value of 4% compounded annually.

Costs: There are no enrollment fees or annual maintenance fees. The purchase price of a contract is based on current average tuition as adjusted for actuarial considerations and expenses ($24.64 per unit for 2001-2002). Rather than making additional purchases of units in the future, a quantity of units may be purchased under an installment payment arrangement. Installment payments are computed with an effective 6.78% cost for making payments over time and a small transaction fee.

Maximum contributions: Accepts contributions until balances in all Colorado accounts for the same beneficiary reach $235,000.

Minimum initial contribution: $1000 (or $25 per month for a five year period).

Account changes: Accepts requests to change beneficiary ($25 fee), transfer account ownership, name a successor owner, rollover/transfer to another 529 plan, and change investment option once per calendar year.

State backing: Contracts are not backed by the full faith and credit of the state of Colorado. The program has a "stabilization reserve" to protect against shortfalls in the program fund.

Special considerations:
- Payments are fully deductible in computing Colorado taxable income. Deductions may be subject to recapture if non-qualified withdrawals are taken in a subsequent year.
- Qualified withdrawals, whether from this program or any other 529 plan, are exempt from Colorado income tax.
- If favorable investment performance causes the assets of the program to grow to a level in excess of the amount needed to cover contract obligations (as determined by actuarial estimates) the policy of the program is to allocate the excess to existing contracts.

- There is a $50 refund fee, and a $50 cancellation fee if the refund results in the termination of the account.

STATE: COLORADO

PROGRAM NAME:	CollegeInvest - Scholars Choice College Savings Plan
529 TYPE:	Savings
STATE AGENCIES:	Colorado Student Obligation Bond Authority (CSOBA) and State Treasurer
PROGRAM MANAGER:	Salomon Smith Barney
INITIAL YEAR OF OPERATION:	1999
TELEPHONE:	1-888-5-SCHOLAR (1-888-572-4652)
INTERNET:	www.scholars-choice.com (national); www.collegeinvest.org (Colorado residents)

Who can open an account? U.S. residents, UTMA/UGMA custodians, and legal entities.

Time or age limitations on beneficiary or on use of account assets: None.

Age-based investment options: The Age-Based and Years to Enrollment options contain up to seven portfolios of underlying mutual funds. Contributions are initially placed into the portfolio corresponding to the beneficiary's age, or expected years to enrollment, and later reassigned to more conservative portfolios as the beneficiary ages.

Static investment options: There are three supplemental portfolios: the Balanced Portfolio (50% equity and 50% fixed income), the All Equity Portfolio, and the Fixed Income Portfolio.

Underlying investments: Mutual funds from Salomon Brothers, Smith Barney, AFG, and MFS.

Fees and expenses: For accounts that are not opened through a broker, there is a 1.09% annualized program management fee charged against value of account, that includes the expenses of the underlying mutual funds. There are no enrollment or annual account maintenance fees, except that an account that does not have a Colorado resident as owner or beneficiary may be charged a $30 fee in June of each year.

Broker distribution: Accounts opened through a financial advisor will be subject to one of three alternative expense structures that will determine any initial sales charge, contingent deferred sales charge, and/or additional asset-based fees.

Maximum contributions: Accepts contributions until all Colorado account balances for the same beneficiary reach $235,000.

Minimum initial contribution: $25 (no set minimum for non-broker accounts with automatic contributions).

Account changes: Accepts requests to change beneficiary, name a successor owner, rollover/transfer assets within the program or to another 529 plan, and change investment option once per calendar year. Does not accept requests to transfer account ownership.

Special considerations:

- Contributions are fully deductible in computing Colorado taxable income. Deductions may be subject to recapture if non-qualified withdrawals are taken in a subsequent year.
- Qualified withdrawals, whether from this program or any other 529 plan, are exempt from Colorado income tax.

STATE: **CONNECTICUT**

PROGRAM NAME:	The Connecticut Higher Education Trust (CHET) Program
529 TYPE:	Savings
STATE AGENCY:	The Connecticut State Treasurer
PROGRAM MANAGER:	TIAA-CREF Tuition Financing, Inc.
INITIAL YEAR OF OPERATION:	1997
TELEPHONE:	1-888-799-CHET (1-888-799-2438)
INTERNET:	www.aboutchet.com

Who can open an account? Individuals living in the U.S. who have reached the age of majority, UTMA/UGMA custodians, and legal entities.

Time or age limitations on beneficiary or on use of account assets: None.

Age-based investment option: The Managed Allocation Option contains 11 portfolios of underlying mutual funds. Contributions are placed into the portfolio corresponding to the age of the beneficiary. Each portfolio shifts to a more conservative investment allocation over time.

Static investment options: There are two supplemental investment options: a High Equity Option (80% to equity and 20% fixed income and money market), and a Principal

Plus Interest Option. The Principal Plus Interest Option is invested in an instrument that guarantees principal and a minimum 3% annual rate of interest (actual rate is declared quarterly).

Underlying investments: TIAA-CREF institutional mutual funds and TIAA-CREF Life Guaranteed Funding Agreement.

Fees and expenses: 0.79% annualized program management fee charged against the value of the account, including the expenses of the underlying mutual funds. The State Treasurer may also charge an administrative fee of up to 0.02% annually. There are no enrollment or annual account maintenance fees.

Broker distribution: None.

Maximum contributions: Accepts contributions until all account balances for the same beneficiary reach $235,000.

Minimum initial contribution: $25 ($15 with automatic payroll deduction).

Account changes: Accepts requests to change beneficiary, transfer account ownership, name a successor owner, rollover/transfer assets within the program or to another 529 plan, and change investment option once per calendar year.

Special considerations:
- Qualified withdrawals from this program are exempt from Connecticut income tax. Connecticut treatment of withdrawals from other 529 plans depends on state conformity to the federal tax law changes.

STATE:	**DELAWARE**
PROGRAM NAME:	Delaware College Investment Plan
529 TYPE:	Savings
STATE AGENCY:	Delaware College Investment Board
PROGRAM MANAGER:	Fidelity Investments
INITIAL YEAR OF OPERATION:	1998
TELEPHONE:	1-800-544-1655
INTERNET:	www.fidelity.com/delaware

Who can open an account? U.S. citizens and resident aliens at least 18 years of age, UTMA/UGMA custodians, state/local government agencies, and 501(c)(3) organizations.

Time or age limitations on beneficiary or on use of account assets: None.

Age-based investment option: The Age-Based Strategy contains eight portfolios of under-lying mutual funds. Contributions are placed into the portfolio corresponding to the age of the beneficiary or as determined by the account owner. Seven portfolios shift to a more conservative investment allocation over time, eventually transferring to the "College" portfolio.

Static investment options: The Static Portfolios consist of three portfolios: 100% Equity, 70% Equity, and Conservative (100% fixed income and money market).

Underlying investments: Fidelity Investments mutual funds.

Fees and expenses: $30 annual account maintenance fee (waived for accounts with a bal-ance of at least $25,000 or enrolled in the automatic investment plan), 0.30% annualized program management fee charged against value of account, and underlying fund expenses ranging from approximately 0.65% to 0.80% (portfolio weighted average). There is no enrollment fee.

Broker distribution: None.

Maximum contributions: Accepts contributions until all account balances for the same beneficiary reach $250,000.

Minimum initial contribution: $500 ($50 per month for automatic investment plan).

Account changes: Accepts requests to change beneficiary, name a successor owner, rollover/transfer assets within the program or to another 529 plan, and change invest-ment option once per calendar year. Does not accept requests to transfer ownership prior to death or incapacity.

Special considerations:

- Delaware does not provide specific state tax incentives for residents in this pro-gram, but its tax law generally conforms to federal tax law and so qualified with-drawals that are exempt from federal income tax should be exempt from Delaware income tax as well.

STATE: **FLORIDA**

PROGRAM NAME: Florida Prepaid College Program
529 TYPE: Prepaid contract
STATE AGENCY: Florida Prepaid College Board
INITIAL YEAR OF OPERATION: 1987
TELEPHONE: 1-800-552-GRAD (1-800-552-4723)
INTERNET: www.floridaprepaidcollege.com

Who can purchase a contract? Individuals at least 18 years old and legal entities. The beneficiary must be a Florida resident or child of a divorced parent who is a Florida resident. Children of military personnel with Florida as their home of record are also eligible.

Enrollment period: The 2001-2002 enrollment period ended January 25, 2002. The next enrollment period will be Fall 2002.

Time or age limitations on beneficiary or on use of benefits: The beneficiary must be under 21 years of age and below the 12th grade at the time of enrollment. Contract benefits must be used within 10 years after graduation, although extensions are permitted. Years in military service are not counted toward the 10-year limit.

Contract benefits: Covers the undergraduate tuition at Florida public institutions, with optional plans that cover local fees and/or dormitory housing. If the beneficiary attends an accredited, not-for-profit, four-year, degree-granting independent college or university in Florida, or a qualified out-of-state college, the program will transfer an amount equal to current rates paid to a public university in Florida.

Contract options: There are three options. The Four-Year University Tuition Plan covers 120 semester credit hours at a state university in Florida. The 2 + 2 Tuition Plan covers 60 semester credit hours at a community college and 60 semester credit hours at a state university in Florida. The Two-Year Community College Tuition Plan covers 60 semester credit hours at a community college in Florida.

Costs: There is a one-time $42 enrollment fee. In the enrollment period that ended January 25, 2002, lump-sum contract prices for a child in the 11th grade ranged from $2,751 for the two-year community college tuition plan to $7,836 for the four-year university tuition plan. Prices are discounted for younger beneficiaries. Contract payments may be made in a lump sum, under a 5-year monthly payment plan, or in monthly installments through the year of projected enrollment. Monthly installment payments are computed to include an additional cost for making payments over time.

Cancellation provisions: Contracts can be cancelled at any time. The refund amount will be the money paid into the program, less a cancellation fee of $50 or 50 percent of the amount paid into the program (waived for contracts held for more than two years), whichever is less. In the case of death or disability, the cancellation fee will be waived, and the purchaser will be refunded an amount equal to the current rates at state post-secondary institutions.

Contract changes: A contract may be transferred prior to matriculation to a brother, sister or first cousin of the original beneficiary, or to a grandchild of the purchaser. Transfers to other relatives or persons unrelated to the original beneficiary are not permitted. Owner-ship of the contract can be transferred, and a successor owner may be named. There are no operational provisions concerning a rollover to another state's 529 plan. A rollover would be subject to the contract cancellation provisions.

State backing: Full faith and credit backing of the state of Florida.

Special considerations:
- The beneficiary will be eligible to attend Florida state universities and community colleges as a resident for tuition purposes even if he or she moves away from Florida prior to enrollment.
- Payments in the program are exempt from forfeiture under Florida law. This exemp-tion may be recognized by a bankruptcy court if claimed by the debtor.
- There are no state income tax incentives because Florida does not have a personal income tax.

STATE:	**FLORIDA**
PROGRAM NAME:	Florida College Savings Program
529 TYPE:	Savings
STATE AGENCIES:	Florida Prepaid College Program Board
PROGRAM MANAGER:	TIAA-CREF Tuition Financing, Inc.
INITIAL YEAR OF OPERATION:	Targeted for first quarter 2002
TELEPHONE:	1-800-552-GRAD
INTERNET:	www.floridaprepaidcollege.com

Who can open an account? U.S. residents, UTMA/UGMA custodians, and legal entities.

Time or age limitations on beneficiary or on use of account assets: None.

Age-based investment options: Yes.

Static investment options: Fixed Income Option, Guaranteed Option, Balanced Option, and 100% Equity Option.

Underlying investments: TIAA-CREF institutional mutual funds.

Fees and expenses: 0.75% annualized program management fee charged against value of account, including expenses of underlying mutual funds. There are no enrollment or annual account maintenance fees.

Broker distribution: None.

Minimum initial contribution: $25 ($15 with automatic contributions).

STATE: **GEORGIA**

PROGRAM NAME: Georgia Higher Education Savings Plan
529 TYPE: Savings
STATE AGENCY: Georgia Office of the Treasury and Fiscal Services and Georgia Higher Education Savings Plan
INITIAL YEAR OF OPERATION: Targeted for 2002

Georgia is planning to launch a new 529 savings program in 2002. Negotiations to establish a management contract with a financial services company were under way at the time this book went to press. The program does not have any state residency requirements and Georgia residents are permitted to claim a deduction for up to $2,000 (joint filers) each year. Qualified withdrawals are exempt from Georgia income tax. Georgia law currently limits annual contributions to $8,000 per beneficiary ($120,000 total). There is a catch-up provision that allows contributions of up to a total of $16,000 per year for children 10 years or older for the first three years the plan is in operation.

STATE: **HAWAII**

PROGRAM NAME: Hawaii College Savings Program
529 TYPE: Savings
STATE AGENCIES: The Hawaii Department of Budget and Finance
INITIAL YEAR OF OPERATION: Targeted for 2002
INTERNET: www.state.hi.us/budget/college/college.htm

Legislation for a 529 savings plan in Hawaii was enacted in 1999. The program is expected to launch sometime in 2002. Further details were not available at the time this book went to press.

STATE: IDAHO

PROGRAM NAME:	Idaho College Savings Program (IDeal)
529 TYPE:	Savings
STATE AGENCY:	Idaho College Savings Program Board
PROGRAM MANAGER:	TIAA-CREF Tuition Financing, Inc.
INITIAL YEAR OF OPERATION:	2001
TELEPHONE:	1-866-IDEALED (1-866-433-2533)
INTERNET:	www.idsaves.org

Who can open an account? Individuals, UTMA/UGMA custodians, and legal entities.

Time or age limitations on beneficiary or on use of account assets: None.

Age-based investment option: The Managed Allocation Option contains 11 portfolios of underlying mutual funds. Contributions are placed into the portfolio corresponding to the age of the beneficiary. Each portfolio shifts to a more conservative investment allocation over time.

Static investment options: There are two supplemental investment options: 100% Equity Option (80% domestic equity and 20% international equity) and the Guaranteed Option. The Guaranteed Option invests in an instrument that guarantees principal and a minimum 3% annual rate of interest (actual rate will be declared quarterly).

Underlying investments: TIAA-CREF institutional mutual funds and TIAA-CREF Life Guaranteed Funding Agreement.

Fees and expenses: 0.70% annualized program management fee charged against the value of the account, and the expenses of the underlying funds ranging from 0.16% to 0.23% (portfolio weighted average). There are no enrollment or annual account maintenance fees.

Broker distribution: None.

Maximum contributions: Accepts contributions until all account balances for the same beneficiary reach $235,000.

Minimum initial contribution: $25 ($15 with automatic payroll deduction).

Account changes: Accepts requests to change beneficiary, transfer account ownership, name a successor owner, rollover/transfer assets within the program or to another 529 plan, and change investment option once per calendar year.

Special considerations:

- Contributions of up to $4,000 annually per claimant ($8,000 for joint filers) may be deducted from Idaho taxable income.
- At the time this book went to press, Idaho law required that an Idaho taxpayer include the entire amount of a non-qualified withdrawal in Idaho income, whether or not contributions were entirely deducted, and effectively subjecting the earnings portion to twice the ordinary rate of Idaho income tax.
- Qualified withdrawals are not specifically exempted under state law. The Idaho treatment of withdrawals from this program, and from any other state 529 plan, will depend on Idaho passing conformity legislation for the federal tax law changes (anticipated first quarter 2002).

STATE: **ILLINOIS**

PROGRAM NAME:	College Illinois!
529 TYPE:	Prepaid contract
STATE AGENCY AND PROGRAM MANAGER:	Illinois Student Assistance Commission
INITIAL YEAR OF OPERATION:	1998
TELEPHONE:	1-877-877-3724
INTERNET:	www.collegeillinois.com

Who can purchase a contract? U.S. residents, UTMA/UGMA custodians, and legal entities. However, the purchaser or beneficiary must be an Illinois resident for at least 12 months prior to enrollment.

Enrollment period: Ends March 27, 2002. The next enrollment period is expected to begin in late Fall 2002. Enrollment will be accepted until August 1, 2002 for children less than one year of age.

Time or age limitations on beneficiary or on use of benefits: The contract must be purchased at least three years before benefits can be used to pay for tuition and fees, and the beneficiary must begin using contract benefits within a ten-year period beginning on the date of projected enrollment.

Contract benefits: The contract pays in-state undergraduate tuition and mandatory fees at an Illinois public institution according to the plan and number of years selected. The value derived from the contract will depend in part on the selection of institution, because public institutions in Illinois have different tuition and fee levels. If the beneficiary decides to attend a private college in Illinois or an out-of-state college, the program will pay the equivalent value of the contract based on the average mean-weighted credit hour cost of in-state tuition and fees. A $15 fee will be deducted from the benefit for each institution attended. If the beneficiary receives a scholarship or grant, a semester-by-semester refund of the value of the benefits can be requested, or the benefits can be retained to pay for graduate school or continuing education.

Contract options: One to nine semesters at a public four-year university, one to four semesters at an Illinois community college, or a combination of four semesters at a community college and four semesters at a public university.

Costs: There is a one-time $75 application fee (reduced to $40 for subsequent applications by the same purchaser). In the enrollment period that ends March 27, 2002, lump-sum contract prices for a child in the ninth grade or higher ranged from $943 for the one-semester community college plan to $25,087 for the nine-semester university plan. Prices are discounted for younger beneficiaries grouped in ranges by grade in school. Contract payments may be made in a lump sum, in monthly or annual installments, or by combination of down payment and monthly installments. Installment payments are computed to include an effective annual 8% cost for making payments over time along with a small account maintenance fee.

Cancellation provisions: The contract may be canceled at any time after three years for a refund of all contract payments, plus interest at 2% annually, less a cancellation fee of up to $100. Cancellation within three years will not return any interest. In the event of the beneficiary's death or disability, the refund is based on the average mean-weighted credit hour cost of in-state tuition and fees, and a cancellation fee is not assessed.

Contract changes: Accepts requests to change beneficiary ($15 fee plus possible price adjustment if new beneficiary is older), transfer contract ownership ($15 fee), and name a successor owner. There are no special provisions concerning rollovers/transfers to another 529 plan (cancellation provisions would apply).

State backing: Contracts are not backed by the full faith and credit of the state of Illinois. If the program is discontinued, beneficiaries who are enrolled in college, or will be within five years, are entitled to all contract benefits; others will receive a return of contributions plus interest. The Governor and General Assembly must consider legislative appropriation of funds to the extent needed to cover program liabilities in the event the program is discontinued.

Special considerations:

- Qualified distributions from this program are exempt from Illinois state income tax. Illinois treatment of withdrawals from other 529 plans depends on the extent to which Illinois conforms to federal tax law changes.

- The value of the contract will not be counted in determining eligibility and need for student financial aid programs provided by the state of Illinois.

STATE:	**ILLINOIS**
PROGRAM NAME:	Bright Start College Savings Program
529 TYPE:	Savings
STATE AGENCY:	Office of the State Treasurer
PROGRAM MANAGER:	Salomon Smith Barney
INITIAL YEAR OF OPERATION:	2000
TELEPHONE:	1-877-43-BRIGHT (1-877-432-7444)
INTERNET:	www.brightstartsavings.com

Who can open an account? U.S. residents, UTMA/UGMA custodians, and legal entities.

Time or age limitations on beneficiary or on use of account assets: None.

Age-based investment option: The Age-Based option contains six portfolios of underlying mutual funds. Contributions are initially placed into the portfolio corresponding to the beneficiary's age and later reassigned to more conservative portfolios as the beneficiary ages. For accounts opened through participating Illinois banks, certificates of deposits are substituted for a portion of the fixed income and money market funds.

Static investment options: There are two supplemental portfolios: the Equity Portfolio and the Fixed Income Portfolio. Guaranteed option will be in place in 2002. For accounts opened through participating Illinois banks, the only option is a Fixed Income Portfolio.

Underlying investments: Smith Barney mutual funds. For accounts opened through participating Illinois banks, certificates of deposit comprise 50% of the Fixed Income Portfolio.

Fees and expenses: For accounts that are not opened through a broker, there is a 0.99% annualized program management fee charged against the value of account, that includes the expenses of the underlying mutual funds. There are no enrollment or annual account maintenance fees, except that accounts opened through a participating financial institution may be charged up to $30 as a one-time processing fee.

Broker distribution: Accounts may be opened through Salomon Smith Barney financial advisors and certain third-party selling agents. There are no additional program expenses or sales charges associated with these accounts.

Maximum contributions: Accepts contributions until account balances in all Illinois 529 plans for the same beneficiary reach $235,000.

Minimum initial contribution: $25 (no set minimum for automatic contributions).

Account changes: Accepts requests to change beneficiary, name a successor owner, rollover/transfer assets within the program or to another 529 plan, and change investment option once per calendar year. Does not accept requests to transfer account ownership.

Special considerations:

- Contributions are fully deductible in computing Illinois taxable income.
- Qualified withdrawals from this program are exempt from Illinois income tax. Illinois treatment of withdrawals from other 529 plans depends on state conformity to the federal tax law changes.

STATE:	**INDIANA**
PROGRAM NAME:	CollegeChoice 529 Investment Plan
529 TYPE:	Savings
STATE AGENCIES:	Indiana Education Savings Authority (IESA) chaired by the State Treasurer
PROGRAM MANAGER:	One Group Administrative Services, Inc.
INITIAL YEAR OF OPERATION:	1997 (substantially revised in 2002)
TELEPHONE:	1-866-400-PLAN (1-866-400-7526)
INTERNET:	www.collegechoiceplan.com

Who can open an account? Individuals at least 18 years old, emancipated minors, UTMA/UGMA custodians, and legal entities.

Time or age limitations on beneficiary or on use of account assets: None.

Age-based investment option: The Age-Based Program contains five portfolios of underlying mutual funds. Contributions are initially placed into the portfolio corresponding to the beneficiary's age, and later reassigned to more conservative portfolios as the beneficiary nears college age.

Static investment options: The Custom Portfolios consist of seven portfolios: the Growth Portfolio (80%-100% equity), the Growth & Income Portfolio (60%-80% equity), the Balanced Portfolio (40%-60% equity), the Conservative Growth Portfolio (20%-40% equity), Tuition Portfolio (100% money market fund), the Equity Index Portfolio (100% equity index fund), and the Bond Portfolio (100% bond fund). Under this option, contributions may be spread among a maximum of three portfolios in any one account.

Underlying investments: One Group Mutual Funds.

Fees and expenses: There is an annual account maintenance fee as follows (but waived for accounts with balances of at least $25,000 or with automatic contributions): $30 for Indiana non-residents, $10 for Indiana residents, and $25 for accounts converted from the Indiana Family College Savings Plan regardless of residence. There is a $10 state authority fee for Indiana non-residents. The underlying expenses of the mutual funds range from approximately 0.35% to 0.97% (portfolio weighted average) In addition, except for accounts converted from the predecessor program (Indiana Family College Savings Plan) and other specified situations, the contributor selects one of three advisor fee structures. Structure A involves an initial 3.5% sales charge and a 0.40% annualized program management/investment fee charged against the value of the account. Structure B (not available if the beneficiary is 15 or older) has no initial sales charge and a 0.95% annualized program management/investment fee. There is a contingent deferred sales charge starting at 2.5% for units withdrawn in the first year declining to 0.50% for units withdrawn in the sixth year. After six years, any units under Structure B automatically convert to Structure A. Structure C (not available if the beneficiary is 17 or older) has no initial sales charge and a 0.65% annualized program management/investment fee. There is a contingent deferred sales charge of 1% for units withdrawn within the first year. Structures B and C are not available in the Tuition Portfolio.

Broker distribution: Accounts may be opened through financial advisors. Any accounts opened directly without a broker will be subject to the same expense structure as broker-sold accounts.

Maximum contributions: Accept contributions until balances in all accounts for the same beneficiary reach $114,548 (increased to $236,750 effective July 1, 2002).

Minimum initial contribution: $50. Accounts with a balance of less than $500 and no contributions or withdrawals within the preceding calendar year may be terminated.

Account changes: Accepts requests to change beneficiary (except that a new beneficiary under Fee Structure C must be less than 17 years old), transfer account ownership, name a successor owner, rollover/transfer assets within the program or to another 529 plan, and change investment option once per calendar year.

Special considerations:

- Qualified withdrawals from this program are exempt from Indiana income tax. Indiana treatment of withdrawals from other 529 plans depends on the state passing conformity legislation for the federal tax law changes.
- The value of the account will not be counted in determining eligibility and need for student financial aid programs provided by the state of Indiana.

STATE:	**IOWA**
PROGRAM NAME:	College Savings Iowa
529 TYPE:	Savings
STATE AGENCY AND PROGRAM MANAGER:	State Treasurer
INVESTMENT MANAGER:	Vanguard Investments
INITIAL YEAR OF OPERATION:	1998
TELEPHONE:	1-888-672-9116
INTERNET:	www.collegesavingsiowa.com

Who can open an account? U.S. residents age 18 or older and UGMA/UTMA custodians.

Time or age limitations on beneficiary or on use of account assets: The beneficiary must be younger than 18 at the time the account is opened. The account must be used by the time the beneficiary reaches age 30.

Age-based investment options: Choose one of four investment tracks that vary in the amount of equity risk assumed. Each track contains as many as five portfolios of underlying stock and bond index funds, ranging from 100% equity to 20% equity. Contributions are initially placed into the portfolio corresponding to the selected track and beneficiary's age, and later reassigned to more conservative portfolios within that track as the beneficiary gets older.

Static investment options: None.

Underlying investments: Vanguard index funds.

Fees and expenses: 0.65% annualized program management fee charged against value of account that includes the expenses of the underlying mutual funds. There are no enrollment or account management fees.

Broker distribution: None.

Maximum contributions: Accepts contributions until all accounts for the same beneficiary reach $146,000.

Minimum initial contribution: $25 (but not less than $50 in any year of contribution).

Account changes: Accepts requests to change beneficiary, transfer account ownership, name a successor owner, rollover/transfer assets within the program or to another 529 plan, and change investment option once per calendar year.

Special considerations:
- Iowa residents may deduct up to $2,180 (in 2002) in contributions per beneficiary from state income tax (must be the account owner).
- Qualified withdrawals from this program are exempt from Iowa income tax. Iowa treatment of withdrawals from other 529 plans depends on the state passing conformity legislation for the federal tax law changes.
- The value of the account will not be counted in determining eligibility and need for student financial aid programs provided by the state of Iowa.

STATE:	**KANSAS**
PROGRAM NAME:	Learning Quest Education Savings Program
529 TYPE:	Savings
STATE AGENCY:	Kansas State Treasurer
PROGRAM MANAGER:	American Century Investment Management, Inc.
INITIAL YEAR OF OPERATION:	2000
TELEPHONE:	1-800-579-2203
INTERNET:	www.learningquestsavings.com

Who can open an account? U.S. citizens or resident aliens, UTMA/UGMA custodians, and legal entities.

Time or age limitations on beneficiary or on use of account assets: A qualified withdrawal may be made only after the account has been open at least 24 months. Proposed removal of the waiting period is under review by Kansas legislature.

Age-based investment options: The program offers a choice between three investment tracks: Aggressive, Moderate and Conservative. Each track contains seven portfolios of underlying mutual funds. Contributions are placed into the portfolio corresponding to the selected track and the age of the beneficiary or as determined by the account owner, and later reassigned to a more conservative portfolio as the beneficiary ages, eventually transferring to the "Short-Term" portfolio.

Static investment options: None.

Underlying investments: American Century mutual funds.

Fees and expenses: $40 annual account maintenance fee ($10 for Kansas residents or if account balance is more than $100,000), 0.39% annualized program management fee charged against value of account, and the expenses of the underlying mutual funds ranging from approximately 0.52% to 0.95% (portfolio weighted average). There is no enrollment fee.

Broker distribution: Accounts may be opened through Charles Schwab & Co. for its retail and investment advisor clients. Advisor shares will be available in mid-2002.

Maximum contributions: Accepts contributions until all account balances for the same beneficiary reach $235,000.

Minimum initial contribution: $500 for Kansas residents (or $25 per month with automatic contributions) and $2,500 for non-residents (or $50 per month with automatic contributions).

Account changes: Accepts requests to change beneficiary, transfer account ownership, name a successor owner, rollover/transfer assets within the program or to another 529 plan, and change investment option once per calendar year.

Special considerations:

- Contributions of up to $2,000 per beneficiary each year are deductible from Kansas adjusted gross income ($4,000 if married, filing jointly). Deductions are subject to recapture if non-qualified withdrawals are taken from the account in a subsequent year.
- Although Kansas does not provide specific state tax exemption for qualified withdrawals, its tax law generally conforms to federal tax law and so qualified withdrawals that are exempt from federal income tax should be exempt from Kansas income tax as well.

STATE:	**KENTUCKY**
PROGRAM NAME:	Kentucky Education Savings Plan Trust
529 TYPE:	Savings
STATE AGENCY:	Kentucky Higher Education Assistance Authority
PROGRAM MANAGER:	TIAA-CREF Tuition Financing, Inc.
INITIAL YEAR OF OPERATION:	1990 (substantially revised in 1999)
TELEPHONE:	1-877-598-7878
INTERNET:	www.kentuckytrust.org

Who can open an account? Individuals living in the U.S. who have reached the age of majority, emancipated minors, UTMA/UGMA custodians, and legal entities. Either the account owner or the beneficiary must have "Kentucky ties", which may include current or former residence or employment, or a family member with current or former residence in Kentucky.

Time or age limitations on beneficiary or on use of account assets: None.

Age-based investment option: The Managed Allocation Option contains 11 portfolios of underlying mutual funds. Contributions are placed into the portfolio corresponding to the age of the beneficiary. Each portfolio shifts to a more conservative investment allocation over time.

Static investment option: The 100% Equity Option invests approximately 80% in the TIAA-CREF Institutional Growth and Income Fund and 20% in the TIAA-CREF Institutional International Equity Fund.

Underlying investments: TIAA-CREF institutional mutual funds.

Fees and expenses: 0.81% maximum annualized program management fee charged against value of account, including expenses of underlying mutual funds. There are no enrollment or annual account maintenance fees.

Broker distribution: None.

Maximum contributions: Accepts contributions until all account balances for the same beneficiary reach $235,000.

Minimum initial contribution: $25 ($15 with automatic payroll deduction).

Account changes: Accepts requests to change beneficiary, transfer account ownership, name a successor owner, rollover/transfer to another 529, and change investment option once per calendar year. Any changes must satisfy the "Kentucky ties" requirement.

Special considerations:

- Qualified withdrawals from this program are exempt from Kentucky income tax. Kentucky treatment of withdrawals from other 529 plans depends on the state passing conformity legislation for the federal tax law changes.
- Beneficiaries with at least eight years of participation as a Kentucky resident, and $2,400 in contributions, can lock in their eligibility for in-state tuition at Kentucky public institutions, even if they later move out of the state.
- The value of the account will not be counted in determining eligibility and need for student financial aid programs provided by the Commonwealth of Kentucky.
- The program guarantees a 4% minimum return on contributions received before October 1, 1999 (this benefit is targeted to participants who saw their accounts converted when TIAA-CREF was hired as program manager).
- Under Kentucky law, the right to benefits is not subject to attachment, garnishment, or seizure by creditors of account owner or the beneficiary.

STATE: **KENTUCKY**

PROGRAM NAME:	Kentucky's Affordable Prepaid Tuition (KAPT)
529 TYPE:	Prepaid contract
STATE AGENCY AND PROGRAM MANAGER:	KAPT Board of Directors and the Office of the State Treasurer
INITIAL YEAR OF OPERATION:	2001
TELEPHONE:	1-888-919-KAPT (1-888-919-5278)
INTERNET:	www.getkapt.com

Who can purchase a contract? Individuals of legal age, UTMA/UGMA custodians, and legal entities. However, the beneficiary must be a Kentucky resident or intend to attend a participating institution in Kentucky.

Enrollment period: Ends April 15, 2002. The next enrollment period is expected to be in Fall 2002.

Time or age limitations on beneficiary or on use of benefits: Contract must be purchased at least two years prior to the beneficiary's proposed college enrollment date.

Contract benefits: The Value Plan will pay tuition and fees at any school in the Kentucky Community and Technical College System. The Standard Plan will pay tuition and fees at whichever Kentucky university is most expensive in the year of attendance. The Premium Plan represents an investment that grows in value at the same rate as tuition increases at the University of Kentucky. The value of any of these contracts can be converted for use at any eligible institution in the country. The value of a contract in excess of actual tuition and fees can be used to pay for other expenses such as books, equipment and room and board. There is a $50 out-of-state transfer fee for beneficiaries that attend school outside Kentucky.

Contract options: There are three tuition plans: Value (one or two years), Standard (one to five years), and Premium (one to five years).

Costs: There is a one-time $50 enrollment fee. In the enrollment period that ended December 3, 2001, lump-sum contract prices ranged from $1,450 to $2,900 in the Value Plan, $3,742 to $18,710 in the Standard Plan, and $11,838 to $59,190 in the Premium Plan. Contract payments may be made in a lump sum or in monthly installments (with or without a down payment) over a variety of terms. Monthly installment payments are computed to include an additional cost for making payments over time along with a small account maintenance fee.

Cancellation provisions: The contract may be canceled at any time for a refund of all contract payments, less a cancellation fee of $150. The refund may be paid in installments. In the event of the beneficiary's death, disability, or receipt of a scholarship, the refund will include a share of earnings and the cancellation fee will be waived.

Contract changes: Accepts requests to change beneficiary ($20 fee, and an additional payment may be required if the new beneficiary is older) and name a successor owner. Contract ownership is not transferable except in limited circumstances. There are no special provisions concerning rollovers/transfers to another 529 plan (cancellation provisions would apply).

State backing: Contracts are not backed by the full faith and credit of the state of Kentucky. 75 percent of the abandoned property fund administered by the State Treasurer would be available to meet any unfunded liability of the program trust.

Special considerations:

- Qualified distributions from this program are exempt from Kentucky income tax. Kentucky treatment of distributions from other 529 plans depends on the state passing conformity legislation for the federal tax law changes.
- The value of the contract will not be counted in determining eligibility and need for student financial aid programs provided by the Commonwealth of Kentucky.

STATE: **LOUISIANA**

PROGRAM NAME:	Student Tuition Assistance and Revenue Trust (START) Savings Program
529 TYPE:	Savings
STATE AGENCIES AND PROGRAM MANAGER:	Louisiana Office of Student Financial Assistance, Louisiana Tuition Trust Authority, and State Treasurer
INITIAL YEAR OF OPERATION:	1997
TELEPHONE:	1-800-259-5626
INTERNET:	www.osfa.state.la.us/start.htm

Who can open an account? Individuals, UTMA/UGMA custodians, and legal entities. The account owner or beneficiary must be a Louisiana resident at the time the account is opened.

Time or age limitations on beneficiary or on use of account assets: At least one year must elapse from the date of the first deposit before withdrawals for qualifying higher education expenses can be taken.

Age-based investment options: None.

Static investment options and underlying investments: All contributions are invested in conservative fixed rate securities by the State Treasurer. Equity investments may become available during 2002.

Fees and expenses: None.

Broker distribution: None.

Maximum contributions: Accepts contributions until all account balances for the same beneficiary reach $173,065.

Minimum initial contribution: $10.

Account changes: Accepts requests to change beneficiary and designate a successor owner, and change investment option once per calendar year. Account ownership may not be transferred prior to the owner's death or incapacity.

Special considerations:

- The state of Louisiana also provides an Earnings Enhancement that matches a portion of contributions into the program. The match percentage ranges from 2% to

14% of contributions based on the account owner's federal adjusted gross income and the classification of the account. Currently, the EE portion of any account must be used for qualified higher education expenses and is not refundable.

- Account owners may deduct up to $2,400 of annual contributions from their Louisiana taxable income for each beneficiary. Any unused portion may be carried forward to subsequent years.
- Qualified withdrawals from this program are exempt from Louisiana state income tax. Louisiana treatment of withdrawals from other 529 plans depends on state conformity to the federal tax law changes.
- The value of the account will not be counted in determining eligibility and need for student financial aid programs provided by the state of Louisiana.
- Under Louisiana law, the right of a beneficiary to the assets of the account are not subject to collation, execution, garnishment, attachment, the operation of bankruptcy or insolvency laws or other process of law.

STATE:	**MAINE**
PROGRAM NAME:	NextGen College Investing Plan
529 TYPE:	Savings
STATE AGENCIES:	Finance Authority of Maine (FAME) and the State Treasurer
PROGRAM MANAGER:	Merrill Lynch
INITIAL YEAR OF OPERATION:	1999
TELEPHONE:	1-877-463-9843
INTERNET:	www.nextgenplan.com

Who can open an account? Individuals, UTMA/UGMA custodians, and legal entities.

Time or age limitations on beneficiary or on use of account assets: None.

Age-based investment options: The Active Allocation Portfolios (Client Direct Series) contain ten portfolios of underlying mutual funds. Contributions are initially placed into the portfolio corresponding to the beneficiary's age or as selected by the account owner. Nine portfolios shift to a more conservative investment allocation over time, eventually transferring to the "college" portfolio. Each of the age-based options available in the Client Adviser series operates in a similar manner.

Static investment options: There are three options in the Client Direct Series: 100% Equity, 75% Equity and Fixed Income. Each of the Client Adviser Series also has three static portfolio options.

Underlying investments: The Client Direct Series uses mutual funds from Merrill Lynch Investment Managers (MLIM). The Client Adviser Series is comprised of four distinct groupings of portfolios, managed separately by AIM, Franklin Templeton, MFS, and MLIM.

Fees and expenses: $50 annual account maintenance fee (waived if either the account owner or beneficiary is a Maine resident, annual contributions are at least $2,500, or the account value is at least $20,000), 0.55% annualized program management fee charged against the value of an account in the Client Direct Series, and underlying fund expenses ranging from approximately 0.76% to 0.95% (portfolio weighted average). For the Client Adviser Series, the annualized program management fee is 0.60% (0.90% for portfolios with a target equity allocation of 40% or more), and the expenses of the underlying mutual funds range from approximately 0.71% to 1.79% (portfolio weighted average). There is no enrollment fee or sales charge.

Broker distribution: Accounts in the Client Adviser Series may be opened through Merrill Lynch Financial Consultants and participating Maine brokers.

Maximum contributions: Accepts contributions until all account balances for the same beneficiary reach $235,000.

Minimum initial contribution: $250 ($50 for automatic contributions).

Account changes: Accepts requests to change beneficiary, transfer account ownership, name a successor owner, rollover/transfer assets within the program or to another 529 plan, and change investment option once per calendar year.

Special considerations:
- Qualified withdrawals from this program are exempt from Maine income taxes, and accounts will also be excluded for purposes of Maine estate tax.
- Under Maine law, accounts are not subject to levy, execution, judgment or other operation of law, garnishment or other judicial enforcement, and accounts are not an asset or property of either the account owner or beneficiary for purposes of Maine insolvency laws.

STATE: **MARYLAND**

PROGRAM NAME:	Maryland College Investment Plan
529 TYPE:	Savings
STATE AGENCY:	Maryland Higher Education Investment Board
PROGRAM MANAGER:	T. Rowe Price Associates
INITIAL YEAR OF OPERATION:	2001
TELEPHONE:	1-888-4MD-GRAD (1-888-463-4723)
INTERNET:	www.collegesavingsmd.org

Who can open an account? U.S. citizens or resident aliens, UTMA/UGMA custodians, and legal entities.

Time or age limitations on beneficiary or on use of account assets: None.

Age-based investment options: The Enrollment-Based Portfolios contain seven portfolios of underlying funds, ranging from 100% equity to 20% equity. Contributions may be initially placed into the portfolio corresponding to the number of years to expected enrollment based on the age of the beneficiary or as selected by the account owner. Seven portfolios shift to a more conservative investment allocation over time, eventually transferring to the "college" portfolio.

Static investment options: Select among three portfolios: the Equity Portfolio, the Bond Portfolio, and the Balanced Portfolio (60% equity and 40% fixed income).

Underlying investments: Mutual funds from T. Rowe Price.

Fees and expenses: There is a one-time $90 enrollment fee that covers all accounts opened by the same person for the same beneficiary. The fee is reduced or eliminated in certain circumstances involving rollovers or participation in other Maryland or T. Rowe Price-managed 529 plans. $30 annual account maintenance fee (waived for accounts with at least $25,000 and for accounts enrolled in an automatic investment or payroll deduction plan), 0.38% annualized program management fee charged against value of account, and underlying fund expenses ranging from approximately 0.35% to 0.99%.

Broker distribution: None.

Maximum contributions: Accepts contributions until all Maryland account balances for the same beneficiary reach $175,000.

Minimum initial contribution: $250 ($25 with automatic investment plan).

Account changes: Accepts requests to change beneficiary, transfer account ownership, name a successor owner, rollover/transfer assets within the program or to another 529 plan, and change investment option once per calendar year.

Special considerations:

- Maryland residents may deduct contributions each year of up to $2,500 from Maryland state income. Contributions in excess of $2,500 may be carried forward and deducted for up to 10 additional years.
- Qualified withdrawals from this program are exempt from Maryland income tax. Maryland treatment of withdrawals from other 529 plans depends on state conformity to the federal tax law changes.

STATE: **MARYLAND**

PROGRAM NAME:	Maryland Prepaid College Trust
529 TYPE:	Prepaid contract
STATE AGENCY AND PROGRAM MANAGER:	Maryland Higher Education Investment Board
INITIAL YEAR OF OPERATION:	1998
TELEPHONE:	1-888-4MD-GRAD (1-888-463-4723)
INTERNET:	www.collegesavingsmd.org

Who can purchase a contract? Individuals, UTMA/UGMA custodians, and legal entities. The purchaser or beneficiary must be a resident of Maryland or the District of Columbia at the time of enrollment.

Enrollment period: The current enrollment period ends March 22, 2002. The next enrollment period is expected to begin in Fall 2002. Newborns may be enrolled year-round at contract prices in effect at the time of enrollment.

Time or age limitations on beneficiary or on use of benefits: The beneficiary must be in ninth grade or younger at the time of enrollment. Benefits must be used within ten years after the projected date of high school graduation plus the number of years of tuition purchased in the contract (not including any time spent as an active duty member of the armed forces).

Contract benefits: Contract pays in-state undergraduate tuition and mandatory fees at a Maryland public institution according to the plan and number of years selected. The value derived from the contract will depend in part on the selection of institution, because public institutions in Maryland have different tuition and fee levels. If the beneficiary decides to attend a private or out-of-state school, the contract will pay the weighted average tuition and mandatory fees of the Maryland public colleges in the tuition plan purchased or the actual tuition and mandatory fees, whichever is less. Currently a $25 fee is charged for each registration to an out-of-state college. If the beneficiary receives a scholarship or grant, any unused benefits can be used for other qualified expenses including tuition charges in excess of weighted average tuition, graduate school tuition, room and board, and books.

Contract options: One to five years at a public four-year university, two years at a Maryland community college, or a community/university combination (two years of each).

Costs: There is a one-time $90 enrollment fee. The fee is reduced to $20 in certain circumstances involving purchase of additional years, rollovers, or participation in the Maryland College Investment Plan. In the enrollment period ending March 22, 2002, lump-sum contract prices for a child in the ninth grade ranged from $5,393 for the two-year community college plan to $26,518 for the five-year university plan. Prices are discounted for younger beneficiaries. Payment options also include annual payments, 60 monthly payments or extended monthly payments, which continue until the beneficiary reaches college age. All installment payments are computed to include an effective annual 7.5% cost of making payments over time.

Cancellation provisions: A contract can be canceled at any time to provide a refund of contract payments less a $75 fee, plus or minus 90% (50% if canceled within three years) of the Trust earnings/losses for the period of enrollment.

Contract changes: Accepts requests to change beneficiary ($25 fee, plus adjustment to the purchase price), transfer contract ownership ($10 fee), and name a successor owner, subject to residency requirements. Contract value can be transferred to the Maryland College Investment Plan at an amount equal to contract payments less a $20 fee, plus or minus 100% of the Trust earnings/losses for the period of enrollment. For rollovers to another state's 529 plan, the fee is $75 and rollover value is equal to payments plus 100% of Trust earnings/losses (75% if the contract is not at least three years old).

State backing: The program has a legislative guarantee. If it is unable to pay benefits in any given year, the Governor must include in the annual budget the amount needed to pay full benefits. However, the Maryland General Assembly has final approval of all state appropriations. Any appropriation would need to be repaid by the Trust, without interest, over the following two years.

Special considerations:
- Tuition benefits will be adjusted to ensure that the minimum benefit is equal to contract payments plus a reasonable rate of return pegged to the one-year Treasury bill

(less 1%). That amount less actual tuition and fees can be used to pay for other qualified higher education expenses.

- Maryland taxpayers may deduct up to $2,500 of their payments, per contract, each year from Maryland taxable income, with carryforward of excess payments until all payments have been deducted. Deductions are subject to recapture if contract pay-ments are refunded.
- Qualified distributions are exempt from Maryland income tax. Maryland treatment of withdrawals from other 529 plans depends on state conformity to the federal tax law changes.
- If favorable investment performance causes projected program assets to exceed projected liabilities by at least 30%, the Board has the option to rebate the excess surplus to program participants.
- Under Maryland law, the right to benefits is not subject to attachment, garnish-ment, or seizure by creditors of the contract owner or the beneficiary.

STATE: **MASSACHUSETTS**

PROGRAM NAME:	U.Fund College Investing Plan
529 TYPE:	Savings
STATE AGENCY:	Massachusetts Educational Financing Authority (MEFA)
PROGRAM MANAGER:	Fidelity Investments
INITIAL YEAR OF OPERATION:	1999
TELEPHONE:	1-800-544-2776
INTERNET:	www.fidelity.com/ufund

Who can open an account? U.S. citizens and resident aliens at least 18 years of age.

Time or age limitations on beneficiary or on use of account assets: None.

Age-based investment option: The Age-Based Strategy contains eight portfolios of under-lying mutual funds. Contributions are placed into the portfolio corresponding to the age of the beneficiary or as determined by the account owner. Seven portfolios shift to a more conservative investment allocation over time, eventually transferring to the "College" portfolio.

Static investment options: The Static Portfolios consist of three portfolios: 100% Equity, 70% Equity, and Conservative (100% fixed income and money market).

Underlying investments: Fidelity Investments mutual funds.

Fees and expenses: $30 annual account maintenance fee (waived for accounts with a balance of at least $25,000 or enrolled in the automatic investment plan), 0.30% annualized program management fee charged against value of account, and underlying fund expenses ranging from approximately 0.65% to 0.80% (portfolio weighted average). There is no enrollment fee.

Broker distribution: None.

Maximum contributions: Accepts contributions until all account balances for the same beneficiary reach $230,000.

Minimum initial contribution: $1,000 ($50 per month for automatic investment plan).

Account changes: Accepts requests to change beneficiary, name a successor owner, rollover/transfer assets within the program or to another 529 plan, and change investment option once per calendar year. Does not accept requests to transfer ownership prior to death or incapacity.

Special considerations:

- Massachusetts does not provide specific state tax incentives for residents in this program. All withdrawals by a Massachusetts resident from any 529 plan will be subject to tax unless Massachusetts passes conformity legislation for the federal tax law changes.

STATE:	**MASSACHUSETTS**
PROGRAM NAME:	U.Plan
529 TYPE:	Prepaid (but not a 529 plan)
STATE AGENCY:	Massachusetts Educational Financing Authority (MEFA)
INITIAL YEAR OF OPERATION:	1995
TELEPHONE:	1-800-449-MEFA (1-800-449-6332)
INTERNET:	www.mefa.org

Who can purchase tuition certificates? Any individual. There are no Massachusetts residency requirements.

Enrollment period: May 1, 2002 to June 30, 2002.

Contract benefits: U.Plan involves the issuance of special purpose Massachusetts general obligation bonds. Participants purchase tuition certificates that may be redeemed at maturity to pay for tuition and fees at participating Massachusetts colleges. They may not be used to pay for other costs such as books or room and board. There are over 80 Massachusetts institutions participating in the program, including many private colleges. Each tuition certificate is worth a predetermined percentage of each institution's tuition and fees, as agreed to by the institutions. If not redeemed for use at a participating Massachusetts institution (for example, the beneficiary attends an out-of-state school), tuition certificates can be redeemed for the principal plus annually compounded interest equal to the Consumer Price Index.

Contract options: There are sixteen years of maturities available for purchase in each enrollment period, with five years being the shortest.

Costs: There is no enrollment fee. The minimum purchase is $300 per maturity year and the maximum purchase is four years of tuition and fees at the highest cost institution participating in the program. For the enrollment period that ended June 30, 2001, the cost of attending one of the participating institutions for four years ranged from $6,240 to $107,884.

Cancellation provisions: Tuition certificates may not be redeemed before their maturity date. If an emergency sale is needed, the program administrator will attempt to find a buyer, with no assurances given.

Contract changes: The beneficiary may be changed within the owner's family.

State backing: Tuition certificates are backed by the full faith and credit of the Commonwealth of Massachusetts.

Special considerations:
- U.Plan does not rely upon the provisions of section 529. This means that the special income tax and gift and estate tax provisions contained in section 529 are not applicable.
- Because the tuition certificate represents a general obligation bond, the interest earned is exempt from Massachusetts state income taxes and presumably exempt from federal income tax, although the IRS has not provided a ruling to this effect. The interest may be taxable as it accrues each year on the state income tax return of an owner who resides outside Massachusetts.

STATE: **MICHIGAN**

PROGRAM NAME:	Michigan Education Trust (MET)
529 TYPE:	Prepaid contract
STATE AGENCIES AND PROGRAM MANAGERS:	MET Board of Directors and Department of Treasury
INITIAL YEAR OF OPERATION:	1988
TELEPHONE:	1-800-MET-4-KID (1-800-638-4543)
INTERNET:	www.treasury.state.mi.us/MET/metindex.htm

Who can purchase a contract? U.S. residents at least 18 years old, UTMA/UGMA custodians, and legal entities. However, the beneficiary must be a Michigan resident at the time of purchase enrollment.

Enrollment period: Ends August 31, 2002. The next enrollment period is expected to begin in late Fall 2002.

Time or age limitations on beneficiary or on use of benefits: The beneficiary must be within the age/grade requirements stated in the program price chart at the time of purchase. A full benefits contract may be purchased for a beneficiary in the eighth grade or younger. A limited benefits or community college contract may be purchased for a beneficiary in the tenth grade or younger. Contract benefits must be used within 9 years after the projected college entrance date.

Contract benefits: The contract pays in-state undergraduate tuition and mandatory fees at a Michigan public institution according to the plan and number of years selected. The value derived from the contract will depend in part on the selection of institution, because public institutions in Michigan have different tuition and fee levels. Unused credit hours may be used toward graduate school or an advanced program at a Michigan public university or college at the undergraduate tuition rate. The value of a contract can be converted for use at an institution other than one that falls into the specific plan selected, although the conversion formula can vary depending on the circumstances.

Contract options: One to four years under the Full Benefits Plan, which covers tuition and fees at any Michigan public institution; one to four years under the Limited Benefits Plan, which covers tuition and fees at Michigan institutions whose tuition does not exceed 105 percent of the weighted average tuition of all Michigan public four-year universities; and one or two years under the Community College Plan, which covers in-district tuition and mandatory fees for one or two years at any Michigan public community college.

Costs: There is a one-time $85 enrollment processing fee reduced to as low as $25 for early application. In the enrollment period that ends August 31, 2002, lump-sum prices range from $5,512 for the one-year contract to $22,048 for the four-year contract under the Full Benefits Plan, $4,440 for the one-year contract to $17,760 for the four-year contract under the Limited Benefits Plan, and $1,643 for the one-year contract and $3,286 for the two-year contract under the Community College Plan. Contract payments may be made in a lump sum, or in monthly installments under specified terms. Monthly installment payments are computed to include an effective annual 8% cost for making payments over time along with a small account maintenance fee.

Cancellation provisions: If the beneficiary decides not to attend college, the "refund designee" will receive a refund in four annual installments equal to tuition at the lowest cost Michigan public four-year university, or the lowest cost community college if the community college contract was purchased. A $100 termination fee is deducted from the first refund payment. Only a beneficiary who has reached 18 years of age can terminate the contract and request a refund. Once the beneficiary completes more than one-half of the credit hours needed for a four-year degree, the contract may not be terminated. Contracts terminated due to the receipt of a full-tuition scholarship will be valued at the average tuition of Michigan's public four-year university.

Contract changes: The beneficiary can transfer contract rights to a spouse, parent, or sibling after reaching age 18 or receiving a high school diploma. The contract purchaser has the ability to make a change only if the original beneficiary dies or becomes disabled. An additional payment may be required if the new beneficiary is older. Beneficiary designation cannot be changed once the original beneficiary completes more than one-half of the four-year degree requirements at a Michigan public institution. The contract purchaser cannot transfer rights in the contract during lifetime. If the contract purchaser dies, the executor of the estate can add an appointee, and change the refund designee (unless the beneficiary is the refund designee). There are no operational provisions concerning rollovers to another state's 529 plan. Any rollover would have to wait until the beneficiary reaches age 18 and would be subject to the contract cancellation provisions.

State backing: Contracts are not backed by the full faith and credit of the state of Michigan. The program trust fund carries a reserve to protect against shortfalls.

Special considerations:
- Note that in this program contract ownership rights are generally held by the beneficiary, not the purchaser, except that the purchaser may initially name a "refund designee" other than the beneficiary.
- All payments towards the cost of the contract are eligible for a state income tax deduction.

- Qualified distributions from this program and all other 529 plans will be exempt from Michigan state income tax only to the extent that Michigan conforms to federal tax law changes.

STATE:	**MICHIGAN**
PROGRAM NAME:	Michigan Education Savings Program
529 TYPE:	Savings
STATE AGENCY:	Michigan Department of Treasury
PROGRAM MANAGER:	TIAA-CREF Tuition Financing, Inc.
INITIAL YEAR OF OPERATION:	2000
TELEPHONE:	1-877-861-MESP (1-877-861-6377)
INTERNET:	www.misaves.com

Who can open an account? U.S. citizens or resident aliens with a valid Social Security number or federal taxpayer identification number.

Time or age limitations on beneficiary or on use of account assets: None.

Age-based investment option: The Managed Allocation Option contains 11 portfolios of underlying mutual funds. Contributions are placed into the portfolio corresponding to the age of the beneficiary. Each portfolio shifts to a more conservative investment allocation over time.

Static investment options: There are two supplemental investment options: the 100% Equity Option (80% domestic equity and 20% international equity) and the Guaranteed Option. The Guaranteed option is invested in an instrument that guarantees principal and a minimum 3% annual rate of interest (actual rate is declared quarterly).

Underlying investments: TIAA-CREF institutional mutual funds and TIAA-CREF Life Guaranteed Funding Agreement.

Fees and expenses: 0.65% annualized program management fee charged against value of account, including expenses of underlying mutual funds. There are no enrollment or annual account maintenance fees.

Broker distribution: None.

Maximum contributions: Accepts contributions until all Michigan account balances for the same beneficiary reach $235,000.

Minimum initial contribution: $25 ($15 with automatic payroll deduction).

Account changes: Accepts requests to change beneficiary, transfer account ownership, name a successor owner, rollover/transfer assets within the program or to another 529 plan, and change investment option once per calendar year.

Special considerations:

- Up to $5,000 ($10,000 for married couples filing joint returns) of total annual contributions to all accounts may be deducted from Michigan taxable income each year. Deductions may not be claimed in the year any withdrawals are made or in any subsequent year.
- Qualified withdrawals from this program are exempt from Michigan income tax. Michigan treatment of withdrawals from other 529 plans depends on state conformity to the federal tax law changes.
- A contribution may be eligible for a matching grant from the state of Michigan if the beneficiary is a Michigan resident under seven years old, and if the federal adjusted gross income of the beneficiary's custodial parent(s) is $80,000 or less. This is a one-time grant per beneficiary.

STATE: MINNESOTA

PROGRAM NAME:	Minnesota College Savings Plan
529 TYPE:	Savings
STATE AGENCIES:	Minnesota State Board of Investment and Minnesota Higher Education Services Office.
PROGRAM MANAGER:	TIAA-CREF Tuition Financing, Inc.
INITIAL YEAR OF OPERATION:	2001
TELEPHONE:	1-877-EDU4MIN (1-877-338-4646)
INTERNET:	www.mnsaves.org

Who can open an account? U.S. citizens or resident aliens with a social security number, including minors (with signature of parent or guardian).

Time or age limitations on beneficiary or on use of account assets: None.

Age-based investment option: The Managed Allocation Option places contributions into one of 11 age-banded portfolios of underlying funds. Contributions are placed into the portfolio corresponding to the age of the beneficiary. Each portfolio shifts to a more conservative investment allocation over time.

Static investment options: There are two supplemental investment options. The 100% Equity Option is invested 80% in a growth and income fund and 20% in an international equity fund. The Guaranteed Option is invested in a funding agreement that guarantees principal and a minimum 3% rate of interest (actual rate is declared quarterly).

Underlying investments: TIAA-CREF institutional mutual funds and TIAA-CREF Life Guaranteed Funding Agreement.

Fees and expenses: 0.65% annualized program management fee charged against value of account, including expenses of underlying mutual funds. There are no enrollment or annual account maintenance fees.

Broker distribution: None.

Maximum contributions: Accepts contributions until all account balances for the same beneficiary reach $122,484.

Minimum initial contribution: $25 ($15 with payroll deduction).

Account changes: Accepts requests to change beneficiary, transfer account ownership, name a successor owner, rollover/transfer assets within the program or to another 529 plan, and change investment option once per calendar year.

Special considerations:
- The state of Minnesota will make annual matching grants of up to $300 for each beneficiary in the program where certain residency requirements are met, a separate application is filed, and the family income of the beneficiary does not exceed $80,000. The matching percentage is 15% for families with incomes of $50,000 or less, and 5% for families with incomes between $50,000 and $80,000. The accumulated grants will be fully or partially forfeited if non-qualified withdrawals are taken and under certain other conditions.
- Minnesota does not provide specific state tax incentives for residents in this program, but its tax law generally conforms to federal tax law and so qualified withdrawals that are exempt from federal income tax should be exempt from Minnesota income tax as well.

STATE:	**MISSISSIPPI**
PROGRAM NAME:	Mississippi Prepaid Affordable College Tuition (MPACT) Program
529 TYPE:	Prepaid contract
STATE AGENCY:	Mississippi Treasury Department
PROGRAM MANAGER:	TIAA-CREF Tuition Financing, Inc.
INITIAL YEAR OF OPERATION:	1997
TELEPHONE:	1-800-987-4450
INTERNET:	www.collegesavingsmississippi.com

Who can purchase contracts? Individuals 18 years or older, UTMA/UGMA custodians, and legal entities. The purchaser or beneficiary must be a Mississippi resident at the time of purchase.

Enrollment period: Ended November 30, 2001. The next enrollment period is scheduled for the Fall 2002. Newborns may be enrolled year-round.

Time or age limitations on beneficiary or on use of benefits: The beneficiary must be 18 years old or younger at the time the contract is purchased. Contract benefits must be used within ten years of beneficiary's projected college entrance date.

Contract benefits: Pays full tuition and mandatory fees at Mississippi's public colleges and universities, up to 160 credit hours (10 semesters). The value derived from the contract will depend in part on the selection of institution, because public institutions in Mississippi have different tuition and fee levels. If the beneficiary receives a scholarship, the unused benefits may be refunded, transferred to another qualified beneficiary, or reserved for future tuition hours. If the beneficiary decides to attend a private college in Mississippi or an out-of-state college, the program will pay the lesser of the weighted average tuition and mandatory fees of the Mississippi public colleges in the tuition plan purchased or the actual tuition and mandatory fees of the institution attended. A one-time $25 administration fee is charged for benefit transfers to a private or out-of-state institution.

Contract options: Nine contracts available for one to five years at junior/community colleges or universities.

Costs: There is a one-time $60 application fee. For the enrollment period that ended November 30, 2001, contract prices for a student in the 12th grade range from $1,392 for a one-year junior/community college contract to $16,250 for a five-year university contract. Contract prices are discounted for younger beneficiaries. The cost may be paid in a lump sum, monthly installments over a variety of terms, or a combination of the two.

Cancellation provisions: The contract may be terminated at any time for a refund. The refund will equal the actual payments made, plus interest computed at prevailing rates for bank savings accounts, less a cancellation fee of $25.

Contract changes: Accepts requests to change beneficiary prior to matriculation to a member of the immediate family ($20 fee, plus an additional payment if the new beneficiary is older), transfer contract ownership ($20 fee), and name a successor purchaser, subject to residency requirements. There are no special provisions concerning rollovers/transfers to another 529 plan (cancellation provisions would apply).

State backing: Contracts are backed by the full faith and credit of the state of Mississippi.

Special considerations:

- Qualified distributions from this program are exempt from Mississippi income tax. Any withdrawals from other state 529 plans could subject a Mississippi resident to state tax as Mississippi does not appear to conform to federal tax exemption for qualified withdrawals.
- All payments into MPACT are deductible from Mississippi state income tax without limit.
- Under Mississippi law, any fund surpluses arising from favorable investment performance cannot be allocated to participant accounts.

STATE:	**MISSISSIPPI**
PROGRAM NAME:	Mississippi Affordable College Savings (MACS) Program
529 TYPE:	Savings
STATE AGENCY:	Mississippi Treasury Department
PROGRAM MANAGER:	TIAA-CREF Tuition Financing, Inc.
INITIAL YEAR OF OPERATION:	2001
TELEPHONE:	1-800-486-3670
INTERNET:	www.collegesavingsms.com

Who can open an account? U.S. citizens and resident aliens with a valid Social Security number or federal taxpayer identification number, UTMA/UGMA custodians, and legal entities.

Time or age limitations on beneficiary or on use of account assets: None.

Age-based investment option: The Managed Allocation Option contains 11 portfolios of underlying mutual funds. Contributions are placed into the portfolio corresponding to the age of the beneficiary. Each portfolio shifts to a more conservative investment allocation over time.

Static investment options: There are two supplemental options: a Money Market Option and a 100% Equity Option. The Money Market Option is invested in the TIAA-CREF Institutional Money Market Fund. The 100% Equity Option invests approximately 80% in the TIAA-CREF Institutional Growth and Income Fund and 20% in the TIAA-CREF Institutional International Equity Fund.

Underlying investments: TIAA-CREF institutional mutual funds.

Fees and expenses: 0.70% annualized program management fee charged against the value of the account, and the expenses of the underlying funds ranging from 0.16% to 0.23% (portfolio weighted average). There are no enrollment or annual account maintenance fees.

Broker distribution: None.

Maximum contributions: Accepts contributions until all account balances for the same beneficiary, including amounts deposited in the Mississippi Prepaid Affordable College Tuition (MPACT) Program, reach $235,000.

Minimum initial contribution: $25 ($15 with automatic payroll deduction).

Account changes: Accepts requests to change beneficiary, transfer account ownership, name a successor owner, rollover/transfer assets within the program or to another 529 plan, and change investment option once per calendar year.

Special considerations:
- Contributions of up to $10,000 annually per claimant ($20,000 for joint filers) may be deducted from Mississippi taxable income.
- Qualified withdrawals from this program are exempt from Mississippi state income tax. Any withdrawals from other state 529 plans could subject a Mississippi resident to state tax as Mississippi does not appear to conform to federal tax exemption for qualified withdrawals.

STATE: **MISSOURI**

PROGRAM NAME:	Missouri Saving for Tuition (MO$T) Program
529 TYPE:	Savings
STATE AGENCY:	Missouri Higher Education Savings Program Board, chaired by State Treasurer
PROGRAM MANAGER:	TIAA-CREF Tuition Financing, Inc.
INITIAL YEAR OF OPERATION:	1999
TELEPHONE:	1-888-414-MOST (1-888-414-6678)
INTERNET:	www.missourimost.org

Who can open an account? U.S. citizens or resident aliens with a valid Social Security number or federal taxpayer identification number, UTMA/UGMA custodians, and legal entities.

Time or age limitations on beneficiary or on use of account assets: None.

Age-based investment option: The Managed Allocation Option contains 11 portfolios of underlying mutual funds. Contributions are placed into the portfolio corresponding to the age of the beneficiary. Each portfolio shifts to a more conservative investment allocation over time.

Static investment options: There are two supplemental investment options. The 100% Equity Option is invested 80% in a growth and income fund and 20% in an international equity fund. The Guaranteed Option is invested in an instrument that guarantees principal and a minimum 3% annual rate of interest (actual rate is declared quarterly).

Underlying investments: TIAA-CREF institutional mutual funds and TIAA-CREF Life Guaranteed Funding Agreement.

Fees and expenses: 0.65% annualized program management fee charged against value of account, including expenses of underlying mutual funds. There are no enrollment or annual account maintenance fees.

Broker distribution: None.

Maximum contributions: Accepts contributions until all account balances for the same beneficiary reach $235,000.

Minimum initial contribution: $25 ($15 with payroll deduction).

Account changes: Accepts requests to change beneficiary, transfer account ownership, name a successor owner, rollover/transfer assets within the program or to another 529 plan, and change investment option once per calendar year.

Special considerations:

- Each account owner may deduct up to $8,000 against Missouri taxable income each year for the contributions made to any accounts established under this program. A married couple can deduct up to $16,000 in a year if they both have Missouri income and separate accounts. Non-qualified withdrawals will be subject to recapture of deductions claimed.
- Qualified withdrawals from this program are exempt from Missouri state income tax. Missouri treatment of withdrawals from other 529 plans depends on state conformity to the federal tax law changes.

STATE: MONTANA

PROGRAM NAME:	Montana Family Education Savings Program
529 TYPE:	Savings
STATE AGENCY:	The Montana Board of Regents of Higher Education
PROGRAM MANAGER:	College Savings Bank
INITIAL YEAR OF OPERATION:	1998
TELEPHONE:	1-800-888-2723
INTERNET:	http://montana.collegesavings.com

Who can open an account? U.S. citizens, UTMA/UGMA custodians, state/local governments, and 501(c)(3) organizations.

Time or age limitations on beneficiary or on use of account assets: Since the underlying investment is a certificate of deposit with maturities ranging from one to twenty-five years, CDs are timed to mature in the years the beneficiary attends college and/or graduate school. The CDs are subject to early redemption penalties of as much as 10% of principal. Montana residents are not subject to CD early redemption penalties for non-qualified withdrawals.

Age-based investment options: None.

Static investment options: Funds are invested in CollegeSure® Certificates of Deposit (CDs).

Underlying investments: CollegeSure CDs earn interest at a rate tied to the year-to-year increase in average national college costs. The interest rate adjusts each July 31. The minimum annual interest rate is 4%.

Fees and expenses: None.

Broker distribution: Accounts may be opened through intermediaries who receive a commission. The commission is paid by College Savings Bank and does not affect investment returns.

Maximum contributions: The maximum lifetime contribution limit is $177,000 per beneficiary. The limit is adjusted each year based on seven times the College Board's Independent College 500 Index.

Minimum initial contribution: $250 ($100 with the automatic investment plan and $50 with a payroll deduction plan).

Account changes: Accepts requests to change beneficiary (one change at no cost, then $50), transfer account ownership (but only to beneficiary, or to owner's spouse as part of a divorce proceeding), and name a successor owner. Under current Montana law, a qualifying rollover to another state's 529 plan will be assessed a 10% penalty on earnings and subject to recapture of any Montana tax deductions claimed for contributions that are transferred.

Special considerations:
- Principal and interest are backed by the full faith and credit of the U.S. Government up to $100,000 per depositor.
- The account is established as a revocable trust with spendthrift provisions, providing additional protection from creditors.
- Montana has obtained from the U.S. Department of Education a letter ruling determining that account balances are generally treated as parental assets rather than a "resource" for purposes of determining eligibility for federal student aid.
- Montana taxpayers are allowed a deduction for state income tax purposes for their contributions of up to $3,000 per year ($6,000 for married couples filing jointly). Only the account owner is eligible for the deduction. Upon withdrawal from accounts opened at least three years, deductions are not subject to recapture if used to pay qualified higher education expenses.
- Qualified withdrawals from this program are exempt from Montana income tax. Montana treatment of withdrawals from other 529 plans depends on state conformity to the federal tax law changes.

STATE: **NEBRASKA**

PROGRAM NAME:	College Savings Plan of Nebraska
529 TYPE:	Savings
STATE AGENCIES:	State Treasurer and Nebraska Investment Council
PROGRAM MANAGER:	Union Bank and Trust Company
INITIAL YEAR OF OPERATION:	2001
TELEPHONE:	1-888-993-3746
INTERNET:	www.PlanForCollegeNow.com

Who can open an account? Individuals with a valid Social Security number or taxpayer identification number, UTMA/UGMA custodians, and legal entities.

Time or age limitations on beneficiary or on use of account assets: None.

Age-based investment options: The Age-Based Portfolios offer a choice between four different schedules: Aggressive, Growth, Balanced, and Conservative. Each schedule contains five portfolios of underlying funds. Contributions are initially placed into the portfolio corresponding to the selected schedule and beneficiary's age, and later reassigned to more conservative portfolios as the beneficiary nears the year of enrollment.

Static investment options: The Target Portfolios offer a choice between six portfolios with varying blends of equity funds, fixed income funds, and money market funds, ranging from a target mix of 100% equities to 100% fixed income and money market.

Underlying investments: Mutual funds from Vanguard, American Century, Fidelity, Janus, State Street, T. Rowe Price and PIMCO.

Fees and expenses: $6 quarterly account maintenance fee, 0.60% annualized program management fee charged against value of account, and underlying fund expenses ranging from approximately 0.32% to .44% (portfolio weighted average). There is no enrollment fee.

Broker distribution: Accounts opened through a financial advisor will be subject to one of three alternative expense structures that will determine any initial sales charge, contingent deferred sales charge, and/or additional asset-based fees.

Maximum contributions: Accepts contributions until all Nebraska account balances for the same beneficiary reach $250,000.

Minimum initial contribution: No set minimum.

Account changes: Accepts requests to change beneficiary, transfer account ownership, name a successor owner, rollover/transfer assets within the program or to another 529 plan, and change investment option once per calendar year.

Special considerations:

- Nebraska taxpayers may deduct up to $1,000 of contributions to one or more accounts each year ($500 for married persons filing separate returns). The contributor must be the owner of the account in order to obtain the tax deduction.
- Qualified withdrawals from this program are exempt from Nebraska income tax. Nebraska treatment of withdrawals from other 529 plans depends on state conformity to the federal tax law changes.
- The program intends to build a separate endowment fund that will earmark earnings to participant accounts. Such earnings can be accessed only if the beneficiary attends a Nebraska college or university.
- The value of the account will not be counted in determining eligibility and need for student financial aid programs provided by the state of Nebraska.
- Under Nebraska law, an account is not susceptible to any levy, execution, judgment, or other operation of law, garnishment, or other judicial enforcement, and the amount is not an asset or property of either the participant or the beneficiary for purposes of any state insolvency laws.

STATE:	**NEBRASKA**
PROGRAM NAME:	AIM College Savings Plan
529 TYPE:	Savings
STATE AGENCIES:	State Treasurer and Nebraska Investment Council
PROGRAM MANAGER:	Union Bank and Trust Company
DISTRIBUTION PARTNER:	A I M Management Group (AIM)
INITIAL YEAR OF OPERATION:	2001
TELEPHONE:	1-877-AIM-PLAN (1-877-246-7526)
INTERNET:	www.aimfunds.com

Who can open an account? Individuals with a Social Security number or taxpayer identification number, UTMA/UGMA custodians, state/local governments and 501(c)(3) organizations.

Time or age limitations on beneficiary or on use of account assets: None.

Age-based investment options: The Enrollment-Based Portfolios contain seven portfolios of underlying funds, ranging from aggressive (100% equity) to conservative (25% equity,

40% fixed income, and 35% money market). Contributions are initially placed into the portfolio corresponding to the number of years to enrollment, and later reassigned to more conservative portfolios as the beneficiary nears the year of enrollment. In lieu of automatic reassignment, account owners may elect to reallocate portfolios on their own.

Static investment options: Choose between three portfolios: Aggressive Growth (100% equity), Growth (85% equity and 15% fixed income), and Balanced (60% equity, 30% fixed income and 10% money market).

Underlying investments: AIM mutual funds.

Fees and expenses: $25 annual account maintenance fee (waived for accounts with balances of at least $50,000, or $25,000 if enrolled in an automatic investment plan), and expenses of the underlying mutual funds ranging from approximately 1.06% to 1.67%. In addition, accounts are subject to one of three alternative expense structures that will determine any initial sales charge, contingent deferred sales charge, and/or additional asset-based fees.

Broker distribution: This program is designed for distribution through financial advisors.

Maximum contributions: Accepts contributions until all Nebraska account balances for the same beneficiary reach $250,000.

Minimum initial contribution: $500 per portfolio ($50 with automatic investment plan).

Account changes: Accepts requests to change beneficiary, transfer account ownership, name a successor owner, rollover/ transfer assets within the program or to another 529 plan ($50 fee), and change investment option once per calendar year.

Special considerations:
- Nebraska residents receive the same state income tax and financial aid benefits described above for the College Savings Plan of Nebraska.
- Under Nebraska law, an account is not susceptible to any levy, execution, judgment, or other operation of law, garnishment, or other judicial enforcement, and the amount is not an asset or property of either the participant or the beneficiary for purposes of any state insolvency laws.

STATE:	**NEVADA**
PROGRAM NAME:	Nevada Prepaid Tuition Program
529 TYPE:	Prepaid contract
STATE AGENCIES AND PROGRAM MANAGERS:	Board of Trustees of the College Savings Plans of Nevada and the State Treasurer's Office
INITIAL YEAR OF OPERATION:	1998
TELEPHONE:	1-888-477-2667
INTERNET:	http://nevadatreasurer.com/prepaid

Who can purchase a contract? Individuals 18 years or older who meet Nevada residency requirements (plus alumni of Nevada colleges and universities and certain military personnel), UTMA/UGMA custodians, and legal entities.

Enrollment period: Ended January 15, 2002. Applications will be accepted after the enrollment period for newborns and under certain other conditions.

Time or age limitations on beneficiary or on use of benefits: The beneficiary must not have completed the ninth grade and must be 18 years of age or less at the time of enrollment. The beneficiary has up to ten years from high school graduation or until age 30 to begin using benefits (extensions are granted for military service).

Contract benefits: Pays undergraduate tuition for up to 120 credit hours (8 semesters) at any Nevada state college or university. If the beneficiary decides to attend a private college in Nevada or an out-of-state college, the program will pay an amount equal to the in-state tuition at a Nevada university or community college, less a $25 fee for each academic term. Special refund provisions apply if the beneficiary receives a scholarship.

Contract options: Two-year, four-year, and "2+2" contracts.

Costs: There is a one-time $60 enrollment fee. For the enrollment period that ended January 15, 2002, lump-sum contract prices for a child in the ninth grade ranged from $2,716 for the two-year community college plan to $9,630 for the four-year university plan. Prices are discounted for younger beneficiaries. The cost may be paid in a lump sum, under a 5-year monthly payment plan, or under an extended monthly payment plan to the year of college enrollment. Monthly payments include an additional amount to reflect the cost of making payments over time. Payments can be as low as $21 per month (newborn under the two-year community college contract).

Cancellation provisions: A contract may be canceled at any time and the program will provide a refund of all contract payments (less a cancellation fee of as much as $100), plus interest at a rate determined by the Board. The cancellation fee is waived in the event of the beneficiary's death, disability, or receipt of scholarship.

Contract changes: Accepts requests to change beneficiary (an additional payment may be required if the new beneficiary is more than three years older), transfer contract owner-ship, and name a successor owner, subject to residency requirements. A $20 fee is charged for certain changes. There are no special provisions concerning rollovers/trans-fers to another 529 plan (cancellation provisions would apply).

State backing: Contracts are not backed by the full faith and credit of the state of Nevada.

Special considerations:

- If the program trust fund builds an excess surplus due to favorable investment results, the Board may decide to allocate such excess to participant accounts.
- There are no state income tax incentives because Nevada does not have a personal income tax.
- The program is compatible with the Nevada Millennium Scholarship Program.
- Under Nevada law, the right to benefits or refunds is not subject to attachment, garnishment, or seizure by creditors of the contract purchaser or beneficiary.

STATE:	**NEVADA**
PROGRAM NAME:	America's College Savings Plan
529 TYPE:	Savings
STATE AGENCY:	Board of Trustees of the College Savings Plans of Nevada, chaired by the State Treasurer
PROGRAM MANAGER:	Strong Capital Management, Inc.
INITIAL YEAR OF OPERATION:	2001
TELEPHONE:	1-877-529-5295
INTERNET:	www.americas529plan.com

Who can open an account? U.S. citizens or resident aliens of legal age, UTMA/UGMA cus-todians, and legal entities.

Time or age limitations on beneficiary or on use of account assets: None.

Age-based investment option: The Age-Based Option contains five portfolios of underlying funds, ranging from a 90%/10% blend of stock and fixed income funds to 100% fixed income. Contributions are initially placed into the portfolio corresponding to the years-to-enrollment, and later reassigned to more conservative portfolios as the beneficiary nears the year of enrollment.

Static investment options: The Fixed Allocation Option offers a choice between three portfolios: Aggressive, Balanced, or All-Bond.

Underlying investments: Strong mutual funds.

Fees and expenses: $20 enrollment fee, $25 annual maintenance fee (waived for accounts with balances over $25,000 or enrolled in an automatic investment plan or payroll deduction plan), and 1.30% annualized program fee charged against the value of the account which includes the expenses of the underlying mutual funds. There is a $25 transaction fee for non-qualified withdrawals and rollovers to other State 529 plans. Portfolios may also bear expense of annual independent audit.

Broker distribution: None.

Maximum contributions: Accepts contributions until all Nevada account balances for the same beneficiary (including accounts in the Nevada Prepaid Tuition Program) reach $246,000.

Minimum initial contribution: $250 ($50 for automatic investment plan).

Account changes: Accepts requests to change beneficiary, transfer account ownership, name a successor owner, rollover/transfer assets within the program or to another 529 plan, and change investment option once per calendar year.

Special considerations:

- Under Nevada law, the right to benefits or refunds is not subject to attachment, garnishment, or seizure by creditors of the purchaser or beneficiary.

STATE: **NEVADA**

PROGRAM NAME:	American Skandia College Savings Program
529 TYPE:	Savings
STATE AGENCY:	Board of Trustees of the College Savings Plans of Nevada, chaired by the State Treasurer
PROGRAM MANAGER:	Strong Capital Management, Inc.
DISTRIBUTION PARTNER:	American Skandia
INITIAL YEAR OF OPERATION:	2002
TELEPHONE:	1-800-SKANDIA (1-800-752-6342)
INTERNET:	www.americanskandia.com

Who can open an account? Individuals of legal age with either a valid social security number or taxpayer identification number, UTMA/UGMA custodians, and certain legal entities.

Time or age limitations on beneficiary or on use of account assets: None.

Age-based investment options: The Enrollment-Based Option offers a choice between three different schedules: Aggressive, Moderate, or Conservative. Each schedule contains five portfolios of underlying funds. Contributions are initially placed into the portfolio corresponding to the beneficiary's anticipated year of enrollment, and later reassigned to more conservative portfolios as the beneficiary nears the year of enrollment.

Static investment options: The Static Allocation Option offers a choice between three options: Aggressive (75% equity), Balanced (55% equity), or Conservative (25% equity).

Underlying investments: American Skandia Advisor Funds and Strong Funds.

Fees and expenses: $30 annual maintenance fee (waived for accounts with balances greater than $25,000 or enrolled in automated investment plan or payroll deduction), and expenses of the underlying mutual funds ranging from .94% to 2.20%. In addition, accounts are subject to one of two alternative expense structures that will determine any initial sales charge, contingent deferred sales charge, and/or additional asset-based fees. There is a $25 transaction fee for non-qualified withdrawals and rollovers to other State 529 plans.

Broker distribution: This program is designed for distribution through financial advisors.

Maximum contributions: Accepts contributions until all Nevada account balances for the same beneficiary (including accounts in the Nevada Prepaid Tuition Program) reach $246,000.

Minimum initial contribution: $250 ($50 for automatic investment plan).

Account changes: Accepts requests to change beneficiary, transfer account ownership, name a successor owner, rollover/transfer assets within the program or to another 529 plan, and change investment option once per calendar year.

Special considerations:

- Under Nevada law, the right to benefits or refunds is not subject to attachment, garnishment, or seizure by creditors of the purchaser or beneficiary.

STATE:	**NEW HAMPSHIRE**
PROGRAM NAME:	UNIQUE College Investing Plan
529 TYPE:	Savings
STATE AGENCY:	State Treasurer
PROGRAM MANAGER:	Fidelity Investments
INITIAL YEAR OF OPERATION:	1998
TELEPHONE:	1-800-544-1722
INTERNET:	www.fidelity.com/unique

Who can open an account? U.S. citizens and resident aliens at least 18 years of age, UTMA/UGMA custodians, state/local government agencies, and 501(c)(3) organizations. Other legal entities are not accepted.

Time or age limitations on beneficiary or on use of account assets: None.

Age-based investment option: The Age-Based Strategy contains eight portfolios of underlying mutual funds. Contributions are placed into the portfolio corresponding to the age of the beneficiary or as determined by the account owner. Seven portfolios shift to a more conservative investment allocation over time, eventually transferring to the "College" portfolio.

Static investment options: The Static Portfolios consist of three portfolios: 100% Equity, 70% Equity, and Conservative (100% fixed income and money market).

Underlying investments: Fidelity Investments mutual funds.

Fees and expenses: $30 annual account maintenance fee (waived for accounts with a balance of at least $25,000 or enrolled in the automatic investment plan), 0.30% annualized program management fee charged against value of account, and underlying fund expenses ranging from approximately 0.65% to 0.80% (portfolio weighted average). There is no enrollment fee.

Broker distribution: None (see separate program below).

Maximum contributions: Accepts contributions until all account balances for the same beneficiary reach $233,240.

Minimum initial contribution: $1,000 ($50 for automatic investment plan).

Account changes: Accepts requests to change beneficiary, name a successor owner, rollover/transfer assets within the program or to another 529 plan, and change investment option once per calendar year. Does not accept requests to transfer ownership prior to death or incapacity.

Special considerations:

- Qualified withdrawals from this program are exempt from the New Hampshire interest and dividends tax. New Hampshire does not have a state income tax.

STATE:	**NEW HAMPSHIRE**
PROGRAM NAME:	The Advisor College Investing Plan
529 TYPE:	Savings
STATE AGENCY:	State Treasurer
PROGRAM MANAGER:	Fidelity Investments
INITIAL YEAR OF OPERATION:	2001
TELEPHONE:	1-800-522-7297
INTERNET:	www.advisorxpress.com (for advisors)

Who can open an account? U.S. citizens, resident aliens and trusts.

Time or age limitations on beneficiary or on use of account assets: None.

Age-based investment option: The Age-Based Strategy contains eight portfolios of underlying mutual funds. Contributions are placed into the portfolio corresponding to the age of the beneficiary or as determined by the account owner. Seven portfolios shift to a more conservative investment allocation over time, eventually transferring to the "College" portfolio.

Static investment options: The Static Portfolios consist of two portfolios: 100% Equity and 70% Equity.

Underlying investments: Fidelity Advisor Funds and Fidelity Cash Reserves Fund.

Fees and expenses: $30 annual account maintenance fee (waived for accounts with a balance of at least $25,000 or enrolled in the automatic investment plan), 0.30% annualized program management fee charged against value of account, and underlying fund expenses ranging from approximately 0.48% to 1.24%. In addition, accounts are subject to one of three alternative expense structures that will determine any initial sales charge, contingent deferred sales charge, and/or additional asset-based fees.

Broker distribution: This program is designed for distribution through financial advisors.

Maximum contributions: Accepts contributions until all account balances for the same beneficiary reach $233,240.

Minimum initial contribution: $1,000 ($50 for automatic investment plan).

Account changes: Accepts requests to change beneficiary, name a successor owner, rollover/transfer assets within the program or to another 529 plan, and change investment option once per calendar year. Account ownership during lifetime may be transferred only to the beneficiary, or to the beneficiary's guardian.

Special considerations:
- Qualified withdrawals from this program are exempt from the New Hampshire interest and dividends tax. New Hampshire does not have a state income tax.
- The program accepts contributions only from the person who opens the account.

STATE:	**NEW JERSEY**
PROGRAM NAME:	New Jersey Better Educational Savings Trust (NJBEST)
529 TYPE:	Savings
STATE AGENCIES AND PROGRAM MANAGERS:	Higher Education Student Assistance Authority (HESAA) and the New Jersey Department of the Treasury, Division of Investment
INITIAL YEAR OF OPERATION:	1998
TELEPHONE:	1-877-4NJBEST (1-877-465-2378)
INTERNET:	www.hesaa.org/students/njbest

Who can open an account? Individuals 18 years or older provided that the account owner or beneficiary is a New Jersey resident at time the account is opened.

Time or age limitations on beneficiary or on use of account assets: None.

Age-based investment program: Contributions are placed into one of five investment portfolios corresponding to the age of the beneficiary. Each portfolio shifts to a more conservative investment allocation over time. Equity concentration currently ranges from 60%-80% for the youngest age group to 0%-20% for the oldest age group.

Static investment options: None.

Underlying investments: Pools managed by the Division of Investment at the New Jersey Department of Treasury.

Fees and expenses: $5 account maintenance fee upon enrolling and annually thereafter, and 0.5% annualized program management fee charged on a monthly basis against the program fund (but limited in any month to the amount of interest, dividends, and realized gains or losses in the program fund).

Broker distribution: None.

Maximum contributions: Total combined contributions to the NJBEST account and any other 529 accounts for the same beneficiary cannot exceed $185,000.

Minimum initial contribution: $25 per month, or $300 per year until account balance reaches $1,200.

Account changes: Accepts requests to change beneficiary, and to rollover/transfer assets within the program or to another 529 plan ($75 fee). Does not accept requests to transfer account ownership. Upon owner's death or incapacity, the beneficiary (or if under 18 the guardian or trustee for the beneficiary) will become the account owner, unless a spouse is designated as successor owner.

Special considerations:
- A beneficiary will receive a scholarship from NJBEST if he or she enrolls as an undergraduate in a New Jersey college or university or a degree-granting program at a New Jersey proprietary school licensed or approved by the New Jersey Commission on Higher Education, and meets certain participation requirements. Scholarship amounts range from $500 (minimum $1,200 in contributions and fours year of program participation) to $1,500 (minimum $3,600 in contributions and 12 years of program participation).
- Qualified withdrawals from NJBEST and any other state's 529 plan are exempt from New Jersey income tax.

- The first $25,000 in NJBEST savings will not be counted in determining eligibility and need for student financial aid programs provided by the state of New Jersey.
- The state of New Jersey has placed a "moral obligation" behind NJBEST accounts. If the value of an account at the time of withdrawal does not at least match the amount of contributions, the NJBEST program will request that the state legislature appropriate additional funds for the account.
- Under New Jersey law, NJBEST accounts are exempt from claims of creditors and are excluded from an estate in bankruptcy, with certain exceptions.
- Recent amendments to the law enable the program to seek a private investment manager for all or part of the program, and would permit nonresidents to participate. The creation of a prepaid program has also been authorized, and it would have its own governing board and staff.

STATE: **NEW MEXICO**

PROGRAM NAME:	The Education Plan's Prepaid Tuition Program
529 TYPE:	Prepaid contract
STATE AGENCY:	The Education Trust Board of New Mexico
PROGRAM MANAGER:	Schoolhouse Capital LLC
INITIAL YEAR OF OPERATION:	2000
TELEPHONE:	1-800-499-7581
INTERNET:	www.tepnm.com

Who can purchase a contract? U.S. residents 18 years or older provided that the account owner or beneficiary is a New Mexico resident at the time of purchase, and U.S. legal entities.

Enrollment period: September 1 to December 31 (newborns anytime).

Time or age limitations on beneficiary or on use of benefits: Beneficiary can be any age but must have a target date for use of a contract that is at least five years after the date of application. Contract benefits must be used within 10 years of the anticipated college enrollment date as specified at the time of purchase (with extensions for time in the military).

Contract benefits: Pays undergraduate tuition and mandatory fees for the normal full-time course load for the number of years of education purchased. For attendance at a private college in New Mexico, an out-of-state college, or graduate school, the program will pay the lesser of: 1) the average in-state tuition and mandatory fees for the school category purchased or, 2) the amount of net principal contributions to the account plus a reasonable rate of interest as determined by the program. If the beneficiary receives a scholarship, grant, or tuition waiver, excess contract value may be applied toward other qualified expenses or withdrawn without penalty.

Contract options: Minimum one-year education increments up to 5 years of education. Can be purchased to cover three categories of New Mexico public colleges: Branch and Community Colleges, Comprehensive Universities, and Research Universities.

Costs: There is no enrollment fee. The per-year cost of a branch/community college contract for the year 2001 enrollment was $899, the per-year cost of a comprehensive university contract was $2,496, and the per-year cost of a research university contract was $3,574. The contract price can be paid in a lump sum, installment payments (with an additional amount at a rate determined by the program to reflect the cost of making payments over time), or a combination of lump sum and installment payments. Contracts purchased through financial advisors are subject to a 3.5% sales charge.

Cancellation provisions: Contract can be canceled at any time for a refund equal to contract payments (less a cancellation fee of as much as $150), plus interest at a rate determined by the Board if cancellation occurs after the fifth anniversary of purchase. The cancellation fee is waived if the withdrawal is due to the beneficiary's death, disability, or receipt of scholarship.

Contract changes: Accepts requests to change beneficiary (the original 10-year time limit for use will not change), transfer account ownership, name a successor owner, and rollover/transfer assets within the program or to another 529 plan. The amount available for rollover consists of the principal payments made plus a reasonable amount of interest for contracts that are at least five years old. A rollover to New Mexico's College Savings Program will be credited with interest without regard to the five-year minimum.

State backing: Contracts are not backed by the full faith and credit of the state of New Mexico. The program has an agreement with an affiliate of the program manager that exchanges all investment returns on program assets for an amount equal to the increase in a national tuition index of four-year public undergraduate institutions.

Special considerations:
- Payments made to the program are deductible from New Mexico taxable income. Any non-qualified withdrawals by New Mexico taxpayers in a later year will result in recapture, unless the withdrawal results from the death or disability of the beneficiary.
- Qualified distributions from this program are exempt from New Mexico income tax. New Mexico treatment of withdrawals from other 529 plans depends on state conformity to the federal tax law changes.

- The value of the contract will not be counted in determining eligibility and need for student financial aid programs provided by the state of New Mexico.

STATE:	**NEW MEXICO**
PROGRAM NAME:	The Education Plan's College Savings Program
529 TYPE:	Savings
STATE AGENCY:	The Education Trust Board of New Mexico
PROGRAM MANAGER:	Schoolhouse Capital LLC
INITIAL YEAR OF OPERATION:	2000
TELEPHONE:	1-877-EDPLAN8 (1-877-337-5268)
INTERNET:	www.theeducationplan.com

Who can open an account? U.S. residents 18 years or older, UTMA/UGMA custodians, and legal entities.

Time or age limitations on beneficiary or on use of account assets: For New Mexico resident account owners, there is a one year waiting period from the time the account is established for withdrawals and rollovers.

Age-based investment option: The Age-Based Choice option contains five portfolios of underlying funds, ranging from an 85%/15% blend of stock and fixed income funds to a 20%/80% blend. Contributions are initially placed into the portfolio corresponding to the beneficiary's age, and later reassigned to more conservative portfolios as the beneficiary nears the year of enrollment.

Static investment options: The Custom Choice option offers eight portfolios: the five portfolios under the Age-Based Choice option, a 100% equity portfolio, a 100% fixed income portfolio, and a 100% short-term yield portfolio.

Underlying investments: Mutual funds from State Street Global Advisors, Janus, Invesco, and MFS Investment Management.

Fees and expenses: $30 annual maintenance fee (waived for New Mexico residents, for accounts with a balance of at least $10,000, and for accounts enrolled in an automatic investment plan or payroll deduction), 0.30% annualized program management fee charged against value of account, and underlying fund expenses ranging from approximately 0.41% to 1.24% (portfolio weighted average). There is no enrollment fee.

Broker distribution: Accounts opened through a financial advisor will be subject to a 3.5% initial sales charge and an additional 0.25% asset-based fee.

Maximum contributions: Accepts contributions until account balances in all section 529 plans for the same beneficiary reach $251,000.

Minimum initial contribution: $250 ($25 for automatic investment plan).

Account changes: Accepts requests to change beneficiary, transfer account ownership, name a successor owner, rollover/transfer assets within the program or to another 529 plan, and change investment option once per calendar year.

Special considerations:

- Contributions are deductible from New Mexico taxable income. Deductions are subject to recapture if non-qualified withdrawals are taken in a later year, unless the withdrawal results from the death or disability of the beneficiary.
- Qualified withdrawals from this program are exempt from New Mexico income tax. New Mexico treatment of withdrawals from other 529 plans depends on state conformity to the federal tax law changes.
- The value of the account will not be counted in determining eligibility and need for student financial aid programs provided by the state of New Mexico.

STATE:	**NEW MEXICO**
PROGRAM NAME:	CollegeSense
529 TYPE:	Savings
STATE AGENCY:	The Education Trust Board of New Mexico
PROGRAM MANAGER:	Schoolhouse Capital LLC
DISTRIBUTION PARTNER:	New York Life Investment Management
INITIAL YEAR OF OPERATION:	2001
TELEPHONE:	1-866-529-SENSE (1-866-529-7367)
INTERNET:	www.collegesense.com

Who can open an account? U.S. residents 18 years or older, UTMA/UGMA custodians, and legal entities.

Time or age limitations on beneficiary or on use of account assets: For New Mexico resident account owners, there is a one year waiting period from the time the account is established for withdrawals and rollovers.

Age-based investment option: The Age-Based Choice option contains five portfolios of underlying funds, ranging from an 85%/15% blend of stock and fixed income funds to a 25%/75% blend. Contributions are initially placed into the portfolio corresponding to the beneficiary's age, and later reassigned to more conservative portfolios as the beneficiary nears the year of enrollment.

Static investment options: The Custom Choice option offers eight portfolios: the five portfolios under the Age-Based Choice option, a 100% equity portfolio, a 100% fixed income portfolio, and a 100% short-term yield portfolio.

Underlying investments: Mutual funds from New York Life Investment Management LLC, State Street Global Advisors, and JPMorgan Fleming Asset Management.

Fees and expenses: $25 annual account maintenance fee (waived for New Mexico residents, accounts with balances of $25,000 or more, and accounts enrolled in an automatic investment plan), and the expenses of the underlying mutual funds. In addition, accounts are subject to one of two alternative expense structures that will determine any initial sales charge, contingent deferred sales charge, and/or additional asset-based fees.

Broker distribution: This program is designed for distribution through financial advisors.

Maximum contributions: Contributions accepted until account balances in all section 529 plans for the same beneficiary reach $251,000.

Minimum initial contribution: $250 ($25 for automatic investment plan).

Account changes: Accepts requests to change beneficiary, transfer account ownership, name a successor owner, rollover/transfer assets within the program or to another 529 plan, and change investment option once per calendar year.

Special considerations:
- New Mexico residents receive the same state income tax and financial aid benefits described above for The Education Plans of New Mexico.

STATE: **NEW MEXICO**

PROGRAM NAME: Scholar'sEdge

529 TYPE: Savings

STATE AGENCY: Education Trust Board of New Mexico

PROGRAM MANAGER: Schoolhouse Capital LLC

DISTRIBUTION PARTNER: OppenheimerFunds

INITIAL YEAR OF OPERATION: 2001

TELEPHONE: 1-866-529-SAVE (1-866-529-7283)

INTERNET: www.scholarsedge529.com

Who can open an account? U.S. residents 18 years or older, UTMA/UGMA custodians, and legal entities.

Time or age limitations on beneficiary or on use of account assets: For New Mexico resident account owners, there is a one year waiting period from the time the account is established for withdrawals and rollovers.

Age-based investment option: The Age-Based Choice option contains five portfolios of underlying funds, ranging from an 85%/15% blend of stock and fixed income funds to a 25%/75% blend. Contributions are initially placed into the portfolio corresponding to the beneficiary's age, and later reassigned to more conservative portfolios as the beneficiary nears the year of enrollment.

Static investment options: The Custom Choice option offers eight portfolios: the five portfolios under the Age-Based Choice option, a 100% equity portfolio, a 100% fixed income portfolio, and a 100% short-term yield portfolio.

Underlying investments: Mutual funds from OppenheimerFunds and State Street Global Advisors.

Fees and expenses: $25 annual account maintenance fee (waived for New Mexico residents, accounts with balances of $25,000 or more, and accounts enrolled in an automatic investment plan), and the expenses of the underlying mutual funds. In addition, accounts are subject to one of two alternative expense structures that will determine any initial sales charge, contingent deferred sales charge, and/or additional asset-based fees.

Broker distribution: This program is designed for distribution through financial advisors.

Maximum contributions: Contributions accepted until account balances in all section 529 plans for the same beneficiary reach $251,000.

Minimum initial contribution: $250 ($25 for automatic investment plan).

Account changes: Accepts requests to change beneficiary, transfer account ownership, rollover/transfer assets within the program or to another 529 plan, and change investment option once per calendar year. The program does not accept a designation of successor owner. Transfer of ownership upon the owner's death is controlled by state law.

Special considerations:

- New Mexico residents receive the same state income tax and financial aid benefits described above for The Education Plans of New Mexico.

STATE:	**NEW YORK**
PROGRAM NAME:	New York's College Savings Program
529 TYPE:	Savings
STATE AGENCIES:	Office of the State Comptroller and NYS Higher Education Services Corporation
PROGRAM MANAGER:	TIAA, part of TIAA-CREF
INITIAL YEAR OF OPERATION:	1998
TELEPHONE:	1-877-NYSAVES (1-877-697-2837)
INTERNET:	www.nysaves.org

Who can open an account? Individuals who are U.S residents, including minors (with signature of parent or guardian). UTMA/UGMA custodians and legal entities may not open accounts.

Time or age limitations on beneficiary or on use of account assets: Withdrawals taken within 36 months of establishing the account will be subject to a program-imposed penalty of 10% on earnings.

Age-based investment options: The program offers a choice between two schedules: the Managed Allocation Option and the Aggressive Managed Allocation Option. Contributions are placed into one of 13 investment pools corresponding to the selected schedule and the beneficiary's age. Each pool shifts to a more conservative investment allocation over time.

Static investment options: There are two supplemental investment options: the High Equity Option and the Guaranteed Option. The High Equity option is invested 75%—100% in an equity index fund with any remainder in a bond and/or money market fund. The Guaranteed Option is invested in an instrument that guarantees principal and a minimum 3% annual rate of interest (actual rate is declared quarterly).

Underlying investments: New York College Savings Growth, Bond and Money Market Funds managed by TIAA-CREF. High Equity Option uses the TIAA-CREF Equity Index Institutional mutual fund and the Guaranteed Option uses the TIAA-CREF Life Insurance Company Funding Agreement.

Fees and expenses: 0.65% annualized program management fee charged against value of account, including expenses of underlying institutional mutual funds. There are no enrollment or annual account maintenance fees.

Broker distribution: None.

Maximum contributions: Accepts contributions up to $100,000 per beneficiary or until all account balances for the same beneficiary reach $235,000.

Minimum initial contribution: $25 ($15 for payroll deduction plan).

Account changes: Accepts requests to change beneficiary, transfer account ownership, name a successor owner, rollover/transfer assets within the program or to another 529 plan, and change investment option once per calendar year.

Special considerations:

- Up to $5,000 ($10,000 for married couples filing joint returns) of total annual contributions may be deducted from New York taxable income each year per beneficiary.
- Qualified withdrawals from this program are exempt from New York income tax. New York treatment of withdrawals from other 529 plans depends on state conformity to the federal tax law changes.
- Any withdrawals within 36 months of initial contribution, and any non-qualified withdrawals after 36 months, are currently subject to a 10% program penalty on earnings. (A federal 10% earnings penalty is also imposed on non-qualified withdrawals.)
- The assets in the account will not be counted in determining eligibility for student financial aid provided by the state of New York.
- Under New York law, up to $10,000 of the aggregate account value is exempt from an application to satisfy a money judgment against the account owner. The entire account is exempt if owned by the minor beneficiary.

STATE: # NORTH CAROLINA

PROGRAM NAME: North Carolina's National College Savings Program

529 TYPE: Savings

STATE AGENCY: North Carolina State Education Assistance Authority

PROGRAM MANAGER: College Foundation, Inc.

INITIAL YEAR OF OPERATION: 1998 (substantially revised in 2001)

TELEPHONE: 1-800-600-3453

INTERNET: www.cfnc.org/savings

Who can open an account? Individuals who have reached the age of majority and emancipated minors, UTMA/UGMA custodians, state/local government agencies, and 501(c)(3) organizations. For non-broker accounts, the account owner or beneficiary must be a North Carolina resident or have a principal place of business or employment in North Carolina.

Time or age limitations on beneficiary or on use of account assets: None.

Age-based investment option: The College*Horizon*Funds option contains 22 portfolios of underlying funds. Contributions are initially placed into the portfolio corresponding to the number of years until anticipated withdrawal, and later reassigned to more conservative portfolios as the beneficiary nears the year of withdrawal.

Static investment options: There are three options that may be selected: the Aggressive Stock Fund (100% stocks), the Balanced Fund (targets 40% stocks and 60% fixed income), and the Dependable Income Fund (money market instruments and U.S. Government securities).

Underlying investments: The College*Horizon*Funds option is invested in mutual funds from J. & W. Seligman & Co. The Aggressive Stock Fund is invested 50% in a separate account in NCM Capital's Focused Equity Discipline and 50% in the Legg Mason Value Trust. The Balanced Fund is invested in mutual funds from Wachovia Bank's Evergreen Funds and a separately-managed portfolio of Treasury Inflation Protection Securities (TIPS). The Dependable Income Fund invests in the North Carolina State Treasurer's Short-Term Investment Portfolio.

Fees and expenses: $25 annual account maintenance fee (waived for accounts with a balance of at least $1,000 and for accounts enrolled in an automatic investment plan), annualized program management fee of up to 0.10% for assets invested in the College-*Horizon*Funds and up to .25% for assets in the other options, and the expenses of the underlying investments and mutual funds. These expenses (based on portfolio weighted average) are approximately 0.58% to 1.16% in the College*Horizon*Funds, 0.65% in the

Aggressive Stock Fund, 0.58% in the Balanced Fund, and 0.05% in the Dependable Income Fund. There is no enrollment fee.

Broker distribution: See separate description for Seligman College*Horizon*Funds distributed through financial advisors. The other portfolio options are scheduled to become available nationally through brokers in 2002.

Maximum contributions: Accepts contributions until all account balances for the same beneficiary reach $268,804.

Minimum initial contribution: $5.

Account changes: Accepts requests to change beneficiary, transfer account ownership, name a successor owner, rollover/transfer assets within the program or to another 529 plan ($50 fee), and change investment option once per calendar year.

Special considerations:

- Qualified withdrawals from this program are exempt from North Carolina income tax. North Carolina treatment of withdrawals from other 529 plans depends on the state passing conformity legislation for the federal tax law changes.
- The program description warns nonresidents of North Carolina that accounts may have sufficient tax situs so as to be subject to North Carolina estate tax.

STATE:	**NORTH CAROLINA**
PROGRAM NAME:	Seligman College*Horizon*Funds
529 TYPE:	Savings
STATE AGENCY:	North Carolina State Education Assistance Authority
PROGRAM MANAGER:	College Foundation Inc.
DISTRIBUTOR PARTNER:	J. & W. Seligman & Co.
INITIAL YEAR OF OPERATION:	2001
TELEPHONE:	1-800-600-3453
INTERNET:	www.seligman529.com

Who can open an account? Individuals who have reached the age of majority and emancipated minors, UTMA/UGMA custodians, state/local government agencies, and 501(c)(3) organizations.

Time or age limitations on beneficiary or on use of account assets: None.

Age-based investment option: Contains 22 portfolios of underlying funds. Contributions are initially placed into the portfolio corresponding to the number of years until anticipated withdrawal, and later reassigned to more conservative portfolios as the beneficiary nears the year of withdrawal.

Static investment options: Any of the portfolios available in the age-based option may be acquired and held as a static investment.

Underlying investments: Mutual funds from J. & W. Seligman & Co.

Fees and expenses: $25 annual account maintenance fee (waived for accounts with a balance of at least $25,000), an additional $25 annual account fee for accounts with a balance under $1,000 unless enrolled in an automatic investment plan, 0.25% annualized program management fee, and the expenses of the underlying mutual funds ranging from approximately 0.58% to 1.16% (portfolio weighted average). In addition, accounts are subject to one of three alternative expense structures that will determine any initial sales charge, contingent deferred sales charge, and/or additional asset-based fees.

Broker distribution: This program is designed for distribution through financial advisors.

Maximum contributions: Accepts contributions until all account balances for the same beneficiary reach $268,804.

Minimum initial contribution: $250 ($100 for automatic investment plan, $25 for payroll deduction plan).

Account changes: Accepts requests to change beneficiary, transfer account ownership, name a successor owner, rollover/transfer assets within the program or to another 529 plan ($50 fee), and change investment option once per calendar year.

Special considerations:
- Qualified withdrawals from this program are exempt from North Carolina income tax. North Carolina treatment of withdrawals from other 529 plans depends on the state passing conformity legislation for the federal tax law changes.
- The program description warns nonresidents of North Carolina that accounts may have sufficient tax situs so as to be subject to North Carolina estate tax.

STATE: **NORTH DAKOTA**

PROGRAM NAME:	College SAVE
529 TYPE:	Savings
STATE AGENCY:	Bank of North Dakota
PROGRAM MANAGER:	Morgan Stanley
INITIAL YEAR OF OPERATION:	2001
TELEPHONE:	1-866-SAVE529 (1-866-728-3529)
INTERNET:	www.collegesave4u.com

Who can open an account? U.S. citizens and resident aliens 18 years or older, UTMA/UGMA custodians, trusts, state/local government agencies, and 501(c)(3) organizations.

Time or age limitations on beneficiary or on use of account assets: None.

Age-based investment options: The Age-Based Portfolios offer a choice between three different schedules—Aggressive, Moderate, and Conservative—and within each schedule there is a choice of portfolios using index equity mutual funds and portfolios using actively managed equity mutual funds. Each schedule contains 5 portfolios of underlying funds. Contributions are initially placed into the portfolio corresponding to the selected schedule, management style, and the number of years to anticipated withdrawal, and later reassigned to more conservative portfolios as the beneficiary nears the year of withdrawal.

Static investment options: The Fixed Portfolios offer a choice between four portfolios: an aggressive portfolio that includes an actively managed equity fund, an aggressive portfolio that includes an index equity fund, a balanced portfolio that includes an actively managed equity fund, and a balanced portfolio that includes an index equity fund. The aggressive portfolios currently target 90% in stock funds and 10% in bond funds. The balanced portfolios currently target 50% in stock funds and 50% in bond and money market funds.

Underlying investments: Mutual funds from Morgan Stanley and Van Kampen.

Fees and expenses: $30 account maintenance fee charged at time account is established and each year thereafter (waived for North Dakota and South Dakota residents), 0.5% annualized program management fee charged against value of account (also waived for North Dakota and South Dakota residents), and expenses of the underlying funds ranging from approximately 0.68% to 1.22% (portfolio weighted average). There is no separate asset-based program management fee.

Broker distribution: There are no additional expenses for accounts opened through a Morgan Stanley advisor or other sales agents.

Maximum contributions: Accepts contributions until account balances in all 529 plans for the same beneficiary reach $177,000.

Minimum initial contribution: $25 ($300 must be contributed within 12 months of opening the account).

Account changes: Accepts requests to change beneficiary, transfer account ownership, name a successor owner, rollover/transfer to within the program or another 529 plan, and change investment option once per calendar year.

Special considerations:

- North Dakota does not provide specific state tax incentives for residents in this program, but its tax law generally conforms to federal tax law and so qualified withdrawals that are exempt from federal income tax will be exempt from North Dakota income tax as well.
- Under North Dakota law, interests of the account owner and beneficiary in an account are not subject to attachment or alienation by third-party creditors.

STATE:	**OHIO**
PROGRAM NAME:	CollegeAdvantage Savings Plan
529 TYPE:	Savings program with a guaranteed savings option
STATE AGENCY:	Ohio Tuition Trust Authority
PROGRAM MANAGER:	Putnam Investments for the "Variable Investment Options"
INITIAL YEAR OF OPERATION:	1989 (substantially revised in 2000)
TELEPHONE:	1-800-AFFORD-IT (1-800-233-6734)
INTERNET:	www.collegeadvantage.com

Who can open an account? U.S. citizens and resident aliens, UTMA/UGMA custodians, and trusts. Either the account owner or the beneficiary must be a resident of Ohio at the time the account is opened. Special rules determine if military personnel, Ohio-based employees, migrant workers, and nonresident children of divorced Ohio residents qualify for participation.

Time or age limitations on beneficiary or on use of benefits: For the Guaranteed Savings option only, withdrawals may not be taken until account owner certifies that beneficiary has reached age 18 or has graduated from high school. Rollovers are permitted prior to age 18.

Guaranteed Savings Option: Each unit in the account is worth 1% of the weighted average tuition of Ohio's 13 four-year public universities if held on account unitil beneficiary is age 18. As of January 2002, this figure is $53.30 per unit. A deposit of "any amount, any time" (subject to a $15 minimum) acquires tuition units at $59.50 per unit. Signing up for monthly deposits through automatic transfer from a bank account or payroll deduction will reduce the per-unit price to $58.50. Larger deposits (at least five units) can bring the per-unit price down to as low as $53.30, depending on the age of the beneficiary. Tuition unit prices are based on actual tuition at Ohio's four-year public universities, past and projected annual returns on investments, program growth, and other key actuarial factors. Tuition units can be used at any accredited college in the country to pay for tuition, fees, room and board, books, and other qualified college expenses. Tuition units are worth the same redemption rate per unit no matter where they are used to pay for college expenses.

Age-based investment option: The Age-Based Fund contains seven core portfolios of mutual funds, ranging from an 85%/15% mix of equity and fixed income to a 15%/85% mix. Contributions are initially placed into a blend of two core portfolios corresponding to the beneficiary's age. A reallocation of each account is made on January 1 every year to a more conservative blend of portfolios.

Static investment options: Choose between three portfolios—the Balanced Fund (targeted 60% equity), the Growth Fund (targeted 85% equity), and the Aggressive Growth Fund (targeted 100% equity) and ten individual asset class options.

Underlying investments: Mutual funds from Putnam Investments.

Fees and expenses: No initial or ongoing expenses for the Guaranteed Savings Option. For the Variable Investment Options (fee structure O) there is a 0.99% annualized program management fee charged against the value of the account. There is no enrollment fee.

Broker distribution: Ohio accounts opened through a financial advisor are subject to a different expense structure. These expenses consist of a $25 annual account maintenance fee (waived for accounts with a balance of at least $25,000 and for accounts enrolled in an automatic investment plan), a 0.20% maximum (currently 0.15%) annualized OTTA fee charged against the value of the account, and the expenses of the underlying mutual funds ranging from approximately 0.49% to 1.23% (portfolio weighted average). In addition, accounts are subject to one of three alternative expense structures that will determine any initial sales charge, contingent deferred sales charge, and/or additional asset-based fees.

Maximum contributions: Accepts contributions until all account balances for the same beneficiary reach $232,000.

Minimum initial contribution: $15 per investment option ($15 for automatic investment plan).

Account changes: Accepts requests to change beneficiary, transfer account ownership, name a successor owner, rollover/transfer assets within the program or to another 529 plan, and change investment option once per calendar year. Rollover withdrawals from a Guaranteed Savings account for a beneficiary under age 18 may be reduced in value if the Guaranteed Fund investment performance lags average tuition increases.

Special considerations:
- Ohio taxpayers may deduct annual contributions up to $2,000 per beneficiary against Ohio income, with unlimited carryforward of any excess contributions. Deductions are subject to recapture if non-qualified withdrawals are taken in later years (except for withdrawals made on account of the beneficiary's death, disability, or receipt of a scholarship).
- Qualified withdrawals from this program and withdrawals due to the beneficiary's death, disability, or receipt of a scholarship are exempt from Ohio income tax. Ohio treatment of withdrawals from other 529 plans depends on state conformity to the federal tax law changes.
- The Guaranteed Savings fund is backed by the full faith and credit of the state of Ohio.
- Under Ohio law, a tuition account or any legal interest therein shall not be subject to attachment, levy, or execution by any creditor of an account owner or beneficiary.

STATE:	**OHIO**
PROGRAM NAME:	Putnam CollegeAdvantage Savings Plan
529 TYPE:	Savings
STATE AGENCY:	Ohio Tuition Trust Authority
PROGRAM MANAGER:	Putnam Investments
INITIAL YEAR OF OPERATION:	2000
TELEPHONE:	1-800-225-1581
INTERNET:	www.putnaminvestments.com

Who can open an account? U.S. citizens and resident aliens, UTMA/UGMA custodians, trusts, and 502(c)(3) organizations.

Time or age limitations on beneficiary or on use of benefits: None.

Age-based investment option: The Age-Based Fund contains seven core portfolios of mutual funds, ranging from an 85%/15% mix of equity and fixed income to a 15%/85% mix. Contributions are initially placed into a blend of two core portfolios corresponding to the beneficiary's age. A reallocation of each account is made on January 1 every year to a more conservative blend of portfolios.

Static investment options: There are thirteen options to select from: three blended portfolios—the Balanced Portfolio (targeted 60% equity), the Growth Portfolio (targeted 85% equity), and the Aggressive Growth Portfolio (targeted 100% equity) —and ten individual asset class options.

Underlying investments: Mutual funds from Putnam Investments.

Fees and expenses: $25 annual account maintenance fee (waived for accounts with balances of at least $25,000 balance and for accounts enrolled in an automatic investment program of at least $50 per month), 0.20% maximum (currently 0.15%) annualized OTTA fee charged against the value of the account, and the expenses of the underlying mutual funds ranging from approximately 0.49% to 1.23% (portfolio weighted average). In addition, accounts are subject to one of three alternative expense structures that will determine any initial sales charge, contingent deferred sales charge, and/or additional asset-based fees.

Broker distribution: This program is designed for distribution through financial advisors.

Maximum contributions: Accepts contributions until all account balances for the same beneficiary reach $232,000.

Minimum initial contribution: $25 per account ($15 for automatic investment plan).

Account changes: Accepts requests to change beneficiary, transfer account ownership, name a successor owner, rollover/transfer assets within the program or to another 529 plan, and change investment option once per calendar year.

Special considerations:
- Ohio residents receive the same state income tax benefits described above for the Ohio CollegeAdvantage Savings Program.
- Under Ohio law, a tuition account or any legal interest therein shall not be subject to attachment, levy, or execution by any creditor of an account owner or beneficiary.

STATE: **OKLAHOMA**

PROGRAM NAME: Oklahoma College Savings Plan

529 TYPE: Savings

STATE AGENCY: Board of Trustees, chaired by State Treasurer

PROGRAM MANAGER: TIAA-CREF Tuition Financing, Inc.

INITIAL YEAR OF OPERATION: 2000

TELEPHONE: 1-877-OK4-SAVING (1-877-654-7284)

INTERNET: www.ok4saving.org

Who can open an account? U.S. citizens or resident aliens 18 years or older, state/local government agencies, and 501(c)(3) organizations.

Time or age limitations on beneficiary or on use of account assets: None.

Age-based investment option: The Managed Allocation Option contains 11 portfolios of underlying mutual funds. Contributions are placed into the portfolio corresponding to the age of the beneficiary. Each portfolio shifts to a more conservative investment allocation over time.

Static investment options: There are two supplemental investment options: the 100% Equity option and the Guaranteed option. The 100% Equity option is invested in a blend of three equity mutual funds—an equity index fund, a growth and income fund, and an international fund. The Guaranteed option is invested in an instrument that guarantees principal and a minimum 3% annual rate of interest (actual rate is declared quarterly).

Underlying investments: TIAA-CREF institutional mutual funds and TIAA-CREF Life Guaranteed Funding Agreement.

Fees and expenses: 0.60% annualized program management fee charged against the value of the account, and the expenses of the underlying funds ranging from 0.18% to 0.22% (portfolio weighted average). There are no enrollment or annual account maintenance fees.

Broker distribution: None.

Maximum contributions: Accepts contributions until all account balances for the same beneficiary reach $235,000.

Minimum initial contribution: $25 ($15 payroll deduction plan).

Account changes: Accepts requests to change beneficiary, transfer account ownership, name a successor owner, rollover/transfer assets within the program or to another 529 plan, and change investment option once per calendar year.

Special considerations:

- Up to $2,500 in contributions per beneficiary are deductible from Oklahoma adjusted gross income each year.
- Oklahoma's tax law generally conforms to federal tax law and so qualified withdrawals that are exempt from federal income tax should be exempt from Oklahoma income tax as well.

STATE: **OREGON**

PROGRAM NAME:	Oregon College Savings Plan
529 TYPE:	Savings
STATE AGENCY:	Oregon Qualified Tuition Savings Board, chaired by State Treasurer
PROGRAM MANAGER:	Strong Capital Management, Inc.
INITIAL YEAR OF OPERATION:	2001
TELEPHONE:	1-86-OR-SAVINGS (1-866-772-8464)
INTERNET:	www.oregoncollegesavings.com

Who can open an account? U.S. citizens or resident aliens of legal age, UTMA/UGMA custodians, and legal entities.

Time or age limitations on beneficiary or on use of account assets: None.

Age-based investment option: The Years-to-College option contains five portfolios of underlying funds, ranging from 90% equity to 90% fixed income and money market funds. Contributions are initially placed into the portfolio corresponding to the year of anticipated withdrawal, and later reassigned to more conservative portfolios, as the beneficiary gets closer to the year of withdrawal.

Static investment options: The Lifestyle Option offers a choice between five portfolios: the Aggressive, Moderate, Balanced, Conservative, or In College portfolios.

Underlying investments: Strong Funds.

Fees and expenses: 0.325% annualized program management fee charged against the account value of the account, and the expenses of the underlying mutual funds ranging from approximately 0.77% to 1.32% (portfolio weighted average). There are no enrollment or annual account maintenance fees.

Broker distribution: Accounts opened through a financial advisor or third-party distributor will be invested in Advisor-class shares, subject to a 0.65% additional annual asset-based fee.

Maximum contributions: Accepts contributions until all account balances for the same beneficiary reach $250,000.

Minimum initial contribution: $250 ($25 for automatic investment plan).

Account changes: Accepts requests to change beneficiary, transfer account ownership, name a successor owner, rollover/transfer assets within the program or to another 529 plan, and change investment option once per calendar year.

Special considerations:
- Up to $2,000 in contributions to one or more accounts may be deducted each year from Oregon taxable income. The limit is reduced to $1,000 for married taxpayers filing separately.
- Qualified withdrawals from this program are exempt from Oregon income tax. Oregon treatment of withdrawals from other 529 plans depends on state conformity to the federal tax law changes.

STATE: **PENNSYLVANIA**

PROGRAM NAME:	Tuition Account Guaranteed Savings Program (TAP)
529 TYPE:	Guaranteed savings
STATE AGENCY AND PROGRAM MANAGER:	Pennsylvania State Treasury
INITIAL YEAR OF OPERATION:	1993
TELEPHONE:	1-800-440-4000
INTERNET:	www.patap.org

Who can open an account? Individuals 18 years or older provided that the owner or beneficiary is a Pennsylvania resident at the time the account is opened, UTMA/UGMA custodians, and legal entities.

Enrollment period: Open.

Time or age limitations on beneficiary or on use of benefits: Contributions must be held in the account for approximately 12 months before being redeemed for qualified expenses.

Guaranteed Savings: Each TAP credit in the account is pegged to one of five average tuition levels, or specific tuition levels for 34 publicly-funded schools. TAP credits can be used at almost all accredited colleges and universities in the country and for many career school programs. TAP credits can also be used for qualified higher education expenses including tuition, fees, room and board, books, and equipment. The five average tuition levels correspond to the approximate average tuition charges for that year at 1) Pennsylvania community colleges, 2) public universities, 3) state-related universities (Penn State, Pitt, Temple, and Lincoln), 4) Ivy League schools, and 5) private four-year colleges. The tuition level used for this purpose is selected by the participant when enrolling. If the account is used for attendance at one of the Pennsylvania publicly funded schools, the tuition level will be automatically changed to the tuition level at that specific school, recalculating the account based on that school's specific tuition increases. For attendance at any other school, a change in the tuition level can be made by the participant retroactive to the first contribution made.

Costs: One-time $50 enrollment fee (reduced to $25 if account is opened within three weeks of materials being sent). Within each tuition level a rate for one TAP credit is established each academic year. The TAP credit rate is currently set at 1/24th of the average tuition of included schools or, in the case of specific school tuition levels, the actual full year tuition.

Maximum contributions: Accepts contributions until all account balances for the same beneficiary reach $260,000.

Minimum initial contribution: $5.

Account changes: Accepts requests to change beneficiary, transfer account ownership, and name a successor owner, subject to residency requirements. A $10 fee may be charged for certain changes. There are no special provisions concerning rollovers/transfers to another 529 plan (Pennsylvania taxpayers may be taxable on earnings).

State backing: TAP credits are not backed by the full faith and credit of the Commonwealth of Pennsylvania. The program trust fund maintains a surplus to protect against shortfalls.

Special considerations:
- Each year the Guaranteed Savings Program fund will be evaluated to determine if the investment performance of the fund has created an excess surplus (above the amount needed to cover future withdrawals as determined by actuarial calculations). The Treasury Department can decide to allocate a portion of the surplus to accounts in the program.

- Qualified withdrawals from this program are exempt from Pennsylvania income tax. Any withdrawals from other state 529 plans could subject a Pennsylvania resident to state tax, as Pennsylvania does not conform to federal tax exemption for qualified withdrawals.
- Accounts are not subject to Pennsylvania inheritance tax. Accounts owned by a Pennsylvania resident in another state's 529 plan could be subject to Pennsylvania inheritance tax.
- The value of the account will not be counted in determining eligibility and need for student financial aid programs provided by the Commonwealth of Pennsylvania.
- Under Pennsylvania law, an account or any legal interest therein shall not be subject to attachment, levy, or execution by any creditor of an account owner or beneficiary.
- Savings in TAP are eligible for earning "Tuition Rewards"—guaranteed tuition discounts at over 140 colleges participating in the privately-run SAGE program.
- A new 529 savings program will be added in 2002. Delaware Investments has been selected as program manager.

STATE:	**RHODE ISLAND**
PROGRAM NAME:	CollegeBoundfund
529 TYPE:	Savings
STATE AGENCIES:	Rhode Island Higher Education Assistance Authority and the State Investment Commission
PROGRAM MANAGER:	Alliance Capital
INITIAL YEAR OF OPERATION:	1998 (substantially revised in October 2000)
TELEPHONE:	1-888-324-5057
INTERNET:	www.collegeboundfund.com

Who can open an account? U.S. citizens and resident aliens, UTMA/UGMA custodians. However, only Rhode Island residents or employees may open accounts without the additional broker-sold account expenses.

Time or age limitations on beneficiary or on use of account assets: None.

Age-based investment options: The Age-Based Portfolios offer a choice between two schedules: Aggressive Growth Emphasis and Growth Emphasis. Each schedule contains seven portfolios of underlying funds, ranging from 100% equity to 24% equity. Contributions are initially placed into the portfolio corresponding to the selected schedule and beneficiary's age, and later reassigned to more conservative portfolios as the beneficiary nears the year of enrollment.

Static investment options: The Additional Portfolios offer a choice between three portfolios: Aggressive Growth, Growth, and Balanced. The Customized Allocation Portfolio offers a choice between nine mutual funds. The Principal-Protection Income Portfolio provides a stable value income option.

Underlying investments: Mutual funds from Alliance Capital and AllianceBernstein.

Fees and expenses: $25 annual maintenance fee (waived for Rhode Island residents, accounts with a balance of at least $25,000, and accounts enrolled in the automatic investment plan or payroll deduction plan). Total program management and fund expenses are currently 0.90%, 1.00%, or 1.10% depending on portfolio. There is no enrollment fee.

Broker distribution: Accounts opened through a financial advisor, including all non-Rhode Island accounts, will be subject to one of three alternative expense structures that will determine any sales load, contingent deferred sales charge, and/or additional asset-based fees.

Maximum contributions: Accepts contributions until all account balances for the same beneficiary reach $265,620.

Minimum initial contribution: $250 for Rhode Island accounts (no minimum with automatic investment plan) and $1,000 for broker-sold accounts ($50 minimum with automatic investment plan).

Account changes: Accepts requests to change beneficiary, transfer account ownership, name a successor owner, rollover/transfer assets within the program or to another 529 plan ($50 fee), and change investment option once per calendar year.

Special considerations:
- Qualified withdrawals from this program are exempt from Rhode Island income tax. Rhode Island treatment of withdrawals from other 529 plans depends on state conformity to the federal tax law changes.
- Under Rhode Island law, an account balance, right or interest of a person in the program is exempt from attachment, with limited exceptions.

STATE: **SOUTH CAROLINA**

PROGRAM NAME: South Carolina Tuition Prepayment Program (SCTPP)

529 TYPE: Prepaid contract

STATE AGENCY AND PROGRAM MANAGER: State Treasurer

INITIAL YEAR OF OPERATION: 1998

TELEPHONE: 1-888-7SC-GRAD (1-888-772-4723)

INTERNET: www.scgrad.org

Who can purchase a contract? U.S. citizens and resident aliens, UTMA/UGMA custodians, and legal entities. However, the beneficiary must be a South Carolina resident for at least 12 months prior to enrollment.

Enrollment period: Ends January 31, 2002. The next enrollment period is expected to begin in October 2002. Enrollment will be accepted at any time (except during month of September) for a newborn beneficiary.

Time or age limitations on beneficiary or on use of benefits: The beneficiary must be in the 10th grade or below at the time of enrollment. Contract benefits must be used by the time the beneficiary is 30 years old (may be extended for up to four years for military service). If the contract is canceled because benefits have not been used by age 30, the value of unused benefits is refunded minus a $100 cancellation fee.

Contract benefits: The contract pays in-state undergraduate tuition and mandatory fees at a South Carolina public institution according to the plan and number of years selected. The value derived from the contract will depend in part on the selection of institution, because public institutions in South Carolina have different tuition and fee levels. If the beneficiary decides to attend a private college in South Carolina or an out-of-state college, SCTPP will pay tuition and fees up to the weighted average tuition charged by in-state public colleges at the time of matriculation. There is a $30 out-of-state school transfer fee charged each semester.

Contract options: Two-year and four-year contracts are available.

Costs: There is a one-time $75 enrollment fee. In the enrollment period that ended January 31, 2002, lump-sum contract prices for a child in the tenth grade ranged from $9,080 for the two-year plan to $17,666 for the four-year plan. Prices are discounted for younger beneficiaries. Contract payments may be made in a lump sum, in 48 monthly installments, or in monthly installments (with or without a down payment) through the year of projected enrollment. Monthly installment payments are computed to include an effective annual 7% cost for making payments over time along with a small account maintenance fee.

Cancellation provisions: The contract may be canceled at any time after one year for a refund of all contract payments, plus a share of the earnings in the program trust, less a penalty of 10% of the earnings. Cancellation within one year will forfeit any share of earnings. Cancellation due to the beneficiary's death, disability, or receipt of scholarship will result in a refund of the lesser of contract payments plus the compounded rate of return earned by the fund or the current tuition charged at colleges and universities in South Carolina. The $100 cancellation fee will be waived. All refunds, except in the event of death, disability, or scholarship, will also incur a $100 fee.

Contract changes: Accepts requests to change beneficiary prior to matriculation to a younger family member ($25 fee), transfer contract ownership ($25 fee), and name a successor owner. There are no special provisions concerning rollovers/transfers to another 529 plan (cancellation provisions would apply).

State backing: Contracts are not backed by the full faith and credit of the state of South Carolina. If the program is discontinued, contract owners are entitled to a refund of all payments plus 4% annual interest. If the program fund does not have sufficient assets to make this payment, the state must consider appropriating the shortfall from the South Carolina general fund.

Special considerations:
- All contributions are eligible for a state income tax deduction.
- Qualified distributions from this program are exempt from South Carolina state income tax. South Carolina treatment of withdrawals from other 529 plans depends on the state passing conformity legislation for the federal tax law changes.
- Under South Carolina law, interests in the program are exempt from attachment under bankruptcy proceedings.

STATE:	**SOUTH CAROLINA**
PROGRAM NAME:	FUTUREScholar 529 College Savings Plan
529 TYPE:	Savings
STATE AGENCIES:	Office of State Treasurer
INITIAL YEAR OF OPERATION:	2002

Legislation for a 529 college savings plan in South Carolina was enacted in 2001. The program is expected to launch in the first or second quarter of 2002. Banc of America Advisors, LLC, an affiliate of Bank of America, has been selected to manage the program and will offer a menu of age-based, fixed allocation and stand-alone investment

portfolios to participants. Present legislature provides for a state tax deduction to qualifying South Carolina taxpayers for their contributions into the plan.

STATE:	**SOUTH DAKOTA**
PROGRAM NAME:	CollegeAccess
529 TYPE:	Savings
STATE AGENCIES:	South Dakota Investment Council
PROGRAM MANAGER:	PIMCO
INITIAL YEAR OF OPERATION:	Targeted for first quarter 2002

Preliminary information: There will be seven investment options in this program. Two of
the options, the age-based option and a fixed income option using treasury inflation protection securities, will be available on both a direct and advisor-sold basis to residents of
South Dakota (direct accounts will have a maximum expense ratio of 0.65%). All seven
options will be available on a nationwide basis through financial advisors. The equity portion of each portfolio will involve a multi-manager approach while the fixed income portion will utilize mutual funds from PIMCO.

STATE:	**TENNESSEE**
PROGRAM NAME:	Tennessee's BEST Prepaid College Tuition Plan
529 TYPE:	Prepaid unit
STATE AGENCY AND PROGRAM MANAGER:	Treasury Department and nine-member Board chaired by State Treasurer
INITIAL YEAR OF OPERATION:	1997
TELEPHONE:	1-888-486-BEST (1-888-486-2378)
INTERNET:	www.treasury.state.tn.us/best.htm

Who can open an account? Individuals with a social security number (including minors)
provided that the purchaser or beneficiary is a Tennessee resident at the time the account
is opened.

Time or age limitations on beneficiary or on use of benefits: There are no age restrictions.
However, tuition units must be on account with BEST for at least two years prior to use.
There is no time limit on the use of units, but the account may be terminated 10 years
after the beneficiary turns 18 if there has been no contact or account activity during that
10-year period.

Contract benefits: Each unit in the account is worth 1% of the weighted average tuition at Tennessee's public four-year universities. Units may be redeemed at any eligible educational institution in the country for any qualified higher education expense that is billed by the institution. The redemption value of a unit based on tuition and fees for the 2001/2002 year is $33.51. If the beneficiary attends an out-of-state or private school, the tuition units will be paid out to the institution at the same rate paid for Tennessee public schools.

Costs: The purchase price of a tuition unit is based on the current tuition as adjusted for actuarial considerations and expenses. As of January 1, 2002, the purchase price is $36.85 per unit. There are no enrollment or account maintenance fees.

Maximum contributions: Accepts contributions until all Tennessee account balances for the same beneficiary reach $235,000.

Minimum initial contribution: One unit.

Cancellation provisions: The designated refund recipient (purchaser or beneficiary) may request a refund of the entire account value, less a $25 fee, after reaching the age of 18 and sending written notarized notice signed by the beneficiary that tuition units will not be used for college.

Contract changes: Under new rules to take affect in 2002, the program will accept requests by the purchaser to change beneficiary, name a successor purchaser, and rollover/transfer assets within the program or to another 529 plan.

State backing: Units are not backed by the full faith and credit of the state of Tennessee. The trustee invests program assets with the goal of creating a reserve to protect against shortfalls in the program fund.

Special considerations:
- Contributions to BEST along with any earnings are exempt from Tennessee state, county, or municipal taxes. Tennessee does not have an income tax.
- Under state law, BEST units are exempt from execution, attachment, garnishment, and bankruptcy proceedings.

STATE: **TENNESSEE**

PROGRAM NAME:	Tennessee's BEST Savings Plan
529 TYPE:	Savings
STATE AGENCIES:	Tennessee Baccalaureate Education System Trust and State Treasurer
PROGRAM MANAGER:	TIAA-CREF Tuition Financing, Inc.
INITIAL YEAR OF OPERATION:	2000
TELEPHONE:	1-888-486-BEST (1-888-486-2378)
INTERNET:	www.tnbest.org

Who can open an account? U.S. citizens and resident aliens, including minors.

Time or age limitations on beneficiary or on use of account assets: None.

Age-based investment program: Contains 11 portfolios of underlying mutual funds. Contributions are placed into the portfolio corresponding to the age of the beneficiary. Each portfolio shifts to a more conservative investment allocation over time.

Static investment options: None.

Underlying investments: TIAA-CREF institutional mutual funds.

Fees and expenses: 0.95% annualized program management fee charged against value of account, including expenses of underlying mutual funds. There are no enrollment or annual account maintenance fees.

Broker distribution: None.

Maximum contributions: Accepts contributions until all Tennessee account balances for the same beneficiary reach $235,000.

Minimum initial contribution: $25 ($15 for payroll deduction plan).

Account changes: Under new rules to take affect in 2002, the program will accept requests by the purchaser to change beneficiary, name a successor purchaser, and rollover/transfer assets within the program or to another 529 plan.

Special considerations:
- Contributions to BEST along with any earnings are exempt from Tennessee state, county, or municipal taxes. Tennessee does not have an income tax.

- Under state law, BEST assets are exempt from execution, attachment, garnishment, and bankruptcy proceedings.

STATE: **TEXAS**

PROGRAM NAME:	Texas Tomorrow Fund
529 TYPE:	Prepaid contract
STATE AGENCIES AND PROGRAM MANAGERS:	State Comptroller's Office and the Texas Prepaid Higher Education Tuition Board
INITIAL YEAR OF OPERATION:	1996
TELEPHONE:	1-800-445-GRAD (1-800-445-4723)
INTERNET:	www.texastomorrowfund.org

Who can purchase a contract? Individuals 18 years or older, UTMA/UGMA custodians, and legal entities. The beneficiary must be either a Texas resident for at least the 12-month period immediately preceding the date of the application or a nonresident child of a purchaser who is a Texas resident.

Enrollment period: Current enrollment ends May 24, 2002.

Time or age limitations on beneficiary or on use of benefits: The beneficiary must not have graduated from high school at the time of enrollment. Contract benefits must be used within a 10-year period beginning on the date the beneficiary is projected to graduate from high school.

Contract benefits: Pays the actual in-state cost (for public school contracts) or the estimated average cost (for private school contracts) of undergraduate tuition and required fees for up to 160 credit hours (10 semesters) at any accredited college or university in Texas. The value derived from the contract may depend in part on the selection of institution, because public institutions in Texas have different tuition and fee levels. The value of the contract benefits based on average in-state tuition and fees can also be transferred to any accredited out-of-state college or university or accredited Texas proprietary school. There is a $25 fee for each academic term that benefits are paid to an out-of-state college. Special refund provisions apply in the event the beneficiary receives a scholarship.

Contract options: One or two year contracts for junior public college plans, one to five year contracts for senior public and private college plans and a four year contract for the junior/senior public college plan.

Costs: There is a one-time $50 application fee. For the enrollment period ending May 24, 2002, lump-sum contract prices for a child in the twelfth grade ranged from $1,820 for the one-year community college plan to $64,202 for the five-year private college and university plan. Prices may be slightly discounted for younger beneficiaries. Payments may be made in a lump sum or in monthly installments over five years, ten years, or an extended term to the beneficiary's projected high school graduation date. Installments are computed to include an effective annual 8% cost of making payments over time.

Cancellation provisions: The contract can be canceled at any time for a refund of at least the amount of your payments, less a cancellation fee of $25 and an account maintenance fee of $3 per month for monthly or annual pay contracts or $20 for lump sum contracts. Cancellations due to the death or disability of the beneficiary or purchaser do not incur the cancellation fee. If the beneficiary is 18 years old or graduated from high school, the refund will be based on the greater of the current average tuition rate or total contract payments made.

Contract changes: Accepts requests to change beneficiary prior to use of any contract benefits by the current beneficiary ($50 fee plus possible increase to contract cost), transfer contract ownership ($20), and name a successor owner, subject to residency requirements. There are no special provisions concerning rollovers/transfers to another 529 plan (cancellation provisions would apply).

State backing: Contracts are backed by the full faith and credit of the state of Texas.

Special considerations:

- A beneficiary who moves to another state after enrolling in the program is still eligible for Texas in-state tuition rates while using program benefits.
- There are no state income tax incentives because Texas does not have a personal income tax.
- Under Texas law, contract benefits are exempt from claims of creditors of a purchaser or beneficiary.

STATE: **UTAH**

PROGRAM NAME:	Utah Educational Savings Plan Trust (UESP)
529 TYPE:	Savings
PROGRAM MANAGEMENT AND OVERSIGHT:	Utah Higher Education Assistance Authority and State Treasurer
INITIAL YEAR OF OPERATION:	1997
TELEPHONE:	1-800-418-2551
INTERNET:	www.uesp.org

Who can open an account? Individuals with a valid social security number or taxpayer identification number, UTMA/UGMA custodians, and legal entities.

Time or age limitations on beneficiary or on use of account assets: Withdrawals must begin by the time the beneficiary reaches the age of 22 years and four months. An automatic extension of time will be granted until the beneficiary's 27th birthday, and the program has the authority to grant further extension.

Age-based investment options: Under Investment Options 2 and 3 contributions are initially invested in a blend of underlying investments corresponding to the beneficiary's expected years to enrollment, and later reassigned to more conservative blends as the beneficiary nears the year of enrollment. Option 2 has a 95% equity investment for the youngest age group and 100% money market investment for the oldest age group. Option 3 is more aggressive, with the equity concentration never going below 65%.

Static investment options: The program offers two options. Option 1 is the State Treasurer's Investment Fund, invested in money market securities. Option 4 is the Vanguard Institutional Index Fund.

Underlying investments: Vanguard institutional index funds and the Utah State Treasurer's Investment Fund.

Fees and expenses: For Options 2, 3, and 4, there is a $25 annual account maintenance fee (reduced to 0.50% of account balance for accounts under $5,000), a 0.25% annualized program management fee charged against the value of the account, and underlying Vanguard mutual fund expenses of 0.06% for the stock index fund and 0.10% for the bond index fund. For Option 1 (Treasurer's Investment Fund), there are no program fees or expenses. There is no enrollment fee.

Broker distribution: None.

Maximum contributions: The cumulative contribution limit is $101,650 per beneficiary, which can be increased to more than $175,000 if an intention to save for a more expensive college outside Utah can be demonstrated.

Minimum initial contribution: $25 per family (minimum of $300 in a year in which any contributions are made except for accounts with $5,000 or more).

Account changes: Accepts requests to change beneficiary, transfer account ownership, name a successor owner, rollover/transfer assets within the program or to another 529 plan, and change investment option once per calendar year.

Special considerations:

- Utah taxpayers may deduct up to $1,410 ($2,820 for a married couple each opening an account) of contributions per year per beneficiary, but only for accounts owned by contributor and that were established before the beneficiary turned age 19. Recapture of deductions is required when non-qualified withdrawals are taken.
- Qualified withdrawals from this program are exempt from Utah income tax. Utah treatment of withdrawals from other 529 plans depends on state conformity to the federal tax law changes.
- The beneficiary's participation in the program for eight consecutive years while a resident of Utah will lock in resident tuition rates at Utah public institutions even if the beneficiary is no longer a state resident at the time of college enrollment.
- If an account is terminated through a non-qualified withdrawal within the first few years, the amount distributed will be the lesser of the amount of contributions made or the value of the account.

STATE:	**VERMONT**
PROGRAM NAME:	Vermont Higher Education Investment Plan
529 TYPE:	Savings
STATE AGENCY:	Vermont Student Assistance Corp. (VSAC)
PROGRAM MANAGER:	TIAA-CREF Tuition Financing, Inc.
INITIAL YEAR OF OPERATION:	1999
TELEPHONE:	1-800-637-5860
INTERNET:	www.vsac.org

Who can open an account? U.S. citizens and resident aliens with a valid social security number or federal taxpayer identification number, UTMA/UGMA custodians, corporations, and certain other legal entities.

Time or age limitations on beneficiary or on use of account assets: None.

Age-based investment option: The Managed Allocation Option contains 11 portfolios of underlying mutual funds. Contributions are placed into the portfolio corresponding to the age of the beneficiary. Each portfolio shifts to a more conservative investment allocation over time.

Static investment options: There are two supplemental investment options: the 100% Equity option and the Interest Income option. The 100% Equity option is currently invested 80% in a growth and income fund and 20% in an international fund. The Interest Income option provides a return at least equal to the 91-day T-bill rate.

Underlying investments: TIAA-CREF institutional mutual funds for the Managed Allocation option and 100% Equity option, and an interest-bearing note (backed by guaranteed student loans) for the Interest Income option.

Fees and expenses: For the TIAA-CREF options only, there is a 0.80% annualized program management fee charged against the value of the account, including the expenses of the underlying mutual funds. There are no enrollment or annual account maintenance fees.

Broker distribution: None.

Maximum contributions: Accepts contributions until all account balances for the same beneficiary reach $240,100.

Minimum initial contribution: $25 ($15 for payroll deduction plan).

Account changes: Accepts requests to change beneficiary, transfer account ownership, name a successor owner, rollover/transfer assets within the program or to another 529 plan, and change investment option once per calendar year.

Special considerations:
- Qualified withdrawals from this program are exempt from Vermont income tax. Vermont treatment of withdrawals from other 529 plans depends on state conformity to the federal tax law changes.

STATE: **VIRGINIA**

PROGRAM NAME: Virginia Prepaid Education Program (VPEP)

529 TYPE: Prepaid contract

STATE AGENCY AND PROGRAM MANAGER: Virginia College Savings Plan Board and its Executive Director

INITIAL YEAR OF OPERATION: 1996

TELEPHONE: 1-888-567-0540

INTERNET: www.virginia529.com

Who can purchase a contract? U.S. citizens and resident aliens 18 years or older, UTMA/UGMA custodians, and legal entities. The purchaser, beneficiary, or parent of a non-resident beneficiary must be a Virginia resident at the time the application is submitted.

Enrollment period: Current enrollment period is January 28, 2002 through May 1, 2002.

Time or age limitations on beneficiary or on use of benefits: The beneficiary must be in ninth grade or younger at the time the contract is purchased. Automatic extensions of the 10-year limit for usage are available upon request.

Contract benefits: Contract pays in-state undergraduate tuition and mandatory fees at a Virginia public institution according to the plan and number of years selected. The value derived from the contract will depend in part on the selection of institution, because public institutions in Virginia have different tuition and fee levels. At any time, contracts may be rolled over from VPEP to VEST (Virginia's 529 savings program) at an amount that includes payments plus the reasonable rate of return (the institutional money-market fund index). If the beneficiary decides to attend an in-state private school, the contract will pay an amount equal to the payments made plus the actual rate of return earned on program fund investments, capped at the highest tuition and mandatory fees at a Virginia public institution. For attendance at an out-of-state school, the contract will pay an amount equal to payments made plus a reasonable rate of interest as declared on an annual basis, capped at the average tuition and mandatory fees at Virginia public institutions.

Contract options: One to five years at a public four-year university, one to three years at a Virginia community college, or any combination of university and community college (maximum of eight years).

Costs: There is a one-time $85 application fee ($25 for each additional Virginia account opened and owned by same person). In the 2002 enrollment period, lump-sum contract prices for a child in the ninth grade ranged from $1,385 for the one-year community college plan to $23,520 for the five-year university plan. Prices are discounted for younger beneficiaries. The contract price may also be paid in 60 monthly installments or over an extended period until the beneficiary reaches college age. All installment payments are computed to include an effective annual 8% cost of making payments over time.

Cancellation provisions: If the contract is canceled within three years the program will provide a refund of contract payments less a $25 cancellation fee. If the contract is canceled after three years the program will provide a refund of contract payments plus the reasonable rate of return (the institutional money-market index) less a $25 cancellation fee. Cancellation fees are waived in the event of the beneficiary's death, disability, or receipt of a scholarship.

Contract changes: Accepts requests to change beneficiary (an additional payment may be required if the new beneficiary is older than the current beneficiary), transfer contract ownership, and name a successor owner, subject to residency requirements. A $10 fee is charged for certain changes. Contract payments, including reasonable interest, may be rolled over to Virginia's VEST program at any time. The program also permits rollover of contract payments to another state's 529 plan, except that interest is included only on contracts that are at least three years old, and a $25 fee is charged.

State backing: If the investment return on program funds is not sufficient to cover the plan's contractual obligations, Virginia law requires that the Governor include in the budget an appropriation providing for such contingency.

Special considerations:
- Virginia taxpayers may deduct up to $2,000 of contract payments, per contract, each year from Virginia taxable income, with unlimited carryforward of excess payments until the full amount has been deducted. The annual limit is removed for individuals who are at least 70 years old. Deductions are subject to recapture if non-qualified withdrawals or rollovers to another state's 529 plan are made in a later year, unless the refund is due to the beneficiary's death, disability, or receipt of a scholarship.
- Qualified distributions, and refunds taken as a result of the beneficiary's death, disability, or receipt of a scholarship, are exempt from Virginia income tax. Virginia treatment of withdrawals from other 529 plans depends on state conformity to the federal tax law changes.
- The value of the contract will not be counted in determining eligibility and need for student financial aid programs provided by the Commonwealth of Virginia.
- Under Virginia law, contracts are protected from the claims of creditors of the purchaser or the beneficiary.

STATE:	**VIRGINIA**
PROGRAM NAME:	Virginia Education Savings Trust (VEST)
529 TYPE:	Savings
STATE AGENCY AND PROGRAM MANAGER:	Virginia College Savings Plan Board and its Executive Director
INITIAL YEAR OF OPERATION:	1999
TELEPHONE:	1-888-567-0540
INTERNET:	www.virginia529.com

Who can open an account? U.S. citizens and resident aliens 18 years or older, UTMA/UGMA custodians, and legal entities.

Time or age limitations on beneficiary or on use of account assets: Qualified withdrawals may only be requested after an account has been open 12 months. Automatic extensions of the 10-year time limit for usage are available upon request.

Age-based investment option: The Age-Based Portfolios contain eight portfolios of underlying investments. Contributions are placed into the portfolio corresponding to the age of the beneficiary. The portfolios shift to a more conservative investment allocation over time.

Static investment options: The Non-Evolving portfolios consist of four portfolios: Aggressive, Moderate, Conservative and Money Market.

Underlying investments: Mutual funds or separate accounts managed by Vanguard, Rothschild Asset Management, Capital Guardian, Franklin Templeton, Western Asset Management, and PRIMCO.

Fees and expenses: $85 one-time account application fee ($25 for each additional Virginia account opened and owned by same person), and management and investment expenses at an annual rate ranging from approximately 0.85% to 1.00% charged against the portfolios. There is no annual account maintenance fee.

Broker distribution: None.

Maximum contributions: Accepts contributions until all Virginia account balances for the same beneficiary reach $250,000.

Minimum initial contribution: $25 (additional contributions to the account must bring the amount contributed to $250 within one year from the date the account was opened).

Account changes: Accepts requests to change beneficiary ($10 fee), transfer account ownership ($10 fee), name a successor owner, rollover/transfer assets within the program or to another 529 plan ($25 fee unless to Virginia's VPEP program), and change investment option once per calendar year.

Special considerations:
- Virginia taxpayers may deduct up to $2,000 of contributions, per account, each year from Virginia taxable income, with unlimited carryforward of excess payments until the full amount has been deducted. The annual limit is removed for individuals who are at least 70 years old. Deductions are subject to recapture if non-qualified withdrawals or rollovers to another state's 529 plan are made in a later year, unless the refund is due to the beneficiary's death, disability, or receipt of a scholarship.
- Qualified distributions, and non-qualified withdrawals attributable to the beneficiary's death, disability, or receipt of a scholarship, are exempt from Virginia income tax. Virginia treatment of withdrawals from other 529 plans depends on state conformity to the federal tax law changes.
- Under Virginia law, accounts are protected from the claims of creditors of the purchaser or the beneficiary.

STATE:	**VIRGINIA**
PROGRAM NAME:	CollegeAmerica
529 TYPE:	Savings
STATE AGENCY AND PROGRAM MANAGER:	Virginia College Savings Plan Board and its Executive Director
INVESTMENT MANAGER:	American Funds
INITIAL YEAR OF OPERATION:	2002
TELEPHONE:	1-800-421-0180, ext. 529
INTERNET:	www.americanfunds.com

Who can open an account? U.S. citizens and resident aliens, UTMA/UGMA custodians, and legal entities.

Time or age limitations on beneficiary or on use of account assets: Account must be used within 30 years of the beneficiary's projected date of high school graduation, or 30 years after the account is opened for a beneficiary who has already graduated from high school, unless an extension is granted by the program.

Age-based investment options: None.

Static investment options: There are 21 individual American Funds available to the participant. Contributions may be directed to one fund or allocated among them.

Underlying investments: American Funds.

Fees and expenses: $10 one-time account application fee and $10 annual account maintenance fee. Accounts indirectly incur the expenses of the underlying mutual funds. In addition, accounts are subject to one of four alternative expense structures that will determine any initial sales charge, contingent deferred sales charge, and/or additional asset-based fees.

Broker distribution: This program is designed for distribution exclusively through financial advisors.

Maximum contributions: Accepts contributions until all Virginia account balances for the same beneficiary reach $250,000.

Minimum initial contribution: $250 per fund.

Account changes: Accepts requests to change beneficiary, transfer account ownership, name a successor owner, rollover/transfer assets within the program or to another 529 plan and change investment option once per calendar year.

Special considerations:
- Virginia taxpayers may deduct up to $2,000 of contributions, per account, each year from Virginia taxable income, with unlimited carryforward of excess payments until the full amount been deducted. The annual limit is removed for individuals who are at least 70 years old. Deductions are subject to recapture if non-qualified withdrawals are taken in a later year, unless the refund is due to the beneficiary's death, disability, or receipt of a scholarship.
- Qualified distributions, and non-qualified withdrawals attributable to the beneficiary's death, disability, or receipt of a scholarship, are exempt from Virginia income tax. Virginia treatment of withdrawals from other 529 plans depends on state conformity to the federal tax law changes.
- Under Virginia law, accounts are protected from the claims of creditors of the purchaser or the beneficiary.

STATE:	**WASHINGTON**

PROGRAM NAME:	Guaranteed Education Tuition (GET)
529 TYPE:	Prepaid unit
STATE AGENCY AND PROGRAM MANAGER:	Washington State Higher Education Coordinating Board
INITIAL YEAR OF OPERATION:	1998
TELEPHONE:	1-877-438-8848
INTERNET:	www.get.wa.gov

Who can open an account? Individuals with a social security number (including minors) and legal entities, provided that the beneficiary is a Washington resident at the time the account is opened.

Enrollment period: Current enrollment is from September 15, 2001 through May 31, 2002.

Time or age limitations on beneficiary or on use of benefits: There are no age restrictions. The first payout date must be at least two calendar years after the purchase of units. Units must be used within 10 years after the beneficiary's projected college entrance year or the first use of units, whichever is later, unless an extension is approved.

Contract benefits: Each unit in the account is worth 1% of the resident undergraduate tuition for one year at the highest-price Washington state public university. Up to 100 units may be redeemed each year to pay for tuition and fees at any eligible institution, and excess units can be used to pay for other qualified higher education expenses. The redemption value of a unit based on tuition and fees at the highest-priced Washington state public university for the 2001/2002 year is $38.98. If the beneficiary attends an out-of-state or private school, the tuition units will be paid out to the institution at the same rate paid to Washington's highest priced public college or university.

Costs: There is a one-time $50 enrollment fee with a maximum fee of $100 per family. The purchase price of a tuition unit is based on the current tuition as adjusted for actuarial considerations and expenses. The purchase price for any units acquired through August 31, 2002 is $42 per unit. Rather than making separate purchases of additional units in the future, a quantity of 50 to 500 units may be purchased at one time under a customized monthly payment arrangement over a maximum 18-year period at an additional cost equivalent to annual interest of 7.5%.

Maximum purchase: Up to 500 units may be purchased for any beneficiary (all accounts with the same beneficiary must be aggregated for this purpose).

Minimum initial purchase: One unit.

Cancellation provisions: The program will consider a request for refund after the account has been open at least two years (exceptions to the two-year period exist in cases of death, disability, and financial hardship). Units are valued at 1% of the current annual tuition at the highest priced Washington state public university when the refund is due to the beneficiary's death, disability, receipt of a scholarship, or graduation or program completion. Units are valued based on weighted average public tuition if a refund is requested because the beneficiary decides not to attend college. A refund penalty will be assessed equal to 10% of the increase in unit value (minimum $100 penalty). A withdrawal made on account of the beneficiary's death or disability, or to the extent the beneficiary receives a scholarship, will not be subject to the penalty.

Contract changes: Accepts requests to change beneficiary, transfer contract ownership, and name a successor owner, subject to residency requirements. There are no special provisions concerning rollovers/transfers to another 529 plan (penalty provisions would apply).

State backing: Tuition units are backed by the full faith and credit of the state of Washington.

Special considerations:

- There are no state income tax incentives because Washington does not have a personal income tax.

STATE:	**WEST VIRGINIA**
PROGRAM NAME:	West Virginia Prepaid College Plan
529 TYPE:	Prepaid contract
STATE AGENCY AND PROGRAM MANAGER:	State Treasurer's Office under the authority of the West Virginia College Prepaid Tuition and Savings Program Board of Trustees
INITIAL YEAR OF OPERATION:	1998
TELEPHONE:	1-800-307-4701
INTERNET:	www.wvtreasury.com/prepaid.htm

Who can purchase a contract? Individuals at least 18 years old and approved legal entities. Either the owner of the contract, the beneficiary, or the parent of the beneficiary must be a West Virginia resident at the time the contract is purchased.

Enrollment period: The most recent enrollment period ended on January 31, 2002.

Time or age limitations on beneficiary or on use of benefits: The beneficiary must be in the ninth grade or younger at the time the contract is purchased. Contract benefits must be used within 10 years after the projected college entrance date.

Contract benefits: Contract pays in-state undergraduate tuition and mandatory fees at a West Virginia public institution according to the plan and number of years selected. If the beneficiary receives a scholarship, any remaining contract value can be refunded or applied to room and board, books, or supplies. The value derived from the contract will depend in part on the selection of institution, because public institutions in West Virginia have different tuition and fee levels. If the beneficiary decides to attend a private college in West Virginia or an out-of-state college, the program will pay an amount up to, but not more than, the weighted average tuition and mandatory fees at West Virginia public four-year institutions.

Contract options: A college and university plan for one to five years, a one or two year community college plan, and the "2+2" plan combining two years of community college with two years of university attendance.

Costs: There is a one-time $70 application fee. Other fees may be imposed if multiple account changes are requested in a year. In the enrollment period that ended January 31, 2002, lump-sum contract prices for a child in the ninth grade ranged from $1,792 for the one-year community college plan to $15,921 for the five-year university plan. Prices are discounted for younger beneficiaries. Payments may be made a single lump sum, 60 monthly installments (only if the beneficiary is in the 7th grade or below), or an extended monthly payment plan that ends in May prior to the projected enrollment year. Installment payments are computed to include an effective annual 8.5% cost of making payments over time.

Cancellation provisions: A contract may be canceled at any time and the program will provide a refund of all contract payments (less a cancellation fee of as much as $150). The cancellation fee is waived in the event of the beneficiary's death, disability, or receipt of scholarship. A refund based on actuarial present value of benefits will be made in the event the beneficiary dies or if the contract benefits have reached maturity.

Contract changes: Accepts requests to change beneficiary (an additional payment may be required if the new beneficiary is older), transfer contract ownership, and name a successor owner, subject to residency requirements. While there are no operational provisions concerning rollovers to other 529 plans, the Board considers rollover requests on a case-by-case basis.

State backing: Contracts are not backed by the state of West Virginia.

Special considerations:

- A deduction may be claimed against West Virginia state income tax for the entire amount of purchase payments each year.
- West Virginia state income tax treatment of qualified distributions from this program and from other 529 plans depends on the state passing conformity legislation for the federal tax law changes.

STATE:	**WEST VIRGINIA**

529 TYPE:	Savings
STATE AGENCY:	State Treasurer's Office
INITIAL YEAR OF OPERATION:	Targeted for 2002
INTERNET:	www.wvtreasury.com/

West Virginia is planning to launch a new 529 savings program in 2002. The Hartford Insurance Company was selected as program manager through a competitive bidding process and negotiations to establish a management contract were under way at the time this book went to press. The program will have no state residency restrictions and West Virginia residents will be permitted to claim a deduction for their contributions to the program. West Virginia law also contains language protecting accounts from the claims of creditors.

STATE:	**WISCONSIN**

PROGRAM NAME:	EdVest College Savings Program
529 TYPE:	Savings
STATE AGENCIES:	Wisconsin College Savings Program Board and the Office of the State Treasurer
PROGRAM MANAGER:	Strong Capital Management, Inc.
INITIAL YEAR OF OPERATION:	1997
TELEPHONE:	1-888-EdVest-WI (1-888-338-3789)
INTERNET:	www.edvest.com

Who can open an account? U.S. citizens or resident aliens of legal age, UTMA/UGMA custodians, and legal entities.

Time or age limitations on beneficiary or on use of account assets: Under the Tuition Unit Option (see below), tuition units must be purchased at least two academic years prior to intended use.

Age-based investment option: The Age-Based Option contains four portfolios of underlying funds, ranging from a 90%/10% blend of stock and fixed income funds to a 100% fixed income portfolio. Contributions are initially placed into the portfolio corresponding to the beneficiary's anticipated year of enrollment, and later reassigned to more conservative portfolios as the beneficiary nears the year of withdrawal.

Static investment options: There is a Variable Investment option and a Tuition Unit option. In the Variable Investment option, five portfolios are offered—the Index, Aggressive, Moderate, Balanced, and Bond portfolios. In the Tuition Unit option, tuition units may be purchased with a guaranteed redemption value in a specific future year (to coincide with anticipated college enrollment). The investment return in the Tuition Unit option can be determined by factoring the difference between current price and future redemption value and the period of time until redemption (much like a zero-coupon bond).

Underlying investments: Strong Funds (except for the Tuition Unit option).

Fees and expenses: $20 one-time enrollment fee (waived for company sponsored programs), $10 annual account maintenance fee (waived for accounts with balances greater than $25,000, and for accounts enrolled in an automatic investment plan or payroll deduction plan), and 1.25% annualized program management fee charged against value of account which includes the expenses of the underlying mutual funds. The program Board may approve an adjustment to the management fee if the underlying fund expenses exceed 1.00% and under certain other circumstances.

Broker distribution: Accounts opened through a financial advisor will be subject to an alternative expense structure that will determine any initial sales charge, contingent deferred sales charge, and/or additional annual program fees.

Maximum contributions: Accepts contributions until all Wisconsin account balances for the same beneficiary reach $246,000.

Minimum initial contribution: $250 ($25 per month for automatic investment plan).

Account changes: Accepts requests to change beneficiary, transfer account ownership, name a successor owner, rollover/transfer assets within the program or to another 529 plan, and change investment option once per calendar year.

State backing (Tuition Unit Option): Tuition units are not backed by the full faith and credit of the state of Wisconsin.

Special considerations:

- Up to $3,000 in contributions per beneficiary (either claimant or claimant's dependent child), per year may be subtracted from Wisconsin state taxable income.
- Qualified withdrawals from this program are exempt from Wisconsin state income tax. Wisconsin treatment of withdrawals from other 529 plans depends on the state passing conformity legislation for the federal tax law changes.
- The value of the account will not be counted in determining eligibility and need for student financial aid programs provided by the state of Wisconsin.

STATE:	**WISCONSIN**
PROGRAM NAME:	tomorrow's scholar
529 TYPE:	Savings
STATE AGENCIES:	Wisconsin College Savings Program Board and the Office of the State Treasurer
PROGRAM MANAGER:	Strong Capital Management, Inc.
DISTRIBUTION PARTNER:	American Express
INITIAL YEAR OF OPERATION:	2001
TELEPHONE:	1-866-677-6933
INTERNET:	www.tomorrowsscholar.com

Who can open an account? Individuals of legal age with either a valid social security number or taxpayer identification number, UTMA/UGMA custodians, and certain legal entities.

Time or age limitations on beneficiary or on use of account assets: None.

Age-based investment options: The Age-Based Option offers a choice between three different schedules: Aggressive Growth, Moderate Growth, or Conservative Growth. Each schedule contains five portfolios of underlying funds, ranging from 90% equity to 20% equity. Contributions are initially placed into the portfolio corresponding to the selected schedule and beneficiary's anticipated year of enrollment, and later reassigned to more conservative portfolios as the beneficiary nears the year of withdrawal.

Static investment options: The Fixed Allocation Option offers a choice between three portfolios—the Aggressive (75% equity), Balanced (50% equity), and Conservative (20% equity) portfolios.

Underlying investments: Mutual funds from American Express and Strong Funds.

Fees and expenses: $20 one-time enrollment fee (waived for company sponsored programs), $10 annual account maintenance fee (waived for accounts with balances greater than $25,000, and for accounts enrolled in an automatic investment plan or payroll deduction plan), and 1.27% annualized program management fee charged against value of account which includes the expenses of the underlying mutual funds (the program Board may approve an adjustment to the management fee if the underlying fund expenses exceed 1.02% and under certain other circumstances). In addition, accounts will be subject to one of three alternative expense structures that will determine any sales load, contingent deferred sales charge, and/or additional annual program fees.

Broker distribution: This program is designed for distribution primarily through American Express Financial Advisors.

Maximum contributions: Accepts contributions until all Wisconsin account balances for the same beneficiary reach $246,000.

Minimum initial contribution: $250 ($25 per month for automatic investment plan).

Account changes: Accepts requests to change beneficiary, transfer account ownership, name a successor owner, rollover/transfer assets within the program or to another 529 plan, and change investment option once per calendar year.

Special considerations:
- Wisconsin residents receive the same state income tax and state financial aid benefits described above for EdVest.

STATE:	**WYOMING**
PROGRAM NAME:	College Achievement Plan
529 TYPE:	Savings
STATE AGENCY:	State Treasurer
PROGRAM MANAGER:	Mercury Advisors
DISTRIBUTION PARTNER:	MFS Investment Management
INITIAL YEAR OF OPERATION:	2000
TELEPHONE:	1-877-529-2655
INTERNET:	www.collegeachievementplan.com

Who can open an account? Individuals with a Social Security number, UTMA/UGMA custodians, and legal entities.

Time or age limitations on beneficiary or on use of account assets: None.

Age-based investment option: The Age-Adjusted option contains nine portfolios of underlying mutual funds. Contributions are placed into the portfolio corresponding to the anticipated number of years to college enrollment. Eight portfolios shift to a more conservative investment allocation over time, eventually transferring to the "Short-term" portfolio.

Static investment options: The Risk-Adjusted option offers a choice between four portfolios: 100% Equity, 75% Equity, Balanced (50% equity), and Fixed-Income.

Underlying investments: Mutual funds from Mercury Funds and MFS Investments.

Fees and expenses: $25 annual account maintenance fee (waived for Wyoming residents, and for accounts with a balance of at least $25,000), 0.95% annualized program management fee charged against value of account, and expenses of the underlying mutual funds ranging from approximately 0.85% to 1.45% (portfolio weighted average).

Broker distribution: Accounts opened through a financial advisor are not subject to an additional expense structure. Brokers receive compensation paid out of the management fee and mutual fund expenses.

Maximum contributions: Accepts contributions until all account balances for the same beneficiary reach $245,000.

Minimum initial contribution: $1,000 ($250 for Wyoming residents).

Account changes: Accepts requests to change beneficiary, transfer account ownership, name a successor owner, rollover/transfer assets within the program or to another 529 plan, and change investment option once per calendar year.

Special considerations:
- There are no state income tax incentives because Wyoming does not have a personal income tax.
- The program description warns that Wyoming residents should be careful to discuss the treatment of an account in this program (or any other 529 plan) with their attorney or other advisor for purposes of the state inheritance tax. The value of the account may be includable as an asset of the account owner for this purpose.

Notes

Notes

Index

Additional Copies

THE BEST WAY TO SAVE FOR COLLEGE
A Complete Guide to 529 Plans

TELEPHONE ORDERS: 1-800-400-9113
Please have your Visa, MasterCard, or American Express ready.

FAX ORDERS: 585-381-3131
MAIL ORDERS: BonaCom Publications
Corporate Crossings
171 Sully's Trail, Suite 201
Pittsford, NY 14534, USA

SOLD TO

Name _____

Company _____

Address _____

City / ST / Zip _____

Phone _____

Email _____

DESCRIPTION	QUANTITY	COST	TOTAL
The Best Way to Save for College	_____	$26.95	_____
ISBN 0-9670322-6-1			
New York State residents, add 8% state sales tax			_____
Shipping and handling*	_____	$4.85	_____
Call for shipping cost on multiple book orders			
TOTAL			▬▬▬

PAYMENT METHOD

❏ Check Enclosed   ❏ VISA   ❏ MasterCard   ❏ American Express

Credit Card # _____

Expiration Date _____

Name on Card _____

Authorized Signature _____

*We offer discounts for purchases of 10 or more books.
Please contact us.*